THE NEW KINSHIP

FAMILIES, LAW, AND SOCIETY SERIES
General Editor: Nancy E. Dowd

Justice for Kids: Keeping Kids Out of the Juvenile Justice System
Edited by Nancy E. Dowd

The New Kinship: Constructing Donor-Conceived Families
Naomi Cahn

The New Kinship

Constructing Donor-Conceived Families

Naomi Cahn

NEW YORK UNIVERSITY PRESS
New York and London

NEW YORK UNIVERSITY PRESS
New York and London
www.nyupress.org

References to Internet websites (URLs) were accurate at the time of writing.
Neither the author nor New York University Press is responsible for URLs that
may have expired or changed since the manuscript was prepared.

Library of Congress Cataloging-in-Publication Data
Cahn, Naomi R.
The new kinship : constructing donor-conceived families / Naomi Cahn.
p. cm. — (Families, law, and society series)
Includes bibliographical references and index.
ISBN 978-0-8147-7203-4 (cloth : alk. paper)
ISBN 978-0-8147-7204-1 (ebook)
ISBN 978-0-8147-9032-8 (ebook)
1. Human reproductive technology—Law and legislation—Social aspects. 2. Parent and
child (Law) 3. Sperm donors—Legal status, laws, etc. 4. Ovum donors—Legal status, laws,
etc. 5. Human reproductive technology—Social aspects. 6. Families. I. Title.
K3611.A77C34 2012
346.01'7—dc23   2012027897

New York University Press books are printed on acid-free paper,
and their binding materials are chosen for strength and durability.
We strive to use environmentally responsible suppliers and materials
to the greatest extent possible in publishing our books.

Manufactured in the United States of America
10 9 8 7 6 5 4 3 2 1

Portions of this book include revised versions of materials from various previously published
articles, including *The New Kinship*, 100 Geo. L.J. 367 (2012); *Accidental Incest: Drawing
the Line—or the Curtain—for Reproductive Technology*, 32 Harv. J. Gender & L. 59 (2009);
and Naomi Cahn and Evan B. Donaldson Adoption Institute, *Old Lessons for a New World:
Applying Adoption Research and Experience to ART*, 24 AAML 1 (2011).

To my kin

CONTENTS

This book is about how families are made and how bonds are created in the brave new world of reproductive technology, and it dramatically reveals the ongoing cultural change in the way we think about family. Anyone—and everyone—who has struggled with questions of how to define themselves in connection with their own biological, legal, or social families will recognize many of the issues explored in this book.

The New Kinship has two purposes. First, it is focused on families and emotional relationships created through donor eggs, sperm, and embryos, and it documents the newly developing connections within and between these families. Second, the book shows how donor families offer lessons for all families, challenging the way we define families by questioning what makes a family. As reproductive technology facilitates the creation of more families, this has, in turn, profoundly affected our expectations of how we experience family life.

Whenever I give a talk about donor conception, I am always asked three things: (1) parents ask me for the best way to disclose to their children that they are donor conceived; (2) both parents and offspring ask how they can find others who have used the same donor; and (3) people not involved in the donor world want to learn more. Sometimes, people talk to me openly with their questions; often, I receive somewhat furtive, sometimes whispered follow-up calls from people who have never disclosed their use of donor gametes.

In response, I tell them that it is never too early to let children know about their origins. I also tell them about studies of people who have connected through their use of the same donor, discussing how these connections have been made and describing the experiences people have had once contact is made. In the past, I have noted that I am writing a book about these issues; I can now refer people to this book!

Over the years, as I have worked on understanding donor-conceived families and their communities, I've explored these topics with numerous colleagues, friends, and family members throughout the world. Thank you to Sonia Allan, John Appleby, Susan Frelich Appleton, Elizabeth Bartholet, Gaia

Bernstein, June Carbone, Glenn Cohen, Maxine Eichner, Martha Ertman, David Fontana, Vivian Hamilton, Joan Hollinger, Clare Huntington, Nancy Levit, and Linda McClain. Thank you to Adam Pertman for supporting my work as a Senior Fellow at the Donaldson Adoption Institute. And Wendy Kramer continues to inspire me with her leadership of the Donor Sibling Registry. Without Nancy Dowd, the editor of New York University Press's Families, Law, and Society series, and Debbie Gershenowitz, my editor at NYU Press, this book would not exist. Debbie's amazing editing over the past five years has deeply influenced my writing. I would also like to thank my research assistants, Melinda Dudley, Lindsay Luken, Alissa Marque and Sarah Rosenbluth, as well as my library liaison, Mary Kate Hunter, who have patiently answered all of my questions and helped me ask more. And I appreciate the strong support of Dean Paul Berman.

Thank you, as always, to my family for giving me the space and support to write this book.

Introduction

How do you know who is in your family? How do you define the group of people whom you label as family members? Do you consider them to be members of your family because you have chosen them or because you were born into a particular family with "your" parents and siblings? Imagine that you are not biologically related to at least one of your parents—or to either of your parents—because he or she used donor sperm, eggs, or a complete embryo. Are you related to the donor? Most donors are anonymous. No federal laws in the United States require that donors or recipients exchange any information, identifying or otherwise. Donors typically enter into contracts with fertility clinics or sperm banks that promise them anonymity. The parents may know the donor's hair color, height, IQ, college, and profession; they may even have heard the donor's voice. But they don't know the donor's name. And, until recently, donor-conceived offspring typically did not know that one of their biological parents was a donor. Should you have any right to know who that donor is? What about other children born using that same donor's eggs or sperm? Are you related to them? How?

Most people don't think about these issues. Nonetheless, each year, there are approximately fifty thousand children born in the United States through the use of donor eggs or sperm, and there are already more than one million people born via these "donor gametes" worldwide.

One in ten heterosexual couples in the United States today struggles with infertility because of a medical inability to conceive, and thousands of single women and men and gay and lesbian couples are unable to conceive children without egg or sperm donors. They may resolve their fertility issues with the help of a large, consumer-driven business. There are more than four hundred fertility clinics in the United States. California Cryobank, one of the larger sperm banks, ships more than twenty-five hundred vials of sperm each and every month. There are dozens of agencies that sell eggs, and dozens more that help people seeking surrogate pregnancies.

Perhaps because of the rapid expansion of the fertility industry, the secrecy surrounding the use of donor eggs and sperm is changing. And, as it does, increasing numbers of parents and donor-conceived offspring are searching for others who share their same biological heritage. For some it is extremely important to learn about their ancestral, genetic, and medical backgrounds. And they are finding each other, developing new forms of families that exist outside of the law.

The New Kinship offers an in-depth look at the new world that has been created when people deliberately produce children who inherit at least half of their genes from an unknown individual. It shows how these new relationships both reinforce and complicate the social, cultural, and economic meanings of family, and where the law fits into all of this. Consequently, at the outset, it is important to identify the two different kinds of new "donor families" that have been formed through the use of third-party gametes. The first, "donor-conceived families," are families created when a single parent, or a couple, chooses to use donor eggs, sperm, or embryos to create a child. This process not only produces a child but also affects the ways in which partners identify with one another regarding their roles as parents and their own emotional intimacy. In these families, the use of donors creates parent and children.

The second type of family, formed through third-party gametes, "donor-conceived family communities" or "donor kin families or networks," involves two different sets of relationships based on shared genes: (a) those between the donor and resulting offspring; and (b) those among all of the offspring produced by that donor's gametes and their discrete families. People within this second category often think of themselves as kin, part of a close or extended family-type community, even though their relationship is based solely on parents who unintentionally used the same donor gametes. These extended donor kin networks could include dozens (or even hundreds) of people who are all linked via the same donor's eggs or sperm. While the individual families are connected by genes, a traditional marker of family, they enact few of the other conventional and legal trappings of family life, such as living in the same house, pooling financial resources, or enjoying the legal protections accorded to family life. There may be no shared cultural orientations and belief systems; different families that have used the same donor are liberal, conservative, Christian, atheist, gay, and straight. Biological connection is, of course, only one of the many methods of forming a family. Yet the genetic ties among the children cause many to feel strong kinship bonds toward each other.

In these new families, parents and children face the unique challenges of redefining their families, and we, as a society, must face decisions on how to approach the bonds created among these newly found family members. *The New Kinship* has three purposes: first, it is one of the only books to date that is focused on families/relationships conceived through donors, and it documents these newly developing connections. Second, it proposes a legal basis for the development of these new communities, exploring what it would mean for the law to consider and support these different sites for forming familial relationships. It provides answers as to why we should support the new kinship. The book is grounded firmly in the importance of family: donor-conceived people are created to expand or create families, which consist of people (not genes). Consequently, the law needs to shift its dominant focus away from medicine and technology (and commodification, too) and toward family and constitutional law. The fertility industry, because it is ultimately about creating families, needs to be subjected to laws that regulate people, not things. Finally, in thinking through the issues in the donor world, the book shows how donor families both reinforce and complicate the meaning of family, offering lessons for all families by questioning what makes a family.

When we think of family, we tend to have certain images in mind (as explored further in chapter 2): we are typically talking about a group defined by its interdependence and emotional intimacy. Within the law, we may also be envisioning a group that is subject to legal protections for privacy, with a specific structure for the parent, child, and state relationship, and with restrictions on who can enter into legally cognizable unions. Donor-conceived "families" confound the legal issues, even as they construct the emotional ties. Indeed, in many ways, assisted reproduction creates families that are unlike others.

To be sure, donor-conceived family communities are not the first to challenge conventional family norms. Adoption, which is discussed extensively in chapter 6, provides a relevant, albeit not exact, template. Adoption is an example of parent-child connections that are not biological, of families formed without sexual reproduction occurring within the family. Since the mid-1800s, adoption has challenged many assumptions concerning the development of kinship through blood-based connections. And, as in the donor-conceived world, adoption involves potential connections among different families as well as offspring lacking information about their genetic heritage. Moreover, the adoption world is becoming more open, as states allow access to original birth records and as fewer adoptions are closed from the outset.

Although adoption provides interesting and useful parallels, as discussed in chapter 6, donor-conceived families and their donor-linked communities also present different challenges. Adoption focuses on the best interest of the child and on creating a legal structure that fosters that relationship; in the donor world, the focus has been on parents' rights and interests in forming a new family, with relatively few laws regulating access to the biological material at the core of these efforts. There is a profound irony that must be acknowledged that sharply differentiates donor families: family law is moving toward a more expansive view of the way families are formed, moving away from biology and marriage as constitutive of family, while it is biology, and biology alone, that connects donor-conceived families.[1]

When people choose to use donor sperm or eggs, they are constructing a family, and, as discussed in chapter 3, creating kinship and connection within their own families and with other families.[2] They are, in some sense, challenging the traditional, biologically constructed family by using third-party gametes but, at the same time, assimilating themselves into the nuclear family model made up of those with genetic bonds. Yet whether these families are celebrated or seen as subversive, they are still defined by reference to the paradigmatic characteristics of the traditionally described family.[3] And as sociologist Judith Stacey reminds us, the traditional norm is strong: "the word *family* continues to conjure an image of a married, monogamous, heterosexual pair and their progeny."[4]

Indeed, recent scholarship on the family has focused on two different themes: (1) the types of relationships entitled to familial privileges, contesting traditional assumptions about the state's role in the family; and (2) the role of the law in nurturing and supporting various kinds of familial relationships, rather than simply intervening once the family dissolves, such as at divorce.[5] This book draws on these two strands in order to examine how, as a society, we might develop a better approach to donor-conceived family networks, questioning whether the state must treat all families equally in order for a group to qualify as a "family," and whether the state should foster different kinds of familial relationships. As these families increasingly find each other, much uncharted territory remains to be explored in defining their new relationships.

JoEllen Marsh is a poster child for these new families—indeed, she is the subject of a 2011 film, *Donor Unknown*. As she was growing up in western Pennsylvania, she knew that her family situation was somewhat unusual.[6] Not only did she have two mothers who separated when she was young, but she also knew that she was the product of an anonymous sperm donor, Donor 150. When she was seven, she saw Donor 150's sperm bank profile, and she wanted to know more. A few years later, she discovered the Donor Sibling Registry, which was founded in 2000 to help individuals conceived as a result of sperm, egg, or embryo donation who want to contact others with whom they share genetic ties. JoEllen registered, but then waited almost three years before she found a half-sister in New York who was also the product of Donor 150. The *New York Times* then ran a story about JoEllen and her half-sibling. The story began, "Like most anonymous sperm donors, Donor 150 of the California Cryobank will probably never meet any of the offspring he fathered through sperm bank donations."[7]

That turned out to be untrue. Jeffrey Harrison, who lived in Venice, California, with four dogs and a pigeon, was one of the people who read the story. More importantly, he was Donor 150. He waited a few months, and, by the time he logged into the Donor Sibling Registry, he found JoEllen and five other offspring. After having met Jeffrey, JoEllen explained her feelings about finding him and her half-siblings:

> It wasn't really like I needed to find him to complete myself. There were a lot of unanswered questions but I was raised in a very loving family with people who cared about me very much, and I think I found my stability in other ways. But meeting this new side of my family has been more meaningful than I could have imagined, and I expect these relationships to last all of my life. After all, family is family—however I define the word.[8]

* * * *

This book is organized chronologically and thematically. In its first section, the book explores the meaning of family and maps the donor world. It argues that both types of donor families should be supported because of their critical connections. In the second section, it documents the formation of donor-conceived families and the development of relationships among those families. It explores who searches for donor-based relationships—and why. The book turns, in the third section, to the law's approach to, and relationship with, donor-conceived families. The final section sets out proposals for legal reform that foster connections, discussing proposed changes and potential objections. It advocates new regulation that supports the potential relationships among donor-conceived family members by establishing a voluntary registry to allow for half-siblings and their families to connect, by supporting any resulting connections, by allowing offspring to learn the identity of their donors when they reach the age of eighteen, and by limiting the number of offspring from any particular donor. The concluding chapter returns to broader issues involving the construction of families over the life course and reinforces that multiple conceptions of family can coexist for one person.

Ultimately, while the book is a descriptive and a jurisprudential exploration of the donor-conceived family world, it also makes a series of practical policy recommendations.

- First, mandate uniform and national data collection concerning all offspring born through donor gametes, including the permanent retention of relevant records about the donor. The government must require the collection of additional information from all clinics and sperm banks, including any birth from donor gametes (clinics are required to report births from donor eggs, but not donor sperm), record keeping on all donors, and updating and sharing of medical information.
- Second, develop and enact uniform laws concerning the parentage of donors, including the termination of all possible parental rights of unknown donors and the enforceability of contracts between known donors and recipients. Not only must donors be protected from any financial responsibility (such as child support) for offspring, but parents must also be protected from any potential custodial claims by donors. Only if donors know that they are not responsible for their offspring can we establish a basis for donors becoming identified.
- Third, establish a national and mandatory donor gamete registry that would allow all offspring at the age of eighteen (or earlier in some cases) to request identifying information and develop procedures to allow donor-conceived people to access this information easily,
- Fourth, facilitate the establishment of voluntary connections among members of donor-conceived family communities. This includes setting up a voluntary national, federally supported registry to allow families created through the same donor to connect with one another, and providing legal support for

genetically connected families, such as allowing voluntary recognition for purposes of family and medical leave.

- Fifth, require education and counseling for donors and future parents about the impact of using donor eggs and sperm. Donors need to understand that they are helping to create babies, not consumer products. Parents should be encouraged to tell their children that they are donor conceived, and this should be done within a culture that encourages disclosure and offers support for infertility.

The Language of the New Kinship

Finally, a note about language: throughout this area, language distorts and misrepresents actual practices. The donor world is characterized by a vocabulary that serves as a cultural clue (and cue) to our interpretation and understanding of these new families. The distinct linguistic choices show just what is at stake, and the syntax reflects broader questions about the donor world.

First, consider how to describe the family members involved with donor gametes. Does using the word "children" infantilize them, support a system in which they are subordinate to their parents? Are the children "donor-conceived offspring"? "Donor adoptees"?[9] Are the parents "donor-conceived parents"? Are people born from the same donor's gametes strangers or siblings? Are the donors a "mother" or a "father" or a stranger?[10] Donor-conceived offspring who share a gamete provider often refer to themselves as "half-siblings," rather than (the more awkward) "individuals who share genetic material." Phrasing a connection in familial terms, such as "sibling," rather than in biological terms, such as "shared genetic material," already suggests the appropriate legal and cultural frameworks.[11]

Second, assisted reproductive technology (ART) covers a variety of techniques that do not necessarily involve donor gametes; in vitro fertilization is most commonly performed using the patients' own gametes. Should the donor world instead be referred to as "third-party reproduction" and made subject to separate regulations? And perhaps artificial insemination might better be labeled as "alternative insemination" as a way of recognizing that many consumers are lesbians[12] and of emphasizing that there are different means of insemination, rather than only one that is "real, genuine, and natural."

Third, consider the use of the word "donor." What has the donor actually *donated*? Goods or services?[13] And sperm and egg donors are, in most cases, actually sperm and egg sellers, although some gamete providers are not paid for their contributions and the practice is popularly imagined as charitable. As discussed in chapter 2, commercialization and commodification exist here,[14] even though, as with baby selling or, perhaps, prostitution, a relationship is being created. It may certainly be appropriate to sell gametes, but the language should reflect what actually happens, rather than trying to shape perceptions.[15]

The mixed messages, and confusing linguistic choices, are evident in this CNN story: "With a full load of classes, two young children and her bills piling up, Michelle decided to face her economic straits in a pretty unorthodox way. She is donating her eggs to an infertile couple."[16] Well, no, she is *selling* her eggs to an infertile couple willing to pay for them, and the couple might even be paying a premium if she has high SAT scores or other highly valued and commodifiable attributes. On the other hand, although she does not intend to become the legal parent of any offspring, she is, in some definitional sense, a "parent" to any resulting offspring, and the offspring (as discussed later) may view her as a parent.

Finally, perhaps the most problematic issue concerns the meaning of "family" in this context, a theme explored throughout this book. The word "family" connotes certain culturally iconic images: interdependence, emotional intimacy, sharing a home, and kinship based on blood or legally recognized affinities, with the law keeping its distance by respecting the private nature of these relationships. The law is, nonetheless, integrally involved in constructing families by defining who can marry whom (from same-sex couples to sixteen-year-olds), assigning parenthood and identifying the father and mother, determining who can make decisions on behalf of a child, establishing when parental rights can and should be terminated, providing legal protections for the privacy of relationships defined as familial and for family members based on their status, and establishing structures to allocate decision making with respect to the parent, child, and state. Even familial relationships that seem to be "outside" of the law are defined by reference to the law.

Ultimately, using the language of family and altruism as framing devices suggests the applicability of existing family laws. The notion of a donor implies, in the modern imagination, some kind of connection between the giver and the recipient: contrast this connotation with the images associated with a "gamete provider" and "product." The children produced through donor gametes remain "donor children," regardless of their age or the fact that parents, regardless of how they became pregnant, *always* donate their gametes to their children. The book generally uses the term "donor-conceived people" (or "offspring") rather than "children" to emphasize their autonomy. Some refer to themselves as "donor-conceived adoptees." Those who share a gamete provider may consider themselves to be "half-siblings," an issue explored further in chapter 4. Indeed, the book carefully considers many of these "linguistic choices," showing how this framing has consequences for the members of these new kinship communities. Language helps shape the development and meaning of connections among donors, offspring, and recipient parents. The language is, however, problematic for many reasons: the word "donor," for example, expresses the views of many recipient parents and the fertility industry, while "donor parent" or "biological parent" may express the views of offspring and the donor may self-perceive as a "producer."

PART I

Explorations

The Meaning of Family and the Terrain of the Donor World

1

Peopling the Donor World

The donor-conceived world is filled with secrets. Unless they're told otherwise, children don't know that half—or in some cases, all—of their genetic heritage came from someone else. And even if they are aware of their genetic origins, they may never know who their donor is. Similarly, the donors who provided the egg or sperm don't know whether they have helped create any children, or whether they have dozens.

Using donor sperm or donor eggs is not a casual decision. Choosing to create children through another person's gametes means entering a world of planned families and, often, of secrecy. Although the donor world is populated by hundreds of thousands of people and run by a multi-billion dollar industry, it has also been characterized by the stigma attached to infertility and male impotency, and by fears that genetic connection, and only genetic connection, can create bonding. Consequently, this world has traditionally been secretive, with few parents even telling their children that they are the products of donor gametes.

This chapter provides a brief overview of the donor-gamete world, beginning with an introduction to the people who use donor eggs and sperm. It explores the many potential recipients of donor gametes, including heterosexual and same-sex couples, as well as single individuals, all of whom are looking for ways to complete their families. The second section gives an overview of the fertility industry, the business that makes it possible for people who want to become parents to procure the gametes and the technology that will allow them to have babies. Although donor insemination (DI) is hundreds of years old, it is only over the past three decades that DI has become an industry, and only over the past two decades that egg donation has become a possibility.[1] In the final section, this chapter introduces the donors, exploring who they are and why they do what they do.

I. Who Uses Donor Eggs and Sperm?

For many people—whether they are single, gay or lesbian, medically infertile themselves, or partnered with someone who is—reproductive technologies provide their only option for childbearing. The number of people using assisted reproductive technology (ART) has increased dramatically over the past several decades. Infertility services are expensive, however, depending on the type of procedures. Vials of sperm can be several hundred dollars; while a syringe for insemination is relatively inexpensive, costs can add up once the sperm is used in medical procedures, such as intrauterine insemination. Donor eggs are thousands of dollars, as is the in vitro fertilization process in which the eggs are fertilized. Reflecting the underlying costs of our health care system, the United States has the most expensive costs for an ART treatment cycle in the developed world; one cycle in Sweden, England, Japan, and numerous other countries costs less than half that of a comparable cycle in the United States.[2] The cost of a single in vitro fertilization cycle in the United States is typically between ten and twenty thousand dollars (not including the donor eggs).

About 8 percent of women in the United States will seek some type of infertility service during their lifetimes, and approximately six million women have problems becoming, or staying, pregnant.[3] Couples may need donor gametes when one of them is medically infertile and unable to produce viable eggs or sperm. (The need for donor sperm among heterosexual couples has decreased with the technological developments of extracting sperm from men with extremely low sperm counts, and then using ICSI—intracystoplasmic sperm injection—to get the sperm into the egg.)[4] Single people and gay and lesbian couples need donor gametes because they have no other source for the gamete. Some people will opt out of the reproductive technology world entirely, and decide to adopt or remain child free.

Several reasons account for the growth of the fertility industry and the increasing use of infertility services. First, over the past century, the reproductive technology industry has become more sophisticated, offering expanded services.[5] Most large cities in the United States had at least one infertility clinic by the late 1930s, and, in the mid-1940s, the first human eggs were fertilized outside of a woman's body, in a petri dish.[6] As technology advanced to allow for freezing sperm, the first commercial sperm bank opened in 1970 and, in 1978, Briton Louise Brown was the first baby born through in vitro fertilization (IVF). IVF then facilitated the growth of a market for donor eggs that could be grown in one woman's body, fertilized in vitro, and then placed in another woman's body, and clinics had begun to realize the possibilities of this market by the early 1990s.[7] Second, the growth is also due to higher demand. The average age of first birth is rising for the country as a whole and is now twenty-five, while the birth rate is increasing for women over the age of thirty.[8] At the same time, women's fertility declines with age: by age thirty, most women retain only 12 percent of their original egg reserves, and by age forty, just 3 percent.[9] Three percent may be still be on average nine thousand eggs—more than enough to get pregnant—but the odds definitely change.[10] Moreover, as women age, so do their eggs, which makes them less capable of fertilization and, once fertilized, less able to be implanted in the uterus; the risk of miscarriage increases as well. For a woman in her twenties, the chance of getting pregnant is 20-25 percent; it drops to 10-15 percent if she is in her thirties and to 5 percent when she is in her forties.[11]

The deferral of childbearing is one aspect of a changing family structure.[12] Women—and men—are adjusting to a new family model geared for the postindustrial economy.[13] This new culture, what June Carbone and I have labeled elsewhere as the "Blue Family" model, emphasizes the importance of women's as well as men's workforce participation, more egalitarian gender roles, and delay of marriage and childbearing until both parents reach emotional maturity and financial self-sufficiency. With fertility rates dropping and the average age of marriage moving into the late twenties, this culture deregulates sexuality, identifies responsibility with financial independence, respects equality and autonomy, and safeguards access to contraception and abortion for teens and adults. There is also greater toleration of nonmarital cohabitation, and attitudes to same-sex couples have changed from recognition to tolerance to acceptance to support. This is by no means the only model for family. The "Red Family" model rejects the new culture. This model emphasizes religious teachings that celebrate the unity of heterosexual sex, marriage, and reproduction. As a result of the emphasis on chastity and the lesser availability of contraception and abortion, however, the red culture is typified by higher teen pregnancy rates, lower average ages of marriage and first births, and the channeling of childbearing into the traditional heterosexual marriage as the only appropriate setting for childbearing.

In those parts of the country where the most fertility clinics are located, women are more likely to be part of the Blue Family model: they marry and have children at older ages.[14] While infertility (typically defined as the failure to become pregnant within a year of ceasing to use contraceptives) is actually higher among women without a college education;[15] these women are less likely and able to seek higher-tech interventions because of the cost.[16] Even in states with mandated insurance coverage, the majority of women accessing such care are white, highly educated, and wealthy.[17] A state's income predicts the availability of infertility services; availability correlates with utilization of those services; and a state's education levels directly predict utilization.[18]

Indeed, regardless of race, women with a higher socioeconomic status, measured by advanced education, household income, and insurance coverage, are more likely to use sophisticated infertility services; among women with infertility, approximately 30 percent of those who were under 300 percent of the poverty level, compared to 50 percent of women above 300 percent of the poverty level, are likely to seek infertility services.[19] While income does not affect the initial decision to seek advice about infertility, income has a clear effect on who seeks access to the more intensive forms of treatment.[20] Women with higher incomes are more likely to choose surgery or some form of ART compared to women of lower income.[21] ART is particularly important because more than 1 percent of all U.S. births result from IVF.[22] The existence of health insurance is similarly an important factor in pursuing treatment options. The fifteen states that have mandated some form of insurance for fertility services seem to be a random assortment that includes Arkansas, California, Connecticut, Hawaii, Illinois, Louisiana, Maryland, Massachusetts, Montana, New Jersey, New York, Ohio, Rhode Island, Texas, and West Virginia. Even if the insurance does not cover all infertility-related medical procedures, it is strongly correlated with treatment—so is income.[23] In states that required the most comprehensive insurance coverage, patients were almost three times as likely to use IVF.[24]

Not all IVF cycles involve donor eggs or sperm. In fact, people strongly prefer *not* to use donor gametes. While heterosexual couples are open to the

Figure 1.1 Types of ART Cycles by Age Group—United States, 2008

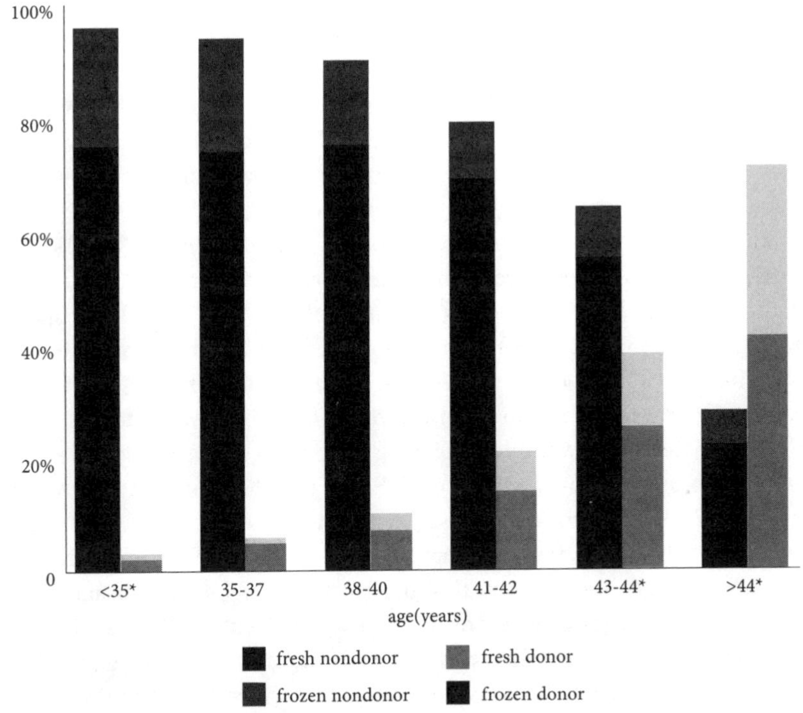

age(years)

fresh nondonor   fresh donor

frozen nondonor   frozen donor

*totals do not equal 100% due to rounding

Source: Centers for Disease Control and Prevention & American Society for Reproductive Medicine, Assisted Reproductive Technology Success Rates: National Summary and Fertility Clinic Reports, 2008 18, fig. 4 (2010), available at http://www.cdc.gov/art/ART2008/PDF/ART_2008_Full.pdf.

possibility of donor eggs or sperm, both men and women are significantly more negative toward the use of donor sperm than toward the use of donor eggs.[25] A study published in 2010 found that both men and women believed that using donor sperm, rather than donor eggs, was more likely to make them feel that they had not experienced some of the joyful feelings of having a child, and they believed it was far more likely that using donor sperm would not only lead to marital conflict but also cause others to be judgmental about their parenting skills.[26] Researchers have speculated that "while many assume a mother would love a child regardless of genetic relatedness, a father does not generate similar feelings of selflessness . . . [and] in patriarchal society where children inherit the father's name, maternal relatedness is less important."[27] Gendered societal norms reinforce the identification of men with their genetic contribution to reproduction.[28] The stigma of infertility for men reflects not just their inability to have a child, but also their perceived lack of virility.[29] Berkeley sociologist Charis Thompson describes a scene at an infertility clinic waiting room in which a nurse hands a man a specimen cup (for sperm production) and he disappears, returns after a few minutes, and is greeted by applause from several of the waiting women patients.[30] She also notes that men with male factor infertility (with insufficient or inadequate sperm for reproduction) felt significantly more stigma than men whose partners were infertile.[31]

This suggests that donor eggs are socially more acceptable than sperm when it comes to the reinforcement of traditional gender roles. And, technological advances have decreased the number of men who need donor sperm with the development in the early 1990s of ICSI, or intracytoplasmic sperm injection. Until then, IVF required that a man produce hundreds of thousands of sperm for an egg to become fertilized. ICSI allows doctors to insert one sperm directly into the egg, meaning that men with extremely low sperm counts can use their own sperm for IVF. The use of donor eggs is, however, increasing. The Centers for Disease Control does not track the use of donor sperm (at all!), but it reported that, in 2009, the latest year for which figures are available, women went through more than eighteen thousand cycles involving donor eggs or embryos, or almost 15 percent of all assisted reproduction cycles that year.[32] That was double the number of donor egg cycles in 1998.[33] Approximately six thousand babies are born each year in the United States through donor eggs, a tiny percentage of the more than four million births per year. As figure 1.2 shows, women over the age of thirty-five are much more likely to use donor eggs.[34]

And, donor eggs work. The success rates for women of all ages who use donor eggs are generally above 50 percent; for example, a 45-year-old woman has a 2.1 percent chance of having a child if she undergoes assisted reproductive technology with her own eggs, but a 53.7 percent chance if she uses donor eggs.[35] Consequently, donor eggs are alluring options, particularly in a society that finds parenthood, rather than marriage, increasingly important. Indeed, 52 percent of the Millennial Generation (those born after 1980) said that being a good parent is "one of the most important things" in life, while only 30 percent rated having a successful marriage as one of the most important things. Moreover, Millennials are more likely to believe that a child does not need a home with both a mother and father, and they are more accepting of single parenthood and nonmarital-couple parenthood.[36] In light of these attitudes, the higher age of marriage, and improving technologies (such as freezing eggs), ART usage is likely to increase.

Figure 1.2 Percentages of ART Cycles Using Donor Eggs, by Age of Woman, 2008.

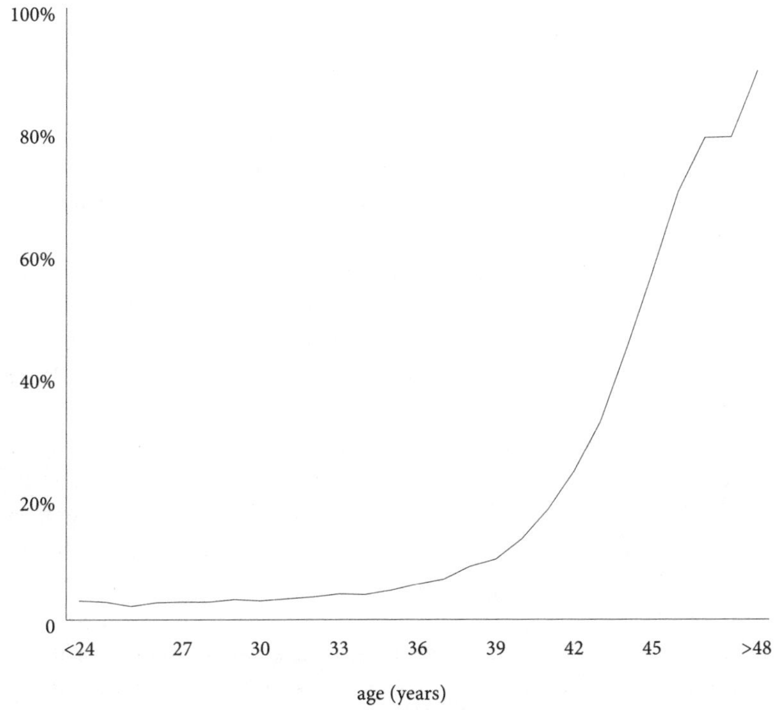

age (years)

Percentages of ART Cycles Using Donor Eggs, by Age of Woman, 2008.
Source: Centers for Disease Control and Prevention & American Society for Reproductive Medicine, Assisted Reproductive Technology Success Rates: National Summary and Fertility Clinic Reports, 2008 60, fig. 46 (2010), available at http://www.cdc.gov/art/ART2008/PDF/ART_2008_Full.pdf.

II. Intermediaries: Sperm Banks and Egg Suppliers

Buying donor sperm is easy. There are more than 150 sperm banks in the United States, and they can ship frozen sperm anywhere. It arrives in nice canisters, and people can use the sperm themselves or go to a fertility clinic for help. It is also comparatively cheap, beginning at less than $350 per vial. Buying donor eggs is more difficult, and more expensive. Until recently, there were relatively few egg brokers, and eggs had to be fresh. With new technology allowing for the successful freezing of eggs, and with increasing demand, there are growing numbers of egg sellers. But, unlike sperm, donor eggs require the use of a fertility clinic and a cycle of in vitro fertilization.

The donor world is medicalized.[37] "Medicalization" refers to "the extension of medical knowledge, practices, and techniques into people's daily lives, including by labeling aspects of social life as 'illness,' or 'disease.'"[38] It occurs when social and legal issues become instead, or simultaneously, medical problems that can be solved by the appropriate professionals. Donor sperm insemination can be a relatively simple technique done at home, but medical professionals have claimed it as a procedure that requires some professional expertise.[39] Sociologist Laura Mamo traces the development of the field of infertility beginning in the late nineteenth century, before which "women did not turn to medical professionals to understand, let alone solve, their inability to conceive; instead, they looked to god and the clergy."[40] Technological advances in understanding the menstrual cycle, developing drugs, and storing sperm helped create infertility as a distinct medical practice.

Of course, the use of medical advances to manage or resolve infertility is not (or should not be) a problem; the problems arise when medicine becomes the primary focus. Once individuals start to use infertility services, they find it difficult to stop, and the central effort becomes curing the illness of infertility rather than, for example, focusing on other means of having children or even the creation of a family without children.[41] Moreover, as bioethicists observe, broader questions, such as the morality of particular technologies (like those that enable parents to create "savior siblings"), also raise challenges. The remainder of this chapter examines the relentless move toward increasingly sophisticated technologies in the medicalization of infertility.

1. Donating to History

The donor world has changed dramatically and fundamentally over the past half-century. In 1948, the influential physician and lawyer Alfred Koerner, who was the executive secretary to the National Research Foundation for Fertility, Inc., wrote one of the first articles in a law journal addressing donor insemination. He observed that it was important for the recipient woman to trust her physician to choose the right donor as well as not to disclose her use of donor sperm.[42] That is, the woman chose her *doctor,* not her *donor.* Technological advances allowing for sperm freezing or cryopreservation occurred during the 1950s, thereby alleviating the need for fresh sperm, and the first for-profit sperm bank did not open until 1972.[43] By the late 1980s, more than four hundred sperm banks were in operation.[44] Banks still sold their wares primarily to doctors. In fact, in 1987, 60 percent of federally surveyed sperm banks would sell *only* to doctors, and none would sell only to recipients.[45]

Sperm banking became increasingly consumer-oriented throughout the 1980s, however. In a series of articles for *Slate* magazine, journalist David Plotz credits the Repository for Germinal Choice (also known as the "Nobel Sperm Bank"), created in the late 1970s, with transforming the sperm banking business by requiring rigorous testing and providing increasing amounts of information to consumers.[46] This gave consumers, rather than doctors, control over the choice of sperm. Other banks began offering the same services to consumers, and the AIDS epidemic added incentives for additional safety tests.[47] Culturally and socially, this coincided with the development of more "single by choice" mothers and lesbian families. While there are no reliable figures on who uses sperm banks, anecdotal evidence suggests that their usage by heterosexual couples is declining, while usage by single women and lesbians is increasing.[48]

2. The Incredible Egg

Egg provision has a far shorter history. The first documented egg donation occurred in 1984.[49] In 2003, clinics implanted more than fourteen thousand embryos created from donated eggs.[50] Egg donation began with identified donors, who were often related to the recipients and voluntarily provided eggs.[51] Today, identified donors constitute a much smaller part of the donation pool and recipients are more likely to use specifically recruited donors.[52] Eggs are typically available under two circumstances: first, women already undergoing an IVF cycle may agree to provide their eggs to other women in exchange for a reduced IVF fee; and second, women from outside of the clinic may be recruited specifically to provide eggs.[53]

Until recently, most donor eggs had to be "fresh."[54] As of 2007, there were only an estimated two hundred children worldwide born from frozen eggs, and egg banks were just beginning to be established.[55] While clinics have long been able to freeze fertilized eggs (embryos), unfertilized eggs are more delicate and more easily damaged. In 2004, the American Society for Reproductive Medicine labeled egg freezing as an "experimental" procedure, meaning that patients had to be informed that it was not an "established medical practice."[56] The technology has exploded due to scientific discoveries, including vitrification, and more than half of American fertility clinics make the procedure available. Clearly, frozen eggs provide opportunities for expanding the market in eggs, perhaps resulting in an increased number of banks. Use of the technology has also expanded as women, worried about their declining fertility, bank their own eggs.

3. Clinically Speaking

Egg and sperm donation programs are structured similarly, with comparable stages for donors and recipients.[57] All programs must first recruit donors, and, second, screen them.[58] The screening process typically includes collection of both medical and personal history data.[59] Aside from the laws governing the various contractual relationships, few of which apply directly to reproductive technology, this is perhaps the only stage where the law plays a direct role in the reproductive industry, mandating certain safety tests of the donated gametic material.

After recruitment and screening, programs help the donor prepare a personal profile to be used to advertise the donor to prospective consumers. Clinics vary considerably as to how much information they include in these profiles. Sites may allow searches based on a variety of characteristics, ranging from hair and eye color to highest educational degree obtained. California Cryobank offers consumers the possibilities of using the featured "Donors of the Month," who are represented by yellow smiley faces and donor numbers.[60] Clicking on a smiley face leads to a cute childhood picture of the donor, along with more (and wholesome) information about the donor's appearance and goals in life. It's not quite the same as the Playboy Playmates of the Month, but there are some presumably deliberate echoes.

While egg donors may initially be identified through a picture and a first name, sperm donors are more typically identified by number until the recipient requests (or pays for) additional information.[61] This distinction may be gendered, appearing to be more revelatory and intimate when it comes to women while more protective of the privacy of men, or it may be due to the comparative number of sperm and egg donors, or the lengthier production process for eggs.

Once the profile is publicly available, the next stage involves matching donors and recipients—and collecting fees, ranging from several hundred to thousands of dollars. Programs are also required by federal law to do some minimal follow-up with sperm donors, such as making sure that they are tested for HIV once they have stopped providing samples.

4. Inspecting Gametes

The medical profession is typically regulated by the states or is self-regulated through physicians' professional organizations, not by the federal government. The American Board of Obstetrics and Gynecology, which is a non-profit organization, administers both an oral and a written test to doctors who want to become certified as obstetricians or gynecologists. Once they become board certified, successful applicants also have the opportunity to become certified—following more examinations and a mandatory research thesis—in the subspecialty of reproductive endocrinology and infertility. Urologists, physicians who specialize in the male reproductive tract, undergo a similar certification process administered by the American Board of Urology. There are continuing obligations imposed on physicians to maintain their certification.[62]

States are generally responsible for any additional oversight of health professionals and procedures, and, in addition to their board specialties, doctors must be licensed to practice in a particular state, rather than nationally. Over the past several decades, however, the federal government has taken a few tentative steps toward the regulation of reproductive technology. Today, it provides monitoring of fertility clinic success rates, and provides some regulation of clinical laboratory services, drugs, and medical devices that are used in IVF treatments, including basis standards for the use of human tissue.

A. SPELLING SUCCESS: CLINICAL STYLE

It was not until 1992, however, that Congress enacted legislation that applied explicitly to the reproductive technology industry itself through the Fertility Clinic Success Rate and Certification Act.[63] (The act was designed to prevent fertility clinics from reporting misleading data about their pregnancy success rates.) Witnesses at the hearings on the bill testified about some clinics' use of deceptive advertising by, for example, reporting on the number of embryos created rather than the number of pregnancies achieved.[64] The law is limited to monitoring clinics' reporting of their success rates. It does not regulate the safety of their practices nor the uses of sperm or eggs or embryos. Instead, it is designed simply to provide access to information about the success rates of fertility clinics. As with other legislation in this area, the 1992 law is focused on market regulation, and even the safeguards it provides concerning the deceptive practices of clinics are relatively minimal.

A second portion of the law required the government to establish a voluntary model program that states could use in certifying embryo laboratories as having satisfied certain safety and other professional quality standards. And, as an example of its extreme deference toward the industry, Congress also refused to let either the federal government or states interfere with doctors' authority over reproductive practices in developing the embryo certification program.[65]

Moreover, implementation of both aspects of this law was neither particularly speedy nor protective of consumers. The first set of data on success rates was not even published until 1997, years after Congress passed the law, and that report included information from 1995.[66] Moreover, if fertility clinics do not provide data about their programs, there are no sanctions beyond the clinic's listing as "nonreporting" in the annual compilation of data. The Model Program for the Certification of Embryo Laboratories was finally released in 1999,[67] and it does not appear that any state has actually adopted it.[68] Indeed, the legislation is hortatory rather than protective; it does not require embryo labs to apply for state certification nor states to enact the model program. And it does not even apply to sperm banks or to clinics that only involve artificial insemination. Instead, it covers only programs that provide treatments involving embryos or eggs.

The reporting requirements are focused on the requirement that clinics practicing assisted reproductive technology provide statistics on their pregnancy success rates to the Centers for Disease Control.[69] Each December, the CDC issues a report available online that provides a national summary of success rates, data on each of the individual clinics that has reported, and a listing at the end of the nonreporting clinics. As the CDC explains, its goal is that the "report should be used to help people considering an ART procedure find clinics where they can meet personally with ART providers to discuss their specific medical situation and their likelihood of success using ART."[70] And the report does offer a comprehensive compilation of information on specific clinics. Its explicit purpose is not, however, to establish uniform standards for ART programs nor to ensure compliance with various safety standards.[71]

B. TESTING, TESTING?

Federal regulations covering the safety of "human cells, tissues, and cellular and tissue-based products" (HCT/Ps), which include donor gametes, were finalized in 2005.[72] By federal law, all gamete providers must be screened, and all of their "products" must be tested.

The FDA guidelines are somewhat limited; they do not regulate the practice of ART, only the collection, processing, storage, and distribution of human gametes as the "articles" of ART. Once a potential donor arrives at a clinic, the clinic must take certain steps to determine the donor's eligibility. To decide on eligibility, the clinic is supposed to review an applicant's medical records for various communicable diseases, such as chlamydia and HIV.[73] Not only must the clinic look to see if the applicant has already experienced one of these diseases, but also the clinic must decide whether the applicant shows risk factors for these diseases. Potential risk factors range from hemophilia to a man having had sex with another man during the previous five years.

If the donor passes the medical records examination, then the clinic must test the actual specimen collected for communicable diseases. The rules generally apply to both egg and sperm donations, with a few minor variations. Beyond the initial screening for various diseases, there must be tests for HIV Type 1 and 2, Hepatitis B and C, syphilis, chlamydia, and gonorrhea (although the last two may be omitted if the specimen is collected in a way that ensures freedom from contamination).[74] All tests must be done using FDA-licensed or -approved screening tests.[75] Further, for anonymous sperm donations, the regulations require that a new, second specimen must be tested at least six months after the date of donation; during this six-month period the anonymous donor's semen is quarantined.[76] Interestingly, the same stipulation does not apply to donated oocytes (immature eggs), which are only required to be withheld until donor eligibility is established, without the comparable necessity of retesting.[77] This different treatment may be due to the difficulties involved in collecting eggs as well as the novelty of egg freezing; fresh eggs needed to be used quickly. However, regardless of these small requirement discrepancies, the most important precautionary measures apply equally to both donor sexes; it is only after both screening and testing (and quarantine, for anonymous donors), that the donor-eligibility determination is made. There are no testing or screening requirements, of course, if the donor and the recipient are already "sexually intimate," so existing partners are exempt from this elaborate screening and testing process.[78]

When specimens are deemed eligible, they are then released for use. Repeat donors need not be completely rescreened; instead an abbreviated process can be used that focuses on any changes in the donor's medical history or relevant social behavior.[79] However, this leniency is only pertinent to donors who have been submitted to complete testing within the previous six months.

In addition to implementing standards for testing donors, the federal regulations require that donation facilities maintain sufficient staff to ensure that they can comply with the federal regulations, and personnel must be competent, with competency being measured by education, experience, and training.[80] Clinics must establish their own internal quality-control program to make sure that any corrective actions are documented, personnel receive proper training and education, periodic audits are performed, and computer software is validated for its appropriate use.[81] Clinics must also set up procedures for all steps involved in the screening, testing, and determination of eligibility.[82] The procedures must be "readily available to the personnel," and must be kept in the area where each step is performed.[83] The regulations are thorough and specific concerning the clinic's monitoring requirements.

To help in explaining how clinics should implement these mandatory screening requirements, the Food and Drug Administration has also issued a "guidance" document that suggests how to determine donor eligibility. It has the enticing title *Guidance for Industry: Eligibility Determination for Donors of Human Cells, Tissues, and Cellular and Tissue-Based Products (HCT/Ps)*. Guidance documents like this one are designed to reflect the FDA's "current thinking on a topic," although they are not legally binding.[84]

There has been an increasing amount of review of establishments,[85] although there is no way to verify much of the information that donors provide. As one potential egg donor found out when she asked the founder of an agency how she could ensure that a woman was honest,

> "Well, we can't," she responded. "It's a matter of having the experience, being able to meet and see them, get a gut feel. It could happen. They forgot to tell us they had two deaf sisters. They don't have medical records—they're 22, 23. We do what we can." [Another agency founder] seems more confident: "I know when a 23-year-old is trying to pull my leg." At Circle Surrogacy in Boston, licensed social workers meet with prospective donors about their goals and motivations. Rachel Campbell is one of them, and she believes that accidental lies by omission are more frequent than outright deception. "It's very, very uncommon that there's nothing in someone's family history—it definitely does tip us off, it makes us press forward. My take is that the donor doesn't know or hasn't asked those questions," Campbell says. "The majority of donors really are very honest—that's why our rejection rates are so high."[86]

In its booklet explaining *What You Should Know* specifically about reproductive tissue donations, the FDA emphasizes that, as a result of its regulation, the tissues are screened for communicable and infectious disease.[87] It does not, however, address any other potential type of testing that might be done, such as testing for risk of transmission of genetic diseases; the focus is on the patient who is receiving the donated products, not on the child who may ultimately be born. Indeed, aside from these safety and market-protection procedures, federal law does not regulate the medical procedures involved in donation. No additional federal restrictions are imposed on clinics. They are not required to prevent discrimination against certain potential recipients or donors,[88] mandate any ongoing obligation of donors to report health information, regulate the disclosure of information to any subsequently born children, or limit the numbers of embryos transferred per cycle, or even the number of times that one person can donate sperm or eggs. As one journalist accurately charged after a thorough report on California Cryobank, the largest sperm bank in the world, "the industry has operated almost completely unmolested. Outside of a mostly inept series of somewhat bizarre FDA rulings, there is no top-down governance in the field. It is, as it has always been, self-policing."[89] For its part, the industry often resists further regulation, claiming that it restricts patient choice.[90] Instead, there are nonbinding industry guidelines that address these issues.

Long before the federal standards became effective, the reproductive technology industry had undertaken self-regulation through the development of organizations such as the American Society for Reproductive Medicine (ASRM) and its affiliate, the Society for Assisted Reproductive Technology.[91] This process is still ongoing, and the industry has established its own voluntary standards and processes of accreditation that coexist with federal and state regulations.[92] The industry has also developed a series of ethical guidelines that, again, are not binding, but that contain advice and standards on a variety of topics that go beyond basic ART medical practice.[93] For example, the ASRM has set out recommendations on when physicians should offer the option of limiting the numbers of embryos that are transferred, advising on the indications for implanting only one embryo in a woman (which depend upon the patient's age and probability for a successful pregnancy), but no law requires observation of this voluntary advice.[94] Some clinics voluntarily limit the number of donations per donor, although no laws exist with respect to this.

5. Fertility Tourism

While in the United States, reproductive technology may be a multi-billion-dollar market on its own, the infertility business is international in its reach. Each year, at least ten thousand people around the world cross international borders to seek access to reproductive technologies in other countries.[95] The phenomenon, known as "fertility tourism" or "reproductive tourism," involves taking advantage of technologies in other countries, with patients using either their own gametes or donor sperm and eggs.[96] India has become a popular destination for individuals in the market for a surrogate, while Spain and Romania have attracted many European and North American tourists seeking IVF treatment and donor eggs.

A variety of factors motivate this type of travel, including the ability to take advantage of less regulated markets and less expensive treatments in other jurisdictions, the desire to escape restrictive laws, a scarcity of techno-logical expertise, or lengthy waiting lists at home. For example, a tightly reg-ulated market in Canada, which bans the commercial sale of donor eggs and places age limits on prospective fertility patients, induces numbers of Cana-dians to seek treatment in the United States or Europe.[97] In France, where lesbian couples were prohibited from obtaining sperm donations, many trav-eled to Belgium to seek treatments there.[98]

Another salient factor that has impelled travel abroad is a lack of donor anonymity in home countries. Some people explain that they do not want to have their children conceived by an identifiable donor, and so they travel to countries that maintain donor anonymity for gamete donation. For example, Denmark, a country that allows donor anonymity, has become a popular destination for prospective fertility patients traveling from nearby Sweden, Switzerland, and the Netherlands, all of which prohibit donor anonymity.[99]

Given the scope of fertility tourism, any examination of the United States ART world must be international in scope.

III. Donors: Egg and Sperm

Egg donors are altruists; sperm donors are in it for the money. This view is reinforced throughout the donor world. When Yale sociologist Rene Almel-ing studied a variety of egg agencies and sperm banks,[100] she found that clin-ics emphasized that egg donation involves caring and helping others, and tried to encourage feelings of altruism even though, as with sperm "dona-tion," this too involves money. The first words on the egg recruitment web-site of Shady Grove Fertility, which has offices in Maryland, Virginia, and the District of Columbia, and claims to be the largest fertility center in the United States, appeal to the potential donor's humanity: "Without the gener-osity and compassion of women like you, many infertile couples will never experience the joy of parenthood."[101] A college newspaper ad might offer "the chance to give 'the gift of life.'"[102]

By contrast to the recruitment of egg donors, sperm donor solicitation is far more explicitly mercenary. If you click on the "become a donor" tab at the NW Andrology & CryoBank website, you are taken to a site that begins by reporting that "[s]perm donors are in high demand" and continues, "As a sperm donor, you can earn as much as $1,000 per month."[103] California Cryobank uses a different strategy, explicitly appealing to the male ego: under the heading, "Do You Have What It Takes to Be a California Cryobank Sperm Donor?," the text explains, "Being a California Cryobank sperm donor means being the best."[104] Notwithstanding the marketing efforts targeted at them, egg and sperm donors generally claim that they are motivated by both money and altruism.[105] Their altruistic motives range from a general feeling of hoping to help others to a more specific wish that others enjoy parenting as they have.[106] The feeling of helping others often remains. Psychologist Andrea Braverman, who is involved in a five-year study of egg donors, found that, after the first year, egg donors continued to feel positive about their actions.[107] They also reported that they were not worried about their potential offspring's health or emotional well-being, and they only occasionally thought of their donations. According to the donors, their dominant motivation was a desire to help others, although money was an important secondary consideration. Braverman also found that, while most donors were open to meeting the recipients of their eggs and participating in a donor registry, women who said the donation process made them feel worthwhile were more receptive to the possibility of meeting their offspring when they reach adulthood than were women with different feelings about the process. Indeed, other donors are not as happy with the process[108] and report that financial motivation is a key component. Not surprisingly, money does affect the supply of egg donors on a national level. As Georgia Tech professor Aaron Levine notes,

[I]n the United Kingdom and Canada the compensation offered to donors is constrained. In these cases, when demand increases, compensation cannot be increased to draw out more supply. . . .

[P]olicy choices, particularly those affecting the compensation of oocyte donors, have influenced the development and use of this technology. . . . The United States, where compensation is only loosely constrained by voluntary guidelines has the highest per capita utilization of oocyte donation services.[109]

Both egg and sperm donors have a variety of concerns about having been a donor. They may worry about having children they will never know, or they may be concerned that, if they choose to try to contact their offspring, they will be unable to do so.[110] After Ruth Ragan donated eggs, like most donors, she never found out whether any children had been conceived; when she sees "awful parents" at a playground, she worries that her eggs may have been used to produce their victimized children. And she has changed:

> Over the years, thoughts about the happiness, safety and well-being of any donor-conceived children have slowly crept into my head, but it wasn't until I became a mother that they invaded. Between age 24 and 39 I changed; I became more loyal, more responsible, more patient and less of a risk-taker. I imagine that most anonymous egg donors, young women in their 20s, also change and grow in the years following their donation.[111]

Although she does not necessarily want to meet any offspring produced by her eggs, she does feel a responsibility to any child who has been born: to prevent accidental incest, to update her medical records, and to know that they are happy.

Those who people the donor world have varying motivations and interests. Clinics, donors, intending parents, and the government are all stakeholders involved in creating the children who will grow up in this world. They are also involved in challenging the definition of family, an issue explored in the next chapters.

2

The Meaning of Family in a Changing World

Are You My Mother?
—P. D. Eastman, 1960

The goal of participating in the donor world is to have a child in order to create, complete, or expand one's family. But changes in the structure of the American family over the past half-century are causing a cultural rethinking of what constitutes a *family*. The donor world helps show that the meaning of family in today's world is changing and becoming more complex. In 1968, famed anthropologist David Schneider was able to proclaim that Americans define "my family" as "a unit which contains a husband and wife and their child or children."[1] Indeed, he noted that living together as a unit was central to the notion of a family, and that married couples who did not have children, or whose children no longer lived with them, do "not quite make a family" in American culture.[2]

Even today, families are typically viewed as establishing and maintaining interdependencies between adult partners and/or their children, living together. Of course, with more than 40 percent of children born in nonmarital families, with the number of cohabitants increasing exponentially, with blended and stepfamilies becoming more pervasive, and with declining rates of marriage, our conceptions of "family" have undergone dramatic changes. Nonetheless, certain core concepts endure. When people are asked in public opinion polls to define a family, they overwhelmingly believe that anyone with a child qualifies.[3] While only 43 percent believe that an unmarried couple is a family, 80 percent believe that an unmarried couple with a child is a family, and 86 percent believe that a single parent with a child constitutes a family. Ninety-nine percent believe that a married couple with children is a family. For many people, having a baby creates kinship: there is an assumption or expectation of the importance of children, along with a norm of creating children through sexual reproduction. Social commentator Pamela Haag observes that children "are in some ways the new spouses. They occupy the psychological and sometimes literal space previously occupied by the spouse, or the marriage itself. They're the ones to whom commitment is made, the ones around whom intimacy is defined, the inviolable bond, the affective and even romantic focus of the family."[4]

This chapter explores changing meanings of the terms "family" and "parents" and then turns to some of the new forms of family that populate the donor-conceived world. After showing how donor-conceived families already complicate the traditional, biologically constructed family form, the chapter next examines other types of bonds that have lent further layers to the meaning of family, such as friendships and parenting relationships. The concept of family becomes more complex as we unravel the different choices made in creating kinship connections through biology, function, and intimacy. Finally, the chapter explores yet another challenge to our concepts of families as intimate havens: the buying and selling of gametes.

I. How Social Science Defines Family and Kinship

Social science is a good starting point for our examination of the meaning of family, especially within the fields of sociology and anthropology. Indeed, "the study of kinship," observe sociologist Sarah Franklin and anthropologist Susan McKinnon, "is itself symbolic of the anthropological tradition."[5] In politics and history, by contrast, the family has served as an assumed subject, less studied albeit relied upon as foundational to the public sphere.[6] Consequently, it is sociologists and anthropologists who are the primary sources of information about donor-related kinships.

According to social scientists, the American concept of kinship, relatives, and family relies on blood and marriage. Indeed, as Janet Dolgin, an anthropologist who is also a lawyer, explains, "in contemporary times family and kin tend to be stabilized and bounded by the sharing of DNA molecules."[7] Given the foundational nature of blood and genes, the increasingly visible use of new reproductive technologies can be seen in several ways. It may be transforma-tive, as anthropologist Nancy Levine explains, in challenging who counts as a family member and how families are formed. Alternatively, it may be conven-tional, drawing on notions of biological kinship and the existence of a child as the foundation of the family.[8] ART enables the formation of families with only one parent, with two parents of the same sex, and without sex. To some extent, as two anthropologists observe, ART has brought "ambiguity and uncertainty into kinship relations, including the fundamental categories of motherhood and fatherhood," and is, accordingly, "undermining the traditional family."[9] On the other hand, as they also note, the emphasis on the biological bond as form-ing a family, which is inherent both in the use of donor gametes and in the search for related family members, can be seen as supporting cultural conven-tions, seeking to replicate the family that would have existed but for the social or medical infertility.[10] Women using donor sperm and/or donor eggs may focus on their pregnancies and birth processes as a way of assimilating their experiences into the "normal" means of having a baby.[11]

The term "recombinant" can be used quite nicely to describe the develop-ment of donor-conceived families, according to famed British anthropologist Marilyn Strathern. Different elements of what constitutes becoming a mother or a father are being recombined in entirely new ways. The social, legal, and biological components of parenthood are separated, for example, when donors become disconnected—legally and medically and socially—from the biology of procreation.[12] Strathern sees similar patterns in the connections between children of divorced parents, who live in different families. Further extrapola-tion from her analysis shows that "recombinant" is also useful in describing the connections within donor-conceived family communities, where there are biological and social familial-type relationships, but no legal recognition.

The views from sociology and anthropology provide useful context for showing the changing, and culturally contingent, "nature" of the family. They help in establishing analogies to existing family types, and in evalu-ating the utility of assimilating donor-conceived families into our collective consciousness of what makes a family. Donor-conceived families and the kin networks they create show the need to reconsider and revise our conceptions of what "family" means. The way the law treats families sheds further light on what it means to be a member of a family.

II. How Law Defines Family and Kinship

Families are both public and private, existing within and outside of the law. Law recognizes some, but not all, intimate relationships, and carefully defines who qualifies as a parent (as discussed in chapter 5). Consider that the biological father of the child of a woman married to another man may have a DNA-based bond with that child, but not be part of that child's legal or social family.

Indeed, law helps in constructing what we mean by family as well as who "belongs" in that family by virtue of defining who qualifies as a legally recognized parent or child or partner. Legal definitions of family can greatly vary. The term "family" appears in zoning ordinances, specifying how many people can live in one unit; in public welfare, through programs such as Aid to Families with Dependent Children and Temporary Assistance to Needy Families; throughout trusts and estates; and even in criminal law. For example, to inherit from a parent, a child must establish that there is a parent-child relationship. Historically, under the common-law approach to inheritance, only a legitimate, blood-related child served as his father's heir, and many children who were genetically connected to their fathers were not entitled to inherit because they were nonmarital. Indeed, this principle was so strongly embedded in the law that illegitimate children were deemed to have "no" blood, and thus to be incapable of inheriting. Nor did legally adopted children always inherit from their adoptive parents or their parents' relatives. Today, a child who is genetically related to the parent, who is legally adopted by the parent, or, in the case of reproductive technology, whose parent has indicated consent to become the parent of an ART child can now establish her right to inherit as a child.[13]

Harvard professor Janet Halley and her colleague, Kerry Rittich, usefully describe four different strata of family law, an analysis that shows the need to look beyond the law of domestic relations for differing conceptions of the family.

Family Law 1—FL1—is what you will find in a modern family law code, course, bar exam, or casebook. It comprises marriage and its alternatives: divorce, parental status, and parental rights and duties.... [Family Law 2 involves] the explicit family-targeted provisions peppered throughout substantive legal regimes that seem to have no primary commitment to maintaining the distinctiveness of the family—regimes ranging from tax law to immigration law to bankruptcy law.... [Family Law 3 consists of] the myriad legal regimes that contribute structurally but silently to the ways in which family life is lived and the household structured.... [I]magine occupancy limits in landlord/tenant law that give more or less protection to incumbents; employment rules that permit dismissal on the part of the employer "at will" or, by contrast, require employers to give notice to employees who are dismissed without cause; rules that exclude house-hold employees from the protective legislation governing workplaces or that craft special regimes governing such employees. . . . [Family Law 4] attend[s] to a wide range of informal norms, as they may substantially alter the impact of FL1, 2, and 3 and, in some cases, effectively "govern" the household.[14]

As this analysis of the layers of family law makes clear, definitions of the family, and regulations structuring the family, appear in numerous places throughout the law and can deeply affect who is considered to be family. They are also historically contingent. In the mid-twentieth century, women who used donor sperm might be accused of adultery, of having sex with a nonfamily member, even when a doctor performed the insemination. The resulting children might then be deemed illegitimate.

While adultery is no longer alleged, and parentage law, as discussed in the next chapter, has changed, there are still multiple meanings and definitions of the deceptively simple word "parent." "Stepparent," "social parent," "legal parent," "functional parent," and "de facto parent" are some of the terms that are used outside of the donor world. Gays and lesbians who adopt their part-ners' children are engaging in "second parent" adoptions. Indeed, legal defi-nitions of the meaning of family have changed dramatically over time.

If the word "parent" is capable of legal definition, manipulation, and vari-ation, so too is the word "child." While, as discussed in the parentage chapter, varying definitions arise in custody and caretaking disputes, this is also true in inheritance law. The legal question of who constitutes a "family member" is essentially a question of *status.* Certain people are entitled to inherit from a person who has died because they are legally connected, so children inherit from their parents because of the relational status conferred on them. (Of course, parents can always disinherit their children by writing a will, but unless the parents provide otherwise, various default rules decide who is a child. Even when parents write a will, there may still be questions about non-marital children.)

Relational status has typically been based on biology or adoption and, more recently, on functioning as a parent by providing care for a child. Today, as the donor world shows, even a biological relationship does not nec-essarily confer child status; issues involving an individual's status as a "child" also arise when children are conceived after the death of a genetic parent, using gametes stored by the parent before his or her death. Even though the genetic parents may have been married to one another, gametes from the dead spouse may be treated in the same way as those of an anonymous donor, so the biological child is not the husband/donor's legal child. That's what happened to W.M.S., the biological child of Don Schafer, Jr. Don and Janice were married in June 1992. Four months later, Don learned that he had cancer and that his cancer treatments might leave him sterile. He deposited sperm samples in a long-term storage facility in December 1992, and died in early 1993. In 1999, six years after her husband's death, Janice used Don's stored sperm and became pregnant through IVF. She gave birth to W.M.S. in January 2000, and then sought Social Security benefits for her child. In April 2011, a federal court finally held that W.M.S. was not a "child" of Don for purposes of receiving Social Security, even though he apparently intended that Janice use his sperm to give birth to their child.[15]

Blended families with stepchildren or with foster children may involve no legally enforceable relationship between the child and her parents. By contrast, when a stepparent adopts a child, the child may still be able to inherit through the biological parent whose rights were terminated. The changing inheritance laws show that the possibilities of deciding who is a "child" are contingent not just culturally but also legally.

III. Beyond Biology: Alternative Family Forms

Changing family forms have an impact on cultural definitions of how to define a family as well as on legal terminology and rights. Donor-conceived families are just one type of newly developing family form. Other challenges to the conventional family involve new types of adult relationships as well as new ways of establishing parenthood without marriage, and they too show the need to adjust existing laws and cultural notions.

Sociologists have labeled relationships involving intimate adult partners who do not live in the same household but who think of themselves as a couple as "living apart together relationships" (or LATs).[16] While LATs involve the establishment of kinship without children and do not involve a genetic tie, unlike donor-conceived families, they nonetheless show how the traditional definition of family is being challenged from numerous directions and by multiple forms of family. This new family form provides insight into the contemporary search for, and the meaning of, family bonds, showing how even intimate partners may never live together and that the recognition of family ties can transcend separated residences.

The term "LAT" itself appears to have originated in a 1978 Dutch newspaper article,[17] and has now become internationally recognized. Members of the couple may live in the same city, or may maintain their households at a distance from one another; nonetheless, they self-define as intimate partners.

The term describes a residential arrangement rather than a legal relationship; indeed, some LATs are married and may be raising children together. "LAT" may actually be more descriptive of status for approximately one-third of people identified as "single" in various demographic surveys.[18] In one of the few in-depth studies, the researchers found similarities and differences between LATs and other intimate partnerships. For example, although everyone could rely on his or her partner for support, "the predicted probability of being able to rely on a partner 'a lot' for help with a serious problem is .87 for a married person, .82 for a cohabiter, and .59 for someone in a LAT union."[19] Moreover, in contrast to married couples, heterosexuals who were in LAT unions valued independence more highly, and were more likely to expect egalitarianism with respect to both paid work and family care.[20]

This does not necessarily mean that LAT relationships should be excluded from the application of traditional family law, but it might suggest somewhat different presumptions on issues like property division or maintenance upon dissolution. LATs exist outside of the traditional ideal of settled romantic and intimate love, but they are nonetheless framed by those traditions.[21]

A second challenge to the traditional family is based on a recognition of relationships that are not intimate sexually and are not based on shared genetics but are intimate emotionally, relationships that exist on a continuum of family and friendship. People may clearly distinguish between their expectations of friends and family. Indeed, many people continue to live in families where the primary focus is interacting with other kin; that is, some families, especially in the working-class world, live in communities that revolve around kin interaction.[22] In the alternative, friends and family may "play[] rather similar roles,"[23] and the two roles may be blurred together ("she's like a sister to me"). It is this latter category, where friends and family are comparable, that provides space for donor-conceived family communities.

Sociologists have studied the changing boundaries between friendship and kinship, noting that, in order to determine whether boundaries have shifted, there must be some clarity as to the meanings of both terms. In their study of friendship, British sociologists Ray Pahl and Liz Spencer noted that, notwithstanding the range in types of relationships labeled as friendships (from coworkers to soul mates), "friends were perceived as playing family-like roles and family as playing friend-like roles. For example, where there was generalized rather than specific reciprocity, where a strong sense of obligation and utter dependability existed between friends, where they loved as well as liked each other and the relationship had lasted many years, the ties were referred to as family-like."[24] In their in-depth study of friendships, sociologists Sasha Roseneil and Shelley Budgeon found that communities of friends may be more important to daily life than sexual partnerships, such that "[c]are and support flow between individuals with no biological, legal, or social recognized ties to each other."[25] They characterize some of the friendships as "ethical practices," with a corresponding series of responsibilities toward one another.[26] The second place for blurred boundaries involves "families of choice," a term with particular salience to gay and lesbian couples and to others who build "kinship" without biological relationships.[27]

Friendship itself is a positive good; the psychological and social support from friendship can provide tangible benefits beyond the emotional ones. An individual's happiness is affected by the happiness of others in the same social network.[28] When people are surrounded by many other happy people, and when they are central in their network, then they are also more likely to become happy in the future.[29] For example, researchers asked study participants to estimate the steepness of a hill. Participants who were accompanied by a friend estimated the incline to be lower than participants who were alone.[30] And ultimately, friends help friends live longer. In a review of 148 studies involving 308,849 participants, the researchers found a 50 percent increased chance of survival for those with strong social relationships.[31]

Of course, friendship can also be powerful in creating negative consequences; for example, social influence is one explanation for the obesity epidemic in the United States.[32] Friends can similarly impact depression: researchers have found that "not only may depressed mood spread across social ties, but also that depression depends on how connected individuals are and where they are located within social networks."[33]

The strength and power of such support might even provide the basis for imposing fiduciary obligations on close friendships as recognition of the expectations of loyalty, good faith, and confidentiality.[34] The care that could become subject to such obligations might be between adults or between adults and children, and might, for example, involve contracts providing rights to a nonparent for ongoing caregiving to a child.[35] Indeed, recognition of friendship would mean "that marriage need not be the only site for emotional care and support,"[36] thereby opening up other possibilities.

A final, and related, challenge to traditional presumptions of how families are created involves establishing legal parenthood for men who have never lived with their children or the mother, or for coparents who have no biological relationship to a child but have lived with the child. In the first category of cases, there is a biological tie, but no residential one, and there may be limited emotional bonds; in the second category of parenthood cases, there is no biology, but there is coresidence and strong emotional connection. The general rule for establishing paternity if the parents were not married at the time of the child's conception or birth allows for fatherhood to be established voluntarily or in other ways, such as if the man "held out" the child as his own, and lived with the child for at least two years.[37] Cohabiting is thus an important element in establishing (or disestablishing) paternity. Nonetheless, men who have not lived with their children have been deemed fathers. If, for example, the biological father does not live with the mother and child, and waits a substantial period of time before asserting paternity, then states may find the social, de facto father who has cohabited with the mother and held out the child to be his own to also be the legal father. Nonetheless, while social parenthood can win out over biological parenthood, in the absence of a social parent, the biological father with little or no emotional connection may be labeled the legal father. The second category of cases involves non-marital couples who raise children together. When the adults have a long-term relationship, the children often consider both partners to be their parents. Based on equitable doctrines, courts have become increasingly likely to allow biological "strangers" to establish legally recognized relationships in some situations, regardless of the lack of biological connection.

These alternative forms of family provide empirical, real-life grounding for developing legal categories that recognize additional members of the family circle. While the traditional family deserves protection, these other relationships, either not based on cohabitation or not involving dependency, may also merit protection. Together, they open up some space to expand our notions of, and protections for, a wider range of kinship forms.

IV. Buying and Selling Genetic Connection

As we consider this wider range of kinship forms, there is a potentially disturbing paradox in the donor world: both egg and sperm "donors" are selling their bodily products to people willing to pay for them, and these bodily products result (ideally) in the creation of babies. Consequently, the fundamental question of how the donor world affects the meaning of family is raised quite clearly by the involvement of commercial transactions, with payment obviously implicating the very creation of familial relationships.

While some countries have banned payment for gametes, and while some providers truly donate their gametes without receiving any payment, most gametes in the United States are bought and sold through specific banks, agencies, or fertility clinics. Gamete provision explicitly mixes money, emotion, and dreams. The simultaneous outrage about higher payments, yet the willingness to make those payments, for specific attributes—high SATs, willingness to be known—reflects both an antipathy to assigning monetary value to these attributes and an acknowledgment that they are more valuable in our culture. (It may also reflect envy and disgust at creating designer babies.)

V. Donor Payment

The Ethics Committee of the American Society for Reproductive Medicine (ASRM) has developed guidelines on payments to gamete donors, observing that while payment may raise some ethical issues, compensation can nonetheless be supported. While there are no specific amounts for sperm donors, the ASRM has suggested that payments to egg donors that exceed five thousand dollars require justification while payments above ten thousand dollars are inappropriate.[38] To develop these suggestions, the ethics committee compared the processes of egg and sperm donation. Based on an estimate that oocyte donors spent fifty-six hours in the medical setting while sperm donors spent only one hour, earning approximately sixty to seventy-five dollars, the committee extrapolated from that amount to arrive at the appropriate payment for egg donation of $3,360 to $4,200. In recognition of the greater discomfort and risks for egg donors, together with their longer time commitment, the committee found a slightly higher payment for egg donors to be justified. The compensation scale, it noted, should ensure that women are not unduly induced to downplay the potential risks.

While the recommendations have not been entirely successful in limiting payments to egg donors, they have resulted in a court case claiming that the guidelines constitute illegal price fixing. Lindsay Kamakahi, an egg donor, filed a lawsuit in May 2011 on her own behalf and also on behalf of anyone else who had sold donor services during a four-year period against the American Society for Reproductive Medicine and other fertility-related organizations who had agreed to comply with the egg donor financial guidelines. Legal scholar Kim Krawiec observes that while the lawsuit is fairly straightforward, and in the antitrust context, doesn't raise particularly challenging issues because "it's a naked horizontal agreement to fix prices and is thus per se illegal," she nonetheless believes that "romanticism and/or paranoia" have tended

to distort discussions of this market. In other words, very few observers have analyzed the oocyte trade for what it is—a profitable industry. Instead, the starting assumption seems to be that the egg market must differ from other markets because egg donors are engaged in a form of philanthropy that distinguishes them from suppliers in other industries.[39]

That is, the language of altruism should not distort the existence of a market and the price-fixing efforts to control that market in a way that reinforces the misleading characterization of the underlying transactions.

Indeed, the attempt to control the price paid to egg donors does not protect egg donors, but might instead be seen as an attempt by the fertility industry to show that it is capable of responding to public concerns about fertility treatments, and should not be subject to additional regulation.[40]

And, indeed, some argue that there is nothing unethical about paying for eggs. "It may lead some women to become egg donors who would not otherwise do so, but that does not mean that they have been exploited, much less unfairly induced," wrote law professor John A. Robertson of the University of Texas. As he noted, banning payments to egg donors could drastically reduce the number of eggs that are donated. He criticized the ASRM for not explaining what is inappropriate about "paying women who are healthier, more fertile, have a particular ethnic background, a high IQ, or some other desirable characteristics. . . . After all, we allow individuals to choose their mates and sperm donors on the basis of such characteristics. Why not choose egg donors similarly?"[41]

Some countries have banned payment for gametes, while others have developed niche markets based on relatively lax regulation and low prices.[42] The underlying issues concern attitudes toward paying for body parts, issues that arise not just in prostitution but also in the surrogacy market. Sociologists, feminist economists, and lawyers have begun to excavate the different meanings of money, questioning its allegedly essentializing nature. They have identified two different "discourses of money" that ascribe enormous power to the influence of money on social transactions: one discourse in which money leads to debasement of what is measured in economic terms and a second in which money leads to liberation.[43] Clearly, both discourses have been used when it comes to housework. But, more importantly, these writers have also begun to critique a focus solely on money as the instrument through which debasement or liberation occurs, suggesting instead that money interacts with social forces, and vice versa—that is, that money cannot be isolated as the only factor that determines value and meaning.[44] The mere introduction of money into a relationship does not necessarily remove intimacy, and donor-conceived families, where parents purchase missing gametes, are clear illustrations of how money can—literally—buy intimacy for the parents. The purchase for money may cause more ambivalence for donor-created offspring, who may instead see the gamete producer as a biological parent, while it may help the gamete producer feel distance from "products."

Not surprisingly, and simultaneously with this understanding of the inter-relationship between the market and the family, there has developed some-thing identified as commodification anxiety,[45] or concern about placing eco-nomic value on activities as a means of removing all of the emotional value associated with those activities. Commodification, here, can be thought of as the transformation of a good or service that is not generally considered something that can be bought or sold into precisely that kind of product. According to this perspective, a market in gametes not only treats the goods themselves as commodities but also commodifies the humans who produce the gametes and in so doing, plays a crucial role in creating families.

The Canadian ethicist Margaret Somerville asks,

> How will the child feel knowing that [his or her] genetic parent sold—and that [his or her] social parent bought—what is (as one donor-conceived woman put it) "the essence of [their] life for $25 to a total stranger, and then walked away without a second look back? What kind of a man sells himself and his child so cheaply and so easily?" Is there something gravely ethically wrong with the commercialization of the miracle of the passing on of human life?[46]

The answer, for some people and in some countries such as Canada and the United Kingdom, is yes: selling gametes is unethical or illegal. Indeed, in recommending that Australia continue to ban payment for donors, a Senate committee noted its concern that donors might provide gametes only for the money, and pointed out that several donor-conceived people mentioned the harmful effects of knowing that their donor was paid.[47]

Yet commodifying gametes can also lead to positive outcomes that rein-force or foster the creation or meaning of families. Denying the possibility of payment also, arguably, denies the possibility of economic value for work performed. Moreover, a market means less control, thereby allowing the pos-sibility of alternative families.[48] And, as law professor Martha Ertman points out, a market in sperm empowers women, turning men, rather than women, into sex objects.[49]

The question, then, is not whether to commodify the family but what to commodify, and how this affects the definition of the family. Introducing eco-nomic concerns into the family does not necessarily "impoverish" family life by corrupting it with cold cash.[50] Money is already present in the family; to deny this buys into assumptions that, because caretaking is a labor of love, it is not labor at all.[51] This does not mean that many of us do not have a vis-ceral reaction against quantifying every action that occurs within the family.

Professor Milton Regan uses a scene from Amy Tan's novel *The Joy Luck Club* to dramatize the awkwardness of autonomy without community in marriage. The mother of Lena, the main character, notices that her daughter and son-in-law have developed a careful accounting of expenses with a bottom line that her daughter will owe money to her son-in-law; Lena explains that she and her husband want to "eliminate false dependencies . . . be equals . . . love without obligation."[52] As Professor Regan observes, this couple is missing the richness and interdependence of relationship that is inherent in our cultural concept of family. Keeping track of each expenditure, accounting for each caretaking activity, does seem contrary to the very notion of intimate relationships.

In other family settings as well, we may wonder about the impact of commodification. Years ago, Professor Margaret Radin asked, "If a free-market baby industry were to come into being, with all of its accompanying paraphernalia, how could any of us, even those who did not produce infants for sale, avoid measuring the dollar value of our children? How could our children avoid being preoccupied with measuring their own dollar value?"[53] The answer to that is simple: I buy life insurance, valuing my life (at my death) in a certain way that has relatively little to do with how I think of myself on a day-to-day basis. That is, putting a price on something does not necessarily destroy its intrinsic (nonmonetary) value, or indicate that it is measured only by its economic price.[54] Indeed, as sociologist Viviana Zelizer demonstrates in the context of children's value, as children became less economically valuable because they were increasingly excluded from the workplace, there was a corresponding increase in their financial and emotional value.[55] (Although Professor Zelizer does not fully explain why children became more emotionally valuable, certainly part of the explanation must come from the declining birth rate, and the decreasing number of children in each family; the ideology of motherhood that exalted white, middle-class, stay-at-home moms also needed an appropriate object for their energy.) And, cash price is inevitably influenced by values outside of the market. Moreover, as Professor Radin also points out, it is possible for both market and nonmarket understandings to coexist.[56] Indeed, the literature on tort remedies as well as the equitable distribution shows how economic valuation of household services can exist simultaneously with noneconomic understandings of caretaking and intimacy.[57] Commodification anxiety actually covers up the fact that many family services are already paid for, simply at an inadequate rate; it is only when we try to commodify work performed by parents or spouses themselves[58] that the anxiety suddenly appears.

Like family, money has different meanings, depending on the context. Paying a woman to take care of children could be seen as domestic wages or a domestic gift, or an early payment by the children, or one gift in recognition of another.[59] Providing for economic recognition of child care and housework services—without necessarily taking the form of paying directly for that work—does not remove the many other motivations inherent in this work, and may serve only to reinforce them.[60] Even when people are paid to take care of someone else, this work requires some connection between the one providing the care and the one cared for, or else it would not be care work.[61] Correspondingly, suggesting that people work only for the money (while certainly true in some cases) overlooks the many other values that influence people's choice of occupations—a job doing child care may pay the same as, or even less than, a job a McDonald's, but each involves different choices and priorities. Because of the requirements of caring work, many workers are not simply motivated by money, thus providing one alleged, ironic, and illegitimate justification for why their wages are depressed: they don't need to be paid as much because of the intangible rewards they get from their work.

Donors are often motivated by altruism—by the desire to help others—but the money is also an important inducement. When we leave out money, when we refuse to value the work that is done, or when we reduce all work to money, we essentialize the complex transactions that characterize family, and work, life. Indeed, behind each gamete, there are actually two sales transactions: a sperm bank typically pays some money for each ejaculation and, in turn, sells that sperm to the intending parents. A woman can sell her eggs to an in vitro fertilization program for thousands of dollars, although some women may receive tens of thousands of dollars. By allowing the sale of sperm and eggs, we are, in a sense, treating them, as a "product."

Interestingly enough, allowing payment for services and making the services quantifiable revisits the distinction between goods and services established by Article 2 of the Uniform Commercial Code: services are not covered, but goods are. In the domestic context, perhaps this distinction is backward. We may be unable to value appropriately a good child or a clean house, and we probably should not, but we can attempt to value the services involved in producing these goods. Or, we could distinguish between the goods: children are not fungible, the cleanliness of a house is. (And, of course, art is not fungible either, and we allow the sale of that.) If babies and children can be sold, then how much are they worth? Is a surrogate selling gestational services, or is she selling a child? Law professor Radhika Rao suggests that body parts can be sold so long as the person does not have a relationship to the part; thus, spare embryos can be sold, but contested embryos, where both parents want custody, require heightened scrutiny.[62]

Debates about the impact of money, in a culture that values money, can have a real effect on poor people who are, almost inherently, defined by their lack of money. Recognizing the value of work performed in their own homes by poor women can transform the controversies over public welfare while providing better care for the children of poor mothers. The movement to understanding market relationships as more than economically based, as social,[63] helps us, simultaneously, in understanding that social relationships, such as the family, are not just socially based but are economic as well. Moreover, money is not fungible. Money as payment for services seems to imply alienation of labor, while money as a gift seems to reward a voluntary undertaking, and is not treated as the basis for a contract. Both, however, can be rewards for the same conduct, although only the former is typically thought of as adequate for a contract.[64]

So the question is how "to structure social relationships that involve elements of both,"[65] rather than banning financial transactions altogether. Coherent discussions of commodification should begin with parsing out the stakes and interests of each market participant and examining why regulation might be appropriate. Yes, money does make sperm and eggs available, allowing children to be created from DNA that is purchased. And yes, money seems to help ensure a viable supply of gametes. Consider what happened in Canada once the government banned compensation for donors: the supply dried up.[66] Similarly, Australia has seen its supply of donors decrease dramatically on the basis of a prohibition on payment. Yet in the United States, payment has not prevented donors from feeling responsibilities to those using, or conceived from, their gametes. Restructuring gamete sales may mean continuing to allow payment but also requiring that donors provide updated medical information and agree to limited disclosure of their identities once offspring reach a certain age. Today, most goods and services are sold with warranties. Additional requirements on donors recognize that a product is being sold but also recognize the special nature of that product; it doesn't just prolong life, it creates life. Paying for eggs or sperm to create a familial relationship is not inherently a paradox, but is instead approached far more flexibly by participants in the donor world.

As part 1 has shown, donor-conceived families and their kin networks call for a deeply nuanced understanding of the meaning of family relationships, even as they affirm and challenge concepts of genetically based relationships. Part 2 provides further depth to the concept of family by unpacking how donor-conceived families are created, and the larger communities they form.

PART II

Creating Donor-Conceived Families and Communities

3

Creating Families

When people enter the donor world, they are looking for children. And, almost always, they are hoping for children who will be genetically related to them or to their partner and for children who will have "good genes." Indeed, as they create families, they do so in a cultural context where biogenetic relationships are central, almost "mythical."[1]

This chapter explores the first type of new kinship that is created through the use of third-party gametes: the kinship created between parent and child and, in two-parent families, the development of new connections between partners who must now see themselves as parents as well as intimate partners. Having a child changes the relationship between the parents, so, when a donor-conceived family is created, not only does this form a new parent-child relationship, but it also can transform the bonds between the parents. The first part of this chapter explores donor-gamete shopping as a way of appreciating the complicated status of genes before turning, in the second part, to examining how using a third party's gametes can foster ties between within a family.

I. Connection Shopping

When people shop for a donor, they may turn to friends or acquaintances who agree to serve as known donors. Known donors allow the recipient a great deal of control over the choice of gametes and make questions about potential health issues easier to handle. In the 2010 movie *The Switch*, Kassie (played by Jennifer Aniston) hires Roland, a blond stud who is also a feminist studies professor, to produce the sperm that ultimately results in the birth of her son, Sebastian. Years later, Roland and Kassie reconnect, and they begin dating. Roland can't understand why Sebastian prefers Wally, Kassie's brown-haired, somewhat neurotic best friend, to him. And Wally does bond, intensely, with Sebastian, even—or especially—when Wally turns out to be responsible for delicing Sebastian. As Roland is about to propose to Kassie, Wally confesses that he had drunkenly purloined Roland's cup of sperm and replaced it with his—even though Kassie had flatly rejected him as a potential donor. Kassie is furious, but the movie ends with Kassie and Wally reconciling.[2]

Many relationships with known donors are, indeed, successful. Sociologist Judith Stacey, for example, describes the formal and informal arrangements between Paul, a gay man, and Nancy, a lesbian, who signed a "coparenting agreement" and shared primary parenting responsibilities, as well as a house, with their two children and with Nancy's partner.[3] Their initial parenting agreement, Stacey notes, has become a model for others, and it sets out arrangements for a variety of otherwise potentially divisive issues, ranging from naming rights to support obligations. In England, co-parentmatch.com describes itself as a site that allows people to connect either with a potential coparent or with a sperm donor or recipient.[4] Several other sites facilitate this kind of "platonic parenting," and people have arranged long-term relationships with elaborate visitation schedules.[5] These private arrangements, involving no sexual intimacy between the parents, provide concrete examples of the way ART creates new types of kinship.

Nonetheless, some known sperm donor arrangements disintegrate into messy court cases when the donor seeks to assert too many legal rights or there has been no advance negotiation of potential roles. Reproductive endocrinologists have told me numerous stories of women who, as they are lying down to be inseminated, explain the role of a known sperm donor: "He'll do anything I ask him to do," they might say. Well, maybe. While a known donor assures that any resulting child will always have access to information about the genetic parent and, perhaps, to the parent as well, there is no guarantee that the donor will, in fact, do anything, that is asked.

Given the potential complications of known donors, many shoppers go to the Internet to search for anonymous donors. Online, they can learn an enormous amount about their potential donor, about the donor's genes, about the donor's education, and even about the donor's politics. Gamete shopping occurs primarily on the Web, where sites invite prospective parents to consider ethnicity, SAT scores, hair color, and personality tests. As Cheryl Shuler, a single-mother-by-choice, explained the process, "For anyone who has trouble choosing among the moo-goo-gai-pan, moo shu pork or sweet and sour shrimp at a Chinese restaurant, selecting the father of your child could be a really tough one."[6] Many banks even offer childhood photos or tape recordings of the donor's voice or even handwriting samples—for a fee. On the World Egg Bank website, potential egg recipients can learn the following about potential donor 4158 in addition to her date of birth and the fact that she is attending college:[7]

TABLE 3.1

Eye Color: Brown
Ethnicity: Italian
Height: 5'6"
Hair Color: Brown
Eggs Available: Now
Weight: 124

The initial screening for the sperm donor program at Growing Generations includes verifying the donor's GPA as well as administering a test that measures the donor's general intellectual abilities. Only a few of the people who express interest in becoming donors—approximately 1-2 percent—ultimately make the grade.[8]

All of these different attributes and products can be quite appealing, although the market is segmented. Women who are single, explains Trine Rodgard, who helps run a Scandinavian sperm bank in Manhattan, invariably "want the highest-IQ, most good-looking babies."[9] Or, they may want to play the "what if" game, providing their children with the opportunity for blue eyes rather than their brown ones.[10] Others want certain ethnicities or religions, and some are willing to pay more for donors who agree to be identified once a child turns eighteen. Cheryl Shuler developed an elaborate accounting system to help her review potential donors in which she enlisted a friend to help her highlight each potential donor's positive qualities in pink, undesirable attributes in yellow, and then tabulate the results.[11]

The donor profiles promise good genes, and are accompanied by the almost explicit message "that genetics are everything—everything—in the formation of your child." And parents of course believe they owe the child the best genes. As one gay couple put it, "What are you going to do—get someone with a 1550 [SAT score], or are you going to cheat your child and get them a mom with a 1210?"[12]

Indeed, one of the themes discussed throughout this book is the complex role that genes play within the donor world. During the selection process, they are "everything" when it comes to a child's appearance and academic and social success. When you have the option of picking genes (by selecting a donor), then genes can become more important than other things, such as trying to have the healthiest possible baby, as people try to get the closest match to their own biological makeup or to their partner's, and in so doing actually replicate the traditional family model, or as they try to create children with high IQs or who are physically stunning or who don't carry genes for particular diseases. Genes are also critical in explaining the potential development of donor-conceived family communities. But they are not "everything" when it comes to how a child is related to someone who thinks of herself as a parent but is not genetically related. And, while intending parents want to know "everything" about the donor's genes, they do not want to know the identity of the person who contains those genes. Ultimately, however, if intending parents want biologically related children (or at least children who look biologically related) and choose donors on the basis of their genes, then it should not be surprising when the children want to know more about their biological parents and the genes they have inherited.

Choosing genes has become so important that the donor world is in the midst of controversies about "designer babies." California Cryobank places donors in groups according to their resemblance to celebrities such as actor Ben Affleck or football star Brett Favre.[13] Through the trademarked "CCB Donor Look-a-Likes" program, prospective purchasers can click on a link that will take them to photos of two or three celebrities whom the staff has decided are the closest matches to the donor.[14] The director of operations at another sperm banks defends this practice of choosing traits (albeit not necessarily the practice of enabling celebrity look-a-like gene pools):

> This talk is more science fiction than fact because using donor sperm doesn't allow someone to manipulate genes and create the perfect baby or design the baby of their dreams. The use of donor sperm simply allows women the ability to conceive and become pregnant. Being able to select a donor based on his hair color, eye color, ethnicity, education or his

interests doesn't constitute making designer babies and saying so cheapens the emotional experience that many women and couples have when using donor sperm.[15]

The ethical controversy in choosing specific attributes—brains, brawn, or deafness—leads to claims of selective breeding and eugenics,[16] and to questions about the emphasis on good genes. At the same time, the ability to use donor eggs and sperm shows that technological change and interventions can produce family and kinship.[17] As the next sections discuss, the donor selection process produces numerous bonds: between the parents, between the child and the parents, between the donor and donor-conceived family members, and between families who have used the same donor.

II. Creating Connections
1. Supplemental Ties between the Parents

The choice of gametes also creates the possibility for fostering kinship between the intending parents. When recipients are single, they generally contribute their own gametes and then choose a donor on the basis of a variety of different criteria. They may want the child to look like them, or they may want to find someone who complements their strengths or compensates for their weaknesses: a humanities major might seek a donor who is an engineer. Or, they may be looking for the perfect partner: indeed, Fairfax Cryobank explicitly compares choosing a donor to choosing a partner.[18]

When recipients are coupled, the equation changes. There are complex motivations with respect to choosing a donor, but they often center on replicating the genetic makeup of the nonbiological parent and on ensuring that offspring are genetically related to one parent and to any potential siblings. The intending parents may want to create ties that reflect their relationship, creating even more ties between the two of them. Author Amie Miller quite candidly states that she "wanted to find a donor who could be a genetic proxy for Jane, because what we really wanted, truth be told, was to make a baby together. I wanted this anonymous man to be a silent partner, to transmit the qualities Jane would give if we could make a baby ourselves."[19] One gay male couple only hired surrogates who would be willing to carry twins in the hopes that one egg fertilized by each of their sperm would develop so that they could "use reproductive science to come as close as possible to having children together."[20]

In her compassionate book designed to guide people through the donor world, Diane Ehrensaft quotes one woman's explanation of her search for a sperm donor: "'We looked for those [donors] who had characteristics of each of our heritages, facial features, even personalities. We also tried to read between the lines of their answers to questions about favorite color, desire for travel, long-term goals, SAT scores.'"[21] There is an attempt to replicate their "as if" family, albeit with an explicit effort to screen for positive attributes. Finding the right match can help create a tie not only between the nonbiological parent and the child but also among family members. One woman describes her search: "'Did the donor look enough like both of us that the child would look enough like both of us? . . . [W]e thought a donor who also had similar coloring would make us all seem connected, you know.'"[22]

Although using donor gametes inherently includes a third person in the reproductive process, parents often try to erase any signs of that person's independent existence. Choosing a donor who simulates the characteristics of the intending parents can help the parents feel more control over their own procreation, as well as their child's future.[23]

2. Creating Ties between the Parent(s) and the Child

In recognition of the fact that most people do, indeed, want a genetic connection with their child, one therapist warns that before heterosexual families consider using donors, "you will need to grieve the loss of the child you were not able to have with your own genes."[24] She suggests that prospective parents ask themselves a series of questions, such as, "How will we feel about unequal genetic relatedness to our child? Will we feel attached to our child?"[25] For lesbian couples, she includes similar questions, but also asks whether the couple might want to consider using one woman's egg while the other carries the pregnancy;[26] for gay couples, she asks whether each man wants to fertilize the egg.[27] These questions suggest the possibilities of genetic connection between parent and child, even when there are no shared genes, and also promote, rather than challenge, the privileging and prioritizing of genetic ties. Peggy Orenstein was quite candid about needing to grieve the potential loss of genetic connection: as she started taking the hormones for a donor egg cycle, she was filled with "tangled" feelings, including gratitude to her donor as well as "grief that I'd never see my smile on a child."[28]

Couples are quite conscious of creating children who have strong physical ties to them, even if they are not biological. As journalist Melanie Thernstrom described her search, "an egg donor has a striking claim on the imagination: it is the opportunity to choose a genetic replacement for yourself."[29] In fact, she even fantasizes that the woman chosen to be her egg donor "was the person I would have been" had a few things in her life been different.[30] Social worker Iris Waichler explains,

> We chose a donor that had my physical characteristics. Grace was born with dark brown hair like mine. She had dark hazel eyes with wisps of brown. My eyes are brown. Over the 10 years since she was born there have been several comments about how much we look alike. As far as I know she does not have the "cancer gene" that my family members carry.[31]

Grace looks like her mother, but is even better!

There are numerous ways to simulate—or even create real—genetic bonds that reinforce a familial image. Planethospital.com offers a variety of medical services, including fertility procedures, in overseas hospitals, along with "concierge services."[32] Among the packages available are "splitting eggs from the same donor to fertilize with different sperm, so children of gay couples can share a genetic mother."[33] When sociologist Judith Stacey studied family diversity in gay Los Angeles, she found Charles, Eddie, and their three children: Charles had provided sperm for their first child, Heather, and, using the same egg donor and surrogate, Eddie provided sperm that resulted in twin sons.[34] The egg donor believed it was important for her two children to know their genetic half-siblings, so the families remained in contact with one another.[35] Another strategy is for gay men to do a "mixed transfer," in which the eggs are fertilized with sperm from each man to ensure uncertainty about which of them is the biological father.[36] When singer Elton John and his partner, David Furnish, discussed the conception of their son, Furnish confessed. "'We both contributed. For the time being we don't have a clue. We look at him every day and at the moment he has Elton's nose and my hands.'"[37] On the other hand, he continued his explanation by discounting the importance of genes: "'Neither of us care. He's our child. The important thing is that he's healthy and happy and loved.'" The double theme—genes matter, but not really because he's our child regardless—appears explicitly. Even as they challenge traditional methods of creating the "natural" family, consumers of donor gametes often "buy into" traditional conceptions of the roles of genes and heredity.[38] As she tried coming to terms with her potential use of donor eggs, journalist Peggy Orenstein found herself

> toying with a new narrative, one that felt revolutionary rather than compensatory. With a donor egg I could still feel a baby grow inside me, experience its kicks and flutters. I could control—that sweetest of words—the prenatal environment, guard against the evils of drug and drink. I could

give birth to my own baby, breastfeed it. Who knew? Maybe for the child, that would make up for the genetic disconnect.[39]

In the absence of a genetic connection, Orenstein would still have a gestational connection with her baby. Being pregnant and giving birth provide an opportunity to form a biological, albeit not a genetic, connection with the child.[40] Indeed, science supports the importance of the gestation process. What happens during that time period has a profound impact on the baby; it is not just "the evils of drug and drink" that are significant in pregnancy but also the health of the mother's uterus, which can be critical to the baby's health.[41]

3. Imagining the Donor

Within the donor world, people may use words like "gamete providers," "donors," "biological parent," and "donor parent" to describe the person who provides egg or sperm to the intending or recipient parents, trying to debunk any romantic images of the donor. Moreover, each of these terms cloaks the speaker's legal and cultural judgments as to the donor's appropriate role with respect to offspring.

Where unknown donors are used, both parents and children may develop their own, sometimes shared, fantasies. In talking to their children about the donor, parents use various images. Commonly (as was true of Canadian Olivia Pratten, who sued to prevent donor anonymity), mothers explain that donor men have provided the "seed" that helps them hatch their eggs into children,[42] although the terminology varies by age. They may also then construct "fantasy" images of the donor father, using the absent man as the repository for any characteristics that differ from their own.[43] This same theme, imagining the unknown donor as the perfect partner, as completing their own gene set, of course, also appears before the child's birth, during the moments of gamete shopping. Not surprisingly, there is much less discussion of the fantasy donor in heterosexual families.

Indeed, in some families, the donor's contribution is minimized. Wendy Kramer, the director and cofounder of the Donor Sibling Registry (which serves as a resource for donor-conceived family members), recounts that she has "heard some parents describe their donor as 'just a piece of genetic material' or 'just a donated cell.'"[44] She admonishes, however, that the donor often represents far more than a DNA contribution, an observation that is reflected in the label "father" that donor offspring may use in describing this (unknown) part of their genetic heritage.[45] Indeed, children may have all kinds of fantasies about their donor. In her book, psychologist Diane Ehren-saft notes that one of the most significant questions for parents in the donor world is, "What if my child converts the 'nice man who donated my sperm' into the father of her dreams?"[46] She suggests that the donor

> may play a very active role in your children's fantasy life as they begin to shape their own identity. In my own practice, all the children I have worked with who know they have a donor have shown an interest at one time or another in the person who helped make them. . . . With limited information at their disposal, sometimes they'll feel compelled to construct an actual parent in fantasy.[47]

Similarly, adoptees may have developed fantasies about their biological parents, ranging from hopes that they are the children of royalty to fears that their mothers were prostitutes.[48]

Rainbow Flag Health Services uses known donors, and it explicitly addresses the potential for hagiography—or denigration. The sperm bank discloses the donor's identity to the mother when the baby is three months old, and requests that she contact the donor before the child turns one. Rainbow Flag explains, "Your child will grow up without secrets. They will not grow up fantasizing that their 'father' is the lost King of Bavaria or Charles Manson. Your child will know that their donor is a regular guy who they will meet and maybe become friends with."[49]

Because children may view their donors as fantasy parents, recipient parents may view donors as threatening genetic parents. Because donor-conceived offspring label their gamete providers as "donor parents," they may face disapproval for not being able to distinguish between their true parents and third parties who provided gametes. Lawrie McFarlane, a former deputy minister of health in British Columbia, exhorted, "Someone who donates sperm is no more a father than the lab technician in a fertility clinic," and "bringing anonymous donors into the family circle . . . elbow[s] aside the genuine parents—those who cherish and care for the child."[50] McFarlane's statement suggests that biological progenitors are being conflated with the nurturing and caring adults who actually raise a child, but this is misguided. First, McFarlane entirely overlooks the role of biology; lab technicians may facilitate the creation of children, but they do not contribute to the child's genetic makeup. Second, notwithstanding fantasies about the donor, most donor-conceived people understand the distinction between their biological and legal parents, and, as discussed earlier, when they search for their donors, they are not looking for new parents. Looking for a donor does not negate the role and contributions of the child's parents. To be sure, an oft-articulated fear among donor parents concerns the threats posed by a donor-conceived child searching for contact, and helps explain why parents may not have told their children about their origins. As philosopher David Velleman notes about adoptees, "a child is capable of forming attachments to absent figures, provided that they are present to its thoughts as real objects."[51]

4. Creating Ties between Siblings

Genes also create ties between siblings who grow up in the same family, and parents deliberately foster these bonds. In the popular movie *The Kids Are All Right*, the two moms choose the same donor to ensure biologically related siblings. I know of cases where one child may have the intending mother's egg and donor sperm while a second child has the same donor's sperm but the mother has used a donor egg. The children are genetically related to each other, and one of them is also genetically related to the mother. One of the largest sperm banks in the world, Denmark's Cryos, counsels that using the same donor for subsequent pregnancies might foster positive mental health consequences: "Some children might develop identity problems later in life if they are told about the donor insemination. It might, however, help them if they are 100% genetically related to their brothers or sisters."[52]

Donor parents often discuss their desire to create biologically related siblings, and they may desperately search for vials of sperm from the same donor as their older children. Indeed, sperm banks may suggest that consumers order extra vials of the same donor so that they can produce genetically related siblings,[53] and the Internet is filled with pleas for sperm vials from a retired donor so that families can have more children. The Sperm Bank of California advertises a special "Sibling Inventory" of sperm vials, which is available only to those customers who already have a child from one of the inventory donors.[54] One woman explained her decision to have a second child with the same donor as wanting to ensure that her children "have one other person in this world to whom they are both fully related."[55] As she underwent fertility treatments, Melanie Thernstrom and her husband, Michael, were hoping for twins, not only so that the parents would not have to undergo additional fertility treatments but also so that the children would be companions for one another; instead, they transferred eggs, fertilized by Michael's sperm, to two different women, who gave birth within five days of one another.[56] Jessica McCallin, a British woman who flew to Denmark for her insemination, had decided that, if she had a second child, "'I would use the same sperm donor again as it makes sense for Freya [her daughter, named after the Norse fertility goddess] to have a sibling exactly like her."[57]

Like heterosexuals, gay and lesbian couples may also try to ensure that their children are genetically related to one of them, and also to each other. Oshel and Matan Amir Cohen have children born on the same day in the same hospital with eggs from the same donor; the children, however, were born to different surrogate mothers, and each man is the biological father of one of the children.[58] As one doctor at an Indian fertility clinic explained, "'It is not uncommon among homosexual couples to request the same donor for eggs. They feel the children are related at least from the mother's side. This is the closest to biological relation the children will have.'"[59] One advice book notes that lesbians may each give birth to a child from the same sperm donor so that, if something happens to one of the parents, a court would be unlikely to separate the "biological siblings."[60]

The search for biological kinship is also about reproduction as "biological performance."[61] As medical anthropologist Gay Becker described the process, assisted reproductive technologies "signal a specific cultural ideology, the ideology of the biological child," and, when they result in a child, "they symbolize the return of normalcy."[62] While gay couples may subvert the traditional family form of husband and wife, they nonetheless conform to the "couple plus biological child" family form. In this sense, donor gametes also create community with families outside of the donor world.

The primary goal of using donor eggs and sperm to produce children is to create numerous different forms, and feelings, of kinship within families, as consumers deliberately choose donors who will help them achieve their desired families. Creating kinship in the donor world occurs, however, not just within the family but also with different families who share genes as individual families join with others on the basis of their shared biological heritage to form larger kin networks. It is these larger kin networks, formed on the basis of a common donor, that are the subject of the next chapter.

4

Creating Communities across Families

In a highly acclaimed 2008 book for tweens, *My So-Called Family*, the narrator, Leah, is a thirteen-year-old who feels that something is missing in her life.[1] When she comes home from kindergarten one day after learning that her friend's mother is pregnant, she asks her mother to explain "sex." Once her mother tells her where babies come from, Leah asks why she doesn't have a father. Her mother then "explained that there had been a very nice man who'd known there was a mommy out there who needed his help to have her little girl. She said even though we didn't know him, we should feel thankful to him because he had given her such an important present."[2] Without telling her mother, Leah searches for information about her potential donor siblings, and she ultimately connects with Samantha, a half-sibling. The first phone call, in which they identify themselves as being produced by the same donor, is awkward, but, by the end, Leah observes, "I realized that I had stopped feeling as though I were talking to a stranger."[3] While fiction, the book expresses common feelings among donor-conceived people of the need to search for connection and self-knowledge, and of finding comfort with a genetically related stranger in their search for larger kin networks that are donor based.

Unlike many donor-conceived people, Leah knew from a very young age about Donor 730. Of course, it is only when an individual finds out that she is donor conceived that she can search for connections. The process of telling can be matter-of-fact or it can be traumatic for parents and offspring. Even once children know about their origins, many donor families never seek to establish connections with others who have used the same donor. Nonetheless, studies show that, just as in the adoption context, some donor-conceived offspring rue their lack of connection with at least one-half of their genetic heritage.[4] Because they want knowledge about their biological progenitors, and because of their emotional needs for this knowledge, donor offspring and their parents have started to advocate for disclosure of donor identities. Thousands of people have begun to use the Internet to expand their "kinship circle" and to create what they often think of as an extended family with others who share the same donor, or even with the donor. While the genetic connection between the offspring is the basis for these relationships, the connections are often wider, including the parents and other relatives. As they label themselves family, members of the donor-conceived world are both redefining and negotiating these new relationships.

This chapter explores how people find out that they are donor conceived, and why and how people search for other members of their donor families to form donor-conceived family communities (or "kin networks). It also reviews the research on donor-created communities, which reveals the varying levels and types of connection among families.

I. Stories of Origin

Disclosure is a critical concept in the donor world that can refer to the knowledge of being donor conceived as well as to release of the donor's identity. This section focuses on the first meaning of the term, that is, providing information to offspring that they are donor conceived. This kind of disclosure can provide the basis for developing interfamilial bonds by allowing children a better understanding of their origins and family dynamics, yet many parents explain that they don't disclose because they fear weakening intrafamilial bonds. Accordingly, anonymous gamete donation remains a significant practice, with parents choosing unknown donors and not telling their children that they are donor conceived.[5]

Children born from gamete donors are born into two types of families. In the first type, it is clear that the genetic parent is missing—because there is a single parent or two mothers or two fathers. In the second type, when the child is born into a heterosexual family, it is not clear that the genetic parent is missing. Heterosexual families often keep the secret in order to preserve the interest of the nongenetic parent. Consequently, there is no need to know because the child has no reason to ask. As this section explores, the general donor culture values secrecy, although that secrecy is dissolving, and more parents are telling their children about their origins.

The secrecy is pervasive. At a meeting at the fertility clinic, Peggy Orenstein and her husband were asked whether the blinds overlooking the street should be closed: "'We're not ashamed,'" they explained.[6] Orenstein wondered, "Had I been wrong to feel less furtive?"[7] Similarly, when writer Melanie Thernstrom went egg shopping in the early twenty-first century, the director of one donor agency advised her, "'Tell everyone or tell no one. . . . But if it were me, I'd tell no one,'" she added. "'Look, I run an agency, so it's in my interest to promote these kinds of families, but to be honest, if I couldn't have children naturally—*God forbid*—I wouldn't want anyone to know!'"[8] The notion that blood families trump any other type of family remains deeply embedded in American culture, and this preference for blood ties explains some of the stigma that has accompanied infertility (and, as masculinities studies remind us, failure to reproduce is associated with male impotence and lack of virility).

A second reason that historically led many parents not to disclose was a fear of how doing so would affect the child's development. Children too might suffer from stigma because they were different or they might be confused about the identity of their "real" father.[9] Parents wanted to protect their children from any bewilderment about the identity of their real families, and from any teasing because of the lack of biological relationship.

Studies of families with children conceived through donor gametes have repeatedly shown that many parents are unlikely to tell their children about their donor origins, but that patterns of disclosure vary, depending on the type of family, with heterosexual couples least likely to disclose. Moreover, parents are likely to tell family members or friends, regardless of their intent to tell their children. In one study, a majority of the parents who never intended to disclose the fact of donor conception to their child had, nonetheless, informed at least one outside person, and the researchers note that these results are in line with what others have found.[10] The disclosure decision, it turns out, is complex, encompassing not just whether to disclose but also when, why, and to whom. Literary critic Eve Kosofsky Sedgwick used the phrase "open secret" to discuss homosexuality as "at once marginal and central,"[11] and this concept resonates in the donor-conceived world.

Donor-conceived people feel profoundly the structures surrounding telling or not telling, knowing and not knowing, that pervade the possibilities of understanding their identities.[12] There is often in donor children a sense that something is not right or that there is something more to be known, even in cases where the donor conception has been kept a carefully guarded secret. The metaphor of the "closet," so important in gay and lesbian studies,[13] works, albeit somewhat differently: medically infertile heterosexuals may be closeted about their inability to conceive, donor-conceived people may not even know they are in the closet until they are told, and they may then be reluctant to tell others, and donors may be closeted about their "contributions."

It is, indeed, difficult to study the donor-conceived world given all of the secrecy attached throughout the procedures. The historical legacy of nondisclosure is, however, quite clear, based on studies as well as expert advice. Parents who have used other forms of reproductive technology, such as in vitro fertilization without donor eggs or sperm, may be more likely to tell a child about how she has been conceived than parents who have used donor gametes; they are also more likely to tell others.[14] As the donor gamete technology advances, as it becomes more widespread in all kinds of families, the issues involved in "telling" have taken center stage, with explorations in popular literature and research journals of whether parents do, or do not, tell, of why and how they tell, and of the impact of the different decisions on donor-conceived people.

First, many parents have historically not told their children that they are donor conceived, although this is changing.[15] In 1996, in one of the first studies, Susan Golombok (then at London's City University and now at the University of Cambridge) and other researchers asked 101 European families if they had told their young children, then aged four to eight, that they were donor conceived. None of the parents had done so, and three-quarters of the mothers stated that they never intended to do so.[16] Indeed, almost three-quarters had not told any of their friends that they had used donor insemination.[17] In a follow-up study six years later, Golombok found that only 8.6 percent of parents had told their child about their donor conception,[18] and, even once the children reached the age of eighteen, no more parents had told their children.[19]

Parents may agree in advance not to tell the children, or one might want to while the other is adamantly opposed. The default, when parents disagree on disclosure, is not to tell the children. Along with his colleagues, Ken Daniels, a social worker from the University of Canterbury in New Zealand, interviewed fifty-seven families in 1990 who had used donor sperm, asking whether they intended to disclose their use of donor sperm, and then, fourteen years later, followed up with the same families.[20] When both parents agreed—either to disclose or not to disclose—there was no subsequent change in their intent. However, in families where the parents had initially disagreed, 73 percent opted for nondisclosure.

Of course, even when parents intend to disclose, they do not necessarily follow through with their intentions. In another relatively recent study of fifty couples that began when the sperm donor children were one year old, almost half (46 percent) of the parents stated that they would disclose their use of donor sperm; six years later, only 29 percent of the parents had done so.[21] While the parents may have wanted to wait until the children were older, it turns out (as discussed later) that telling children early helps with their mental health.

In a later study, published in 2011, a total of 101 families (thirty-six donor-insemination families, thirty-two egg-donation families, and thirty-three surrogacy families) were interviewed when the child was aged seven years. Despite a shift in professional attitudes toward openness, about half of the children conceived by egg donation and nearly three-quarters of those conceived by donor insemination remained unaware that the person they knew as their mother or father was not, in fact, their genetic parent; by contrast, more of the surrogacy families had disclosed the means of conception.[22]

The culture in which parents make their disclosure decisions does not necessarily encourage openness. One psychologist acknowledged parents' numerous potential fears, and explained in the American Fertility Association newsletter that, although she believed in disclosure, "it may not be the right decision for every family in every environment."[23] Similarly, although the American Society for Reproductive Medicine encourages parents to tell their children, it also notes that, throughout its history, the use of donor sperm has been associated with secrecy, yet it has resulted in "many stable loving families without significant pathology."[24] The reasons today have not changed from the early days of donor gametes. Parents give numerous justifications for not disclosing their use of donor sperm, including preventing public knowledge of their infertility, or wanting to protect the child from the distress of being unable to gain any information about their donor. Other concerns include the impact that disclosure may have on family relationships, including a parental fear of rejection because of the lack of a biological tie. One mother who used donor embryos (so there was no genetic link between the parents and the child) worried that "'[p]ossibly you'd get the "you're not really my parents," you know, "what right have you got?"'"[25] A father betrayed his own insecurities when he told journalist Liza Mundy, "'It's *not* all right with me [if my children search for their donor]. . . . I'm the dad, damn it. To me, it's an indicator of whether the kids are happy or not.'"[26] Parents can also be unsure about how to tell their child.[27]

The type of family almost certainly affects not just whether the parents are likely to choose an open-identity donor but also whether they are likely to disclose. The absence of a male partner tends to make disclosure more likely, as well as more likely to occur at an earlier age. Single women and lesbian couples who use donor insemination to conceive appear to be more likely to use an open-identity donor as opposed to an anonymous donor, while heterosexual couples are just as likely to use an open-identity donor as they were an anonymous donor.[28] And, offspring of single mothers (regardless of whether they are heterosexual) and of lesbian couples appear to learn that they are donor conceived at an earlier age than do offspring of heterosexual couples.[29] Heterosexual families often keep the secret in order to preserve the interest of the nongenetic parent, to ensure that the bonding process is not disrupted by fantasies about the "real" parent.[30] Indeed, in one large study of donor-conceived people who were recruited primarily from the Donor Sibling Registry, three-quarters of those raised in single-parent or lesbian-coupled families had always known of their origins, compared to less than a quarter of those raised by heterosexual coupled parents. (Just over 24 percent in dual-parent heterosexual couples as opposed to 75 percent in single-parent families and approximately 80 percent in single- and dual-parent lesbian families stated that they had known throughout their lives.[31]) And they are significantly more likely to express an interest in the donor at a younger age. Twice as many LGBT offspring as compared to heterosexual offspring expressed an interest by age eleven; by age eighteen, two-thirds of heterosexual offspring, compared to 95 percent of LGBT offspring expressed this interest.[32]

As parents become increasingly likely to disclose because of changes in the cultural environment and in the types of families formed through donor gametes,[33] they may have a variety of reasons for letting their children know of their origins. They may simply believe in openness and honesty with their children, they may think their children have the right to know of their origins, or they may want to protect against accidental disclosures, preventing their children from learning the information in the midst of a divorce or after a parent has died, or from others who may know the full story. Some parents explain that there is no reason not to tell their children.[34] "'I don't see why it should be a secret, I wouldn't think of it as anything to be concerned about.'"[35] Parents may feel that it is important for the child not to think of the moment of disclosure as a significant event, equivalent to an "aha" or "coming-out" story, but rather as a part of growing up that is just not a big deal.[36]

Accidental disclosure is, however, a real fear; widespread secrets are certainly more difficult to keep. Even if they don't ever intend to tell their children, parents, nonetheless, have often told others, such as family friends or relatives, of their infertility and use of donor gametes. For example, Professor Ken Daniels (who established the Social Work Department at the University of Canterbury in New Zealand and who is a long-time researcher of reproductive technology) and his colleagues found that almost two-thirds of the parents who had no plans to tell their children had told someone else.[37] When offspring find out through others, both the messenger and the message can cause difficulties. As Britta Dinsmore, a psychologist who specializes in women's issues, wrote about disclosure on a website maintained by Parents Via Egg Donation, "Accidental or belated disclosure can cause a tremendous sense of hurt, anger, and betrayal, which almost certainly impacts a child's attachment to his/her parents, and willingness to allow trust and intimacy in future relationships."[38] Indeed, as discussed next, intentional disclosure may help donor offspring feel better about their origins and their families.

The way of telling is also important. As one blogger explained,

> When I was 13 years old, my mother told me, "Daddy's not your real father." . . . Maybe it was apparent I was going to cry. I cried a lot back then. My mother explained, as my dad sat in the next room oblivious to our conversation, that Daddy wasn't my real father because she had been inseminated with sperm from an anonymous donor at her doctor's office.[39]

Other parents have developed methods for telling designed to minimize the trauma and maximize relationships, including, as discussed earlier, the seed story, and numerous books have been written to help guide parents through the process.

II. Donor Offspring, Mental Health, and Disclosure

Donor conception differs from non-third-party reproduction, not just in the process of conception but also in the resulting offspring's genetic links with parents: in non-third-party-formed families, the child is genetically tied to both parents, while in donor families, the child may be tied to one (sometimes neither) parent. Even adoption (discussed later), which might appear to provide an analogy, differs because donor-conceived families generally are created with a genetic link from birth with one parent and because (at least for heterosexual families), they are characterized by the comparative ease of hiding the lack of a link with the other parent. A child who is adopted as an infant has no biological ties with either parent, while an older child, who may be adopted by a stepparent or other relative, probably knows that the adoptive parent is not genetically connected. Accordingly, parenting in donor-conceived families may differ from and be more stressful than in other families as the parents struggle with potential asymmetries based on biological connections when it comes to their relationship with their child; and donor-conceived children may differ psychologically and developmentally from both biological and adopted children. Yet that's not what the research shows.

1. Parenting

In a comprehensive review of twenty-nine studies of families where only one parent was biologically related to children, two Dutch researchers concluded that there were few differences between these families and families where children were biologically related to both parents.[40] The studies included heterosexual and single-mother families who had used artificial insemination, planned gay and lesbian families, and egg-donation and surrogacy families. Through their review, the researchers hoped to examine concerns as to whether it was difficult for the non–genetically related parents (the "social" parents) to develop a good relationship with their children.[41] What they found—contrary to expectations—was that "a number of studies found higher levels of involved parenthood in [new reproductive technology] families than in natural-conception families."[42] In other words, parents in these families often had more positive interactions with their children, and higher emotional satisfaction with parenting itself, perhaps because the deliberate nature in which they became parents makes them particularly committed to parenting.[43]

Other studies confirm the psychological health of donor-conceived families. Susan Golombok, along with a team of other researchers, has followed a sample of approximately one hundred donor-conceived offspring, and concluded that they follow generally normal development patterns.[44] In a large study of children of lesbian parents, the team found that children in planned lesbian families are psychologically stable.[45] Similarly, another comprehensive review of numerous studies found essentially no differences in the psychological development of children raised in donor-conceived or surrogacy families compared to children in natural-conception families.[46]

2. Offspring: The Impact of Disclosure

While researchers are somewhat limited when it comes to recruiting subjects, they have begun to study the impact of disclosure on donor-conceived families.

As discussed above, there are numerous reasons why parents disclose donor conception to their children, and disclosure seems to have a generally positive impact on their psychological relationships. Children in families where the parents are more open about their donor conception may be stronger psychologically than those children who do not know of their origins. It may be that, in those families, informing a person of her origins is a symbol of an open and honest relationship, representing other aspects of family life.

Psychologist Patricia P. Mahlstedt and her colleagues examined mental health issues with people who learned that they were donor conceived at different points in their lives. They recruited eighty-five participants using contact information provided through Internet-based support groups for adults conceived through sperm donation.[47] In their study, children who learned of their donor origins earlier in life had a more positive outlook on the means of their conception than those children who found out later in life.[48] Moreover, donor offspring's perceptions of their conception correlated with their perceptions about their relationships with their mothers and their perceptions about their mothers' mental health.[49] A similar correlation existed with perceptions about their relationships with and the mental health of their fathers, but it was not as strong as the correlation with perceptions about their mothers.[50] The quality of donor offspring's relationships with their legal fathers (whether positive or negative) did not affect the offspring's curiosity about their donor.[51]

Perhaps not surprisingly, offspring of heterosexual parents are more likely to be confused about their means of conception. The largest study of donor-conceived offspring—more than 750 participants—showed that heterosexual families have a tougher time dealing with disclosure and honesty about donors, even if the child knows the truth. When their children expressed curiosity about the donor, fewer than one-fifth of fathers were supportive, compared to a majority of all mothers—whether they were single, or in heterosexual or lesbian couples.[52]

Studies as well as anecdotes show that children seem to benefit from open discussion of their donor status. When Susan Golombok and her colleagues examined the mother-child relationship in one hundred donor families, and compared the interactions to natural-conception families, they found somewhat less positive interactions in families without disclosure compared to families where children knew about their donor-conceived status.[53]

This is not surprising given that, in the somewhat comparable context of adoption, psychologists have shown that it is helpful for parents to be open with their children about adoption, including providing any information available about the biological parents.[54] Even if parents never discuss donor conception, children may sense that there is an invisible elephant in the room; parents may subtly indicate, through tone of voice, or body language, that there is something they are not telling their children.[55] Indeed, donor-conceived offspring who are told at an older age—looking back—often explain that they knew something was taboo. As one donor offspring explained, "They say 'As long as you love the child enough and want them badly enough, the truth really won't matter.' But, we're all here to tell you that the truth does matter. Living as a family with a terrible secret robs the family. It's a terrible, terrible thing to have happen. This rottenness just gets worse over the years."[56] Offspring told at later ages report feelings of betrayal that something so important was kept from them, as well as feelings of anger and loss.[57]

How do donor-conceived people feel about their means of conception and the importance of identity disclosure? In the Institute for American Values study, higher percentages of the offspring conceived through donor sperm agreed that assisted reproductive technologies "are good for children because the children are wanted" and that people should be encouraged to donate gametes than did individuals who were adopted or whose parents had not used any reproductive technology.[58] In addition, 80 percent of the donor-conceived offspring, compared to 69 percent of the adopted adults and 59 percent of those raised by their biological parents, believed that telling children about their biological origins at an early age was important in making it easier for children to handle their origins.[59] Nonetheless, almost half (45 percent) said that the circumstances of their conception bothered them.[60] Many more of the donor-conceived offspring than the adopted individuals felt hurt or sad when others talked about their genealogical heritages or when they saw other people with their biological parents.[61] Two-thirds of the donor-conceived offspring (67 percent) felt that they should have the right to know their donor's identity, while bare majorities (52 percent) of the other two groups believed that the donor-conceived offspring should have this right.[62] Finally, almost two-thirds of the donor-conceived offspring believed that they should have the opportunity to develop some sort of relationship with their donor as well as with half-siblings who share the same donor.[63] In the largest study of donor offspring, almost three-quarters recommended that parents use a donor who is willing to be known.[64]

Ultimately, donor offspring themselves believe it is important to be told the truth about their conception at an early age and to have access to identifying information about the donor as well as to any half-siblings that might exist.

Of course, there are limitations in all of these studies. Research on donor-conceived family members can only occur when people know their status, and study participants are often recruited through organizations that are focused on helping people who may have concerns about their donor-based identities.[65] And, as law professor Ellen Waldman observes,

> Studies examining the well-being of donor-gamete children in "open" families versus children in more secretive families reveal that children in open families seem to enjoy more peaceful relationships with their mothers. Having noted this difference, researchers are careful to specify that parent-child relations in families where parents have not discussed the role of a donor remain within the normal and acceptable range. Therefore, the data provides no evidence that donor-gamete children are suffering. Rather, children and mothers in open families may enjoy heightened amicability in their family relations when compared to relations prevailing amidst all family types.[66]

Nonetheless, what is clear from existing studies and from anecdotes is that many offspring do benefit from knowing that they are donor conceived and from being able to get information about their donor and half-siblings.

The movement toward disclosure draws strength, then, from a variety of sources. First, in the analogous context of adoption, disclosure can promote positive identity development, helping children develop a sense of ancestry and family history. Second, secrecy can be an insidious and invidious source of unacknowledged tension in a family. Third, respect for the child's autonomy supports providing information.[67] And finally, as discussed in the next section, without disclosure, connections among families with donor-conceived children are not possible.

III. Searching for Connection

As the number of people choosing to use donor eggs or sperm increases, as the number of offspring who know that they are donor conceived increases, and as the number of opportunities for one individual to donate have increased, there are more families united by having used the same donor. And, as this happens, a growing number of donor-conceived offspring want to know more about their origins and their genetically related relatives—as well as their donors.[68] With the support of technology, not only are donor-conceived offspring searching for their biological siblings as well as their gamete providers; they are all finding each other.

Offspring, their families, and donors have numerous reasons for searching, including seeking medical and biological information as well as looking for potential relationships.[69] Regardless of cultural notions of genetic kinship, the centrality of genetics to one's well-being is widely accepted and increasingly vital.[70] Family health history facilitates the prevention, diagnosis, and treatment of disease and assists in reproductive planning.[71] Genetic information has the potential to aid in the prevention, early detection, presymptomatic diagnosis, and treatment of thousands of inherited diseases.[72]

The search for health and medical information might lead to thoughts (and fears) about genetic essentialism. Genetic essentialism (or determinism) is the belief that our genes and our DNA constitute the essence of who we are, with genetics controlling our personalities and identities.[73] In its purest form, genetic determinism uses genes to explain our past actions and even predict future behaviors as well as health outcomes, essentially overlooking the influence of nurture, culture, and environment. Genes are important, of course, and having a certain gene predicts, but does not necessarily control, ultimate outcomes. Without unduly emphasizing the importance of the genetic connection, however, it is something that should be acknowledged. Knowing about the existence of certain genes allows for preventive actions. While much of the genetic knowledge can be acquired without access to the donor, the donor can provide significant information about other aspects of medical histories and treatments. It wasn't until after 2007, when Alison Davenport was diagnosed with a rare form of lymphoma, that she discovered from her 96-year-old mother that she was donor conceived; now in her sixties, she described that "in a single moment, she felt that she had lost 50% of her understanding of herself and where she came from, and that her sense of self 'disintegrated' as a result. Moreover, because of the anonymity of her donor, Ms. Davenport had great difficulty finding a close enough match for a bone marrow transplant."[74] And, of course, while genes create the connection, donor-conceived individuals have numerous other reasons for seeking contact.

Several studies have examined contact among donor-conceived families and between these families and their donors. Some of the questions examined include (1) the reasons why parents of donor-conceived offspring search for their children's half-siblings and donors; and (2) the motivations of donor-conceived people for searching. These searches are conducted in a variety of ways, and parents and children are generally quite pleased to find other members of their donor-connected family communities.

1. Why Do Parents of Donor Offspring Search?

Parents' main reasons for searching for donor siblings of their children were expressed as various forms of curiosity and a desire to create a larger "family" for their children through connections with others who have shared the same donor. And here, this is an obvious example of how the new kinship networks among donor-conceived families push the contours of the traditional, nuclear heterosexual family through the finding of "relatives" solely on the basis of genetics, without necessarily any shared cultural, religious, or social heritage.

In a small study that involved families who used the California Sperm Bank, 85.7 percent of parents said that one of their motivations for seeking donor siblings was "to create a family—not for them, but for their children."[75] Similarly, according to another survey of almost six hundred people recruited through the Single Mothers by Choice organization, almost two-thirds wanted their "child to have the possibility of a larger extended family," and half were interested in developing a relationship with other children who shared the donor's genes.[76]

Additionally, 42.9 percent said that contact with donor siblings was a way to "acquire further information about the donor and address curiosity about him and the children's shared genetics/ancestry."[77] Less frequently cited reasons from parents related to wanting either to connect with people in a similar situation or to provide their children with such a connection.[78] Single women were overrepresented in the matching service, supporting "the hypothesis that contact is a way to create extended family for their children."[79] Heterosexual couples were the least likely to participate in the family matching service, perhaps because, as the authors speculate, there may be less curiosity about the donor.[80]

In a larger study in which participants were recruited from the Donor Sibling Registry, 85 percent of parents searching for donor siblings identified curiosity about similarities in appearance and personalities (among other things) as one of their reasons, with 27 percent of parents citing curiosity as the main reason for searching.[81] The second most popular reason parents searched for donor siblings in this study was "[f]or my child to have a better understanding of who he/she is" (66 percent cited this as a reason and 18 percent of parents cited this as the main reason).[82] The third most popular reason was "[t]o give my child a more secure sense of identity," with 61 percent of parents citing this as a reason for searching and 17 percent of parents responding that this was the main reason for searching for donor siblings.[83]

In terms of searching for donors themselves, the study found that the most common primary reason was "[f]or my child to have a better understanding of who he/she is," with 73 percent of parents who searched for donors citing this as a reason, and 21 percent of parents citing this as the main reason.[84] The other most popular main reasons were "[t]o give my child a more secure sense of identity" (18 percent), "[c]uriosity about characteristics of my child's donor" (10 percent), and "[w]anting to thank my child's donor" (10 percent).[85] The study found that "[p]arents in households without fathers demonstrated higher levels of curiosity about their child's donor origins, as reflected by the greater proportions searching for donor relations overall."[86]

2. Why Do Donor Offspring Search?

The 2010 movie *The Kids Are All Right*[87] focused attention on why offspring search, and what happens when a donor is found. Laser and Joni have each been conceived using the same donor, and their mothers are married to each other. Laser begs his older sister to search for their donor, and, although Joni is worried about hurting her mothers, it is ultimately surprisingly easy for her to find Paul, the donor. The children don't want to tell their mothers, even after they meet the donor. While meeting the donor does not ultimately result in an expanded kinship network, Paul's presence—and disclosure— probably helped bring many issues to light and helped to resolve deeper conflicts among the family members.

The reality of donor relationships, of course, is often even more complex than what occurs in movies. Nonetheless, like Joni and Laser, the majority of donor offspring do express interest in knowing more about their genetic backgrounds[88] and finding their donor or half-siblings.

Vasanti Jadva, at the Centre for Family Research at the University of Cambridge, led a study looking at the experiences of donor-sperm offspring in searching for, and contacting, their donor siblings and donor. They recruited participants through the Donor Sibling Registry, so there was already some curiosity about their origins. Among the participants, more than three-quarters were searching for either their donor or their half-siblings, although 8 percent were not searching for either.[89]

The most common explanation for why they were searching for *donor siblings* was curiosity about similarities in appearance and personality (94 percent cited this as one of the reasons for searching and 44 percent cited this as the main reason).[90] The next two most popular main reasons were "[t]o know and understand a 'missing' part of me" (16 percent) and "[m]y sibling and/or parent(s) initiated the search" (7 percent).[91] Other popular reasons involved getting to know genetic and ancestral history.[92] Interestingly, there was a strong association between the family type of the respondent and the stated desire "to find a new family member" as a reason for searching for donor siblings, with more children from single-mother families citing this as a main reason.[93] Indeed, as Cheryl Shuler, a mother who wrote about her experiences using donor sperm, explains, her son had always hoped for a big family, so he was excited about searching.[94] Jadva and her colleagues are not sure whether children in single-parent families really are more interested in forming additional familial relationships—or whether offspring in two-parent families (either same-sex or heterosexual) are simply reluctant to upset their parents.

When children searched for *donors*, 89 percent cited curiosity about the characteristics of the donor as a reason, with almost a quarter claiming it was their main reason.[95] Relatively few (only 16 percent) said that their main reason for searching was to meet their donor, and only 12 percent said their main reason was medical.[96] Many of them wanted "[t]o have a better understanding of my ancestral history and family background" (79 percent), "[t]o have a better understanding of my genetic make-up" (79 percent), and "[t]o have a better understanding of why I am who I am" (75 percent).[97]

As with searching for donor siblings, the goal may vary according to family type. In a study that compared searching by offspring in lesbian and heterosexual families, almost all of the offspring were curious about the donor, regardless of their family form. Children raised in two-parent lesbian households were, however, least likely to want to establish a relationship with the donor, followed by children raised in heterosexual households by couples or single parents; more than half of children raised by single lesbians were interested in a relationship.[98] Children in two-parent lesbian households were equally curious about other aspects of their donor, such as his looks. The authors report that "we found it was the presence of a social father that was most strongly associated with lower levels of perceived support and understanding of offspring's curiosity about the donor," perhaps because, they speculate, of the long-standing stigma surrounding infertility that serves as an obstacle to openness.[99] Indeed, studies of donor families have found that mothers are the one who generally disclose and in adoptive families, mothers are the primary "communication brokers."[100]

In terms of what triggered searching for donor siblings or donors, the most popular reason was a change in personal circumstances or a life event, such as "becoming a teenager," "becoming an adult," "getting married or forming a long-term relationship," having "a personal crisis," contracting "an illness or other medical condition," or "planning to have children or having children."[101] For most people, searching for the donor, then, appears to be less about forming a relationship than allowing the offspring to learn more about themselves. As Katrina Clark, a donor-conceived college student, explained her feelings when her biological father first emailed her with his picture, "From my computer screen, my own face seemed to stare back at me. And just like that, after 17 years, the missing piece of the puzzle snapped into place. The puzzle of who I am."[102]

Donor offspring commonly report amazement—and relief—when they find relatives with similar tics. For people who take genetic connectedness for granted, routinely pointing out that excellence in school or in sports is "in the genes," this search for genetic continuity may be somewhat mysterious (a lack of understanding of what it's like *not* to have that connectedness), or completely understandable.

IV. How People Connect

People can search for their donors and half-siblings in a variety of ways. According to studies, the methods used for searching for donor siblings or donors included contacting the sperm bank used[103] and using the Internet to register on websites devoted to facilitating contact between donor parents and their children and donor siblings and donors, such as the Donor Sibling Registry,[104] or using it to find other resources. The Internet has not just facilitated the searching process but also helped to open up the entire donor world by providing an easily accessible forum for exploring emotions and attitudes (just as it has facilitated the search for donor eggs and sperm).

First, the search might start with contacting members of the fertility industry. While they are not required to keep records for any length of time, some physicians, clinics, and banks may retain relevant information, or may facilitate connections in other ways. Sperm banks generally protect the donors and do not release any information, although they may provide the searcher with the donor's number.[105] (The situation differs for those families that have used identity-release donors; offspring can access the information once they have reached the appropriate age.) Sperm banks may also have set up a registry to allow people who have used the same donor to connect. California Cryobank, for example, allows anyone who has used sperm from the bank, along with his or her offspring over the age of eighteen, to register, although donors are not permitted.[106] Fairfax Cryobank offers a "private" forum, based on donor number, to allow those who have used the same donor to connect to one another.[107] And, the Sperm Bank of California, which developed the first open-identity program in the world, maintains a

Family Contact List that allows families to register to connect with others who have used the same donor. One-fifth of their clients have signed up, and more than half of them have matched with another family.[108]

In addition to facilitating contact with others who have used the same donor, the Sperm Bank of California reports that approximately one-third of people who know they were conceived by open-identity sperm donors make a request for the donor's identity by the time they turn twenty.[109] However, given that the first generation of offspring from open-identity donors is just coming of age, the bank's research shows that it is likely that additional offspring will make a request for identity release as they grow older.[110] The offspring who have requested information were respectful of the donor's privacy, and they were not typically looking for a "father figure."[111] According to the California Sperm Bank study, most families initiated contact by phone as opposed to mail or email,[112] though this was a very small sample size.[113]

Notwithstanding the positive experiences with the California Sperm Bank, offspring are often frustrated as they have pursued information from the fertility industry. As Paul, a donor-conceived man, explained,

> I hunted down the OBGYN [obstetrician/gynecologist] who did the procedure, he's actually still alive, for how much longer I don't know. He was completely unwilling to give any information citing the fact that this was done in total secrecy as was quite common back then and that everyone was sworn to secrecy and the donor had wanted it that way as well.[114]

While the physician feels bound to the secrecy of the past, Paul is, obviously, quite frustrated; the physician's obligations are, however, less than clear, given that the recipients were the patients, while the donor may not have established a doctor/patient relationship with him.

Self-help is another option. All Kathleen LaBounty knew about her donor was that he was a Baylor Medical School student, and that her mother had requested someone with blond hair. In 2006, she went to Baylor's med school library and pored over yearbooks from 1979 to 1984. In the beginning, she was naive enough to think he'd jump right out. She paid close attention to eyes and smiles. She photocopied the pages and asked friends to flip through them and star the best candidates. But before she knew it, she had come up with a list of six hundred candidates whom she alphabetized and stuck into binders.[115]

She sent out letters to all six hundred of them, and received responses from almost half; after sixteen DNA tests, she has not found her donor, but she has become friendly with several of the men she had contacted, who call her their "'collective pseudo daughter.'"[116] Donor-conceived people may advertise in newspapers or on the Internet, or, as Olivia Pratten did, they may contact the doctor who performed the ART process to find out if any information remains.

More frequently, however, donor-conceived family members turn to technology, including the Internet or DNA testing, to search for family members. They can easily find two different types of sites that are focused on issues involving the donor conceived: (1) registries that are specifically designed to help members of the donor-conceived community find one another; and (2) links that provide information and support, including organizations addressing infertility as well as personal blogs written by donors, offspring, or intending parents. Some of the registries are government supported, such as the British HFEA Registry and its DonorLink. Perhaps the best-known private registry is the Donor Sibling Registry, but other organizations also maintain registries.

1. The Internet

In addition to specific sites targeted to the donor-conceived community, the Internet and new technologies provide other opportunities to search for connections, to explore emotions, and to find advice. Indeed, the Internet has called into question the meaning of anonymity.

"Joel," who was not even looking for the egg donor who had contributed to the creation of his twin daughters, found her by mistake as he was trying to learn about MySpace.[117] Others have used Google or Facebook, relying on a few of the known details to find the identity of the unknown donor. And, increasingly sophisticated DNA tests allow individuals to swab the inside of their cheeks, send off the sample to a DNA testing company, and receive a report on genetic markers that helps narrow down the donor search.[118] As "Girl Conceived" reports,

> Since I received my Family Finder DNA results I've found myself fixated on downloading and analyzing the lists of genetic relatives. . . . [E]very time I log in and see the long list of names I get a little high. I feel my mouth curl into a smile and my heart races a little. I look at the 100s of names. . . . Adler . . . Goldstein . . . Mitchell and I am in awe. I just cannot believe after 30 years of [expecting] that 50 percent of my identity would forever be unknown I have received this tiny glimpse inside into the unknown.[119]

Indeed, advances in DNA technology may leave anonymity a relic of the past. Michelle Jorgenson, a waitress who had used donor sperm, became concerned that her daughter had a sensory disorder; she was sensitive to sounds and walked on her toes. Using the Donor Sibling Registry, she tracked down other biological siblings of her child, and learned that two were autistic and two others had similar symptoms. Jorgenson continued sleuthing, and obtained permission from another parent to test the Y-chromosome of a half-sibling. The Y chromosome passes from father to son virtually unchanged, so it can help in identifying an individual's paternal line. Other DNA tests can provide additional information. Sending a cheek-swab sample to one of the many DNA testing services can result in finding out all kinds of things, including ancestry. Even if the father himself never registered with the testing service, that is not necessarily a problem: all that is necessary is for someone else with the same paternal line to be registered. Through its "Family Finder" test, Family Tree DNA advertises that it can "provide you a breakdown of your ethnic percentages and connect you with relatives descended from any of your ancestral lines within approximately the last 5 generations."[120]

Ultimately, on the basis of information from the DNA test and other fact finding, Jorgenson thought she had successfully identified the "anonymous" sperm donor. When she called him, he admitted that he had been a sperm donor and agreed to meet with her.[121]

In recognition of the possibilities of technology, some may deliberately avoid collecting this information. After she went donor shopping, Alice Crisci, a social entrepreneur, was relieved that she only had a baby photo of the donor; a later photo would, she decided, have given her too much information, allowing her to use new software to track him down, which "would create a false intimacy between us that I did not want. It would humanize his DNA too much for me."[122]

As an effort to acknowledge that changing technologies may mean the effective end of anonymity, Cryos International, a sperm bank based in Copenhagen, Denmark, now offers "Invisible Donors." Through this program, donors provide a limited number of registered characteristics so they will be more difficult to find, and the bank uses fingerprints, not donor numbers, to keep track of them.

The increasingly sophisticated technologies not only facilitate searching but also provide more possibilities for "knowing" the unknown donor. Photographs, finding others who are genetically related, and DNA tests offer connections not just with biological heritage but also with the donor.

2. Registries

More organized methods allow donor-conceived people to find one another, half-siblings, and their donors. Voluntary, mutual-consent registries, based on matches among participants, facilitate contact. Matches might be based on donor number or even DNA tests.

The largest and most well-known source of connections is the Donor Sibling Registry, a nonprofit organization that operates a voluntary, mutual-consent, Internet-based databank for matching offspring with one another and with their donors.[123] It began when Ryan Kramer wondered about his donor but could not get any information. In 2000, when Ryan was ten, he and his mother, Wendy Kramer, started the Donor Sibling Registry (DSR), so that they could establish an Internet meeting place for voluntary contact between donor-created offspring and their genetic relatives.

Wendy and Ryan created a Yahoo group and posted the group's initial message, indicating that they were looking for Ryan's biological relatives. For the first few years, the site grew slowly. It had only thirty-seven members in early November 2002. Later that month, the Kramers received some local Denver TV and newspaper coverage. As a result of that publicity, in December 2002, Diane Sawyer interviewed Wendy and Ryan live on *Good Morning America*. Since then the Donor Sibling Registry has received tremendous media attention both domestically and internationally, including on numerous national television shows such as the *Oprah Winfrey Show*, *60 Minutes*, and NBC's *Today Show*.

Parents, donor-conceived offspring, and donors are all registered on the site, and the site also serves as a repository for research and advice. It also operates a discussion group for people to share advice and stories. People can use the website to search for anyone who has used the same donor. They fill out a search form with as much information as they have available about the donor, such as the number given the donor by a sperm bank or egg agency or the donor's birthday. Matches can be made among families that have used the same donor as well as between the donor and offspring. As of late 2011, the DSR had facilitated contact among more than eighty-five hundred genetically related people, including donors and half-siblings.

Apparently, it is not just members of donor families who are mesmerized by these contacts. The registry has appeared in hundreds of newspapers and magazines. According to Kramer, when an "anonymous teen" found his donor father using DNA testing, the story broke in U.K.-based *New Science* magazine. Within days, the story appeared in Australia, France, Italy, China, Malaysia, South Africa, India, and hundreds of papers around the world.

After the *Washington Post* broke the story in the United States, it appeared in newspapers from Boston to Chicago to San Jose. When the *New York Times* ran another story in the fall of 2009, two million people came to the DSR website. As publicity allows more people to learn about the possibility of connecting by joining the site, the site has expanded in membership and the number of matches has similarly increased.

The DSR is not the only registry. A comparatively new type of registry uses DNA matches. The private company, Family Tree DNA, has established a project to allow members of the donor-conceived community to find relatives with genetic confirmation of the matches. Only those who have undergone the requisite DNA testing are allowed to register, and the site is growing slowly.[124] The site is particularly useful for people who may not have a donor number; if the same donor provided sperm to numerous banks, then the site allows for "cross-matching" among sibling groups. The success of this site, and, indeed, any voluntary registry, depends on the number of people who sign up to participate.

V. Developing Relationships, Creating Connections

When their searches are successful, each member of these newly formed communities—the parents, the offspring, and the donors—generally feels quite positive about one another. The types of contact and the closeness of the relationships vary.

1. Donor Parents' Rating of Contact

In the small study involving donor-identity families at California Sperm Bank, participants rated their first contact experience with donor-sibling families as moderately or very positive, giving the experience fours and fives on a five-point scale.[125] The children were excited and curious about meeting their half-sibling(s).[126] Some parents felt as though the families "clicked," although a few reported that they did not make a good connection because of differing desires with respect to the amount of contact or differing approaches to disclosure. Parents also believed that there was a difference between the way they and their children viewed the relationship with the donor sibling.[127] While only 28.6 percent of parents described their relationship with the donor sibling family as "family," 64.3 percent reported that "the matched family was family to their child."[128] Indeed, while many of the parents wanted to create families for their children through matching with related donor-conceived families, one mother had not told her child of the possibility of matching because she feared the child would be unable to understand the distinction between her family and the donor-sibling family.

In the larger study using the Donor Sibling Registry, in responding to questions about contacting donor siblings, 80 percent of parents rated their experience meeting donor siblings as very positive and 68 percent of parents rated their children's experience as very positive.[129] Of the remaining parents who rated their and their children's experience of contacting donor siblings, 15 percent rated it as fairly positive for themselves and 14 percent rated it as fairly positive for their children.[130] Additionally, 5 percent rated the experience as neutral for themselves and 13 percent rated the experience as neutral for their children.[131] Only one parent rated the experience as fairly negative for either the parent or the child.[132] In contrast, all parents who met with their child's donor rated the experiences positively for both them and their children.[133]

2. Donor Offspring Rating of Contact

When donor offspring have reported their impressions, they too have generally expressed positive feelings about meeting donor siblings as well as the donors. As one sixteen-year-old boy explained about his contact with his donor siblings, it felt "like we have known each other all our lives even though we did not grow up together."[134] For Ryan Kramer, finding his donor led to a feeling of "'immediate peacefulness,'" his mother explained to the *Denver Post*.

Studies of donor offspring contact support the importance of finding half-siblings and the donor, although reactions are not uniformly positive. In their study, Jadva and her colleagues found that, of the offspring who had made contact with donor siblings, 85 percent (thirty-four people) rated the experience as fairly positive or very positive, 13 percent (five people) rated it as neutral, and 3 percent rated it as fairly negative (one person). When it came to meeting their donors, they were similarly enthusiastic: "I am so glad that I met him, and I would not trade the world for the experience I had," explained one teen boy.[135] Most of the offspring were either "very positive" or "fairly positive" about their meetings, although a few were not. While none of the offspring in lesbian or single-mother families expressed anything but positive feelings, half of the offspring in heterosexual families felt either neutral or somewhat negative about their contact experience with their donor.[136]

3. What about the Donors?

Yale sociologist Rene Almeling, who undertook an extensive survey of banks, egg recruiters, and donors, found that while egg donors rarely think of themselves as mothers to the offspring who are born from their gametes, sperm donors consistently think of themselves as fathers to any resulting children.[137] This may, she speculates, be the result of cultural norms concerning the causal relationship between sperm and fatherhood, which differ when it comes to eggs and motherhood: women experience substantial interventions before an egg turns into a baby (nine months of pregnancy and the birth process).[138] Nonetheless, she found that both sperm donors and egg donors would like more access to information about the results of reproductive efforts that use their genetic material, and most "exhibited a mild curiosity in seeing how the children 'turn out.'"[139] Moreover, a substantial minority felt some sense of responsibility for their donor offspring, which included (potentially) not just providing them with medical information or family histories but also, in some cases, even giving financial help to the child.[140] In general, egg and sperm donors seem quite interested in knowing how many offspring have resulted from their gametes, and express some concern about the well-being of their donor offspring.[141] In one of the few studies of egg donors, the 155 participants overwhelmingly (97 percent) indicated an interest in contact, and none said they were *not* interested in contact.[142] Almeling found that egg donors (more than sperm donors) are quite conscious of the recipients of their gametes, and accord great significance to the role of the woman who actually gestates and bears the child.[143] Indeed, because some women request that their sisters serve as egg donors and because some women donate their eggs to others at the same fertility clinic, this may create "kin-like female alliances"[144]—yet another novel form of the new kinship.

Anecdotally, the media frequently covers happy donors meeting their "families," and there are numerous other stories of donors who appreciate having been found.[145] While these accounts are pervasive, not all stories have happy endings or even happy middles. When Emma, a participant in a small research study, called the man she believed was her donor, he flatly denied that he had donated sperm—but "Emma holds out hope that she might have had the right man, because, as she reports, when she called this man, 'he had to go into another room, like have privacy before he could talk. So that makes me think that he probably has not told his wife or his family members if it is him.'"[146] Lindsay Davenport, who started the "Confessions of a Cryokid" blog, reports that the media are only interested in happy reunions.[147] *Fox News* contacted her and asked to feature her in a story about donor-conceived offspring searching for their donors, but then politely distanced her once the producers realized that she had not, after years of searching, found her donor (In fact, her blog has a plaintive side bar, asking "ARE YOU XYTEX DONOR 2035?" along with a description of the characteristics she knows about him.).[148] And even Wendy and Ryan Kramer have dealt with half-siblings where the parents have not wanted to pursue contact, providing "examples of tightly woven secrets and legal ties that the adults do not want to alter."[149] As donor kin networks develop, members (and potential members) face challenges in developing and defining their new relationships.

VI. Continuum of Connections

Indeed, Wendy Kramer has corresponded with many parents of donor-conceived children who are seeking advice "on how to navigate their new relationships. Some parents in the newly formed donor groups simply want to trade basic information, while others want to form groups that spend holidays together, forming familial-type relationships."[150] These are all "new relationships," and they are developing outside of the way the law has traditionally defined family—as including married biological parents with children—while using genetic connection, a well-recognized basis for creating family, as the starting point for the relationship. The challenge is transforming the mere biological facts of shared genes into a social relationship in the absence of the more traditional contexts of kinship, such as shared residence or culture. People find out that they are related, genetically, to someone they have never met, and, even if they have been searching for their relatives, the reality of starting a new relationship can be very different from the fantasy.

The initial meeting may be somewhat awkward. "Once people connect," Wendy Kramer observed, "it's a delicate dance figuring out, 'Who are we to each other?'"[151] On the other hand, most people feel "overwhelmingly positive" about these new relationships after some ticklish starts. Diane Allen, who runs the Infertility Network in Canada, noted that she doesn't know of anyone who has ever regretted meeting a donor.[152]

Contact might be occasional, at the level of sending holiday greetings, or much closer, with the children growing up together. As one eight-year-old said of his donor-conceived half-sibling, "'I call him brother. . . . We kind of got along right away.'"[153] The half-siblings themselves may develop closer relationships than do their parents.[154] On the other hand, while the offspring might choose contact, their parents may not.[155] Similarly, even once the donor is found, either the donor or the parents may want to discontinue contact.[156]

Many donor-conceived offspring and their parents do want contact, however, rather than simply written information, and these contacts lead them to some kind of "'family feeling.'"[157] People who have connected often feel as though they are starting to create a family.[158] The meaning of family, however, changes depending on the particular donor-conceived community. People engage in varying degrees of contact, from exchanging a few emails to meeting to spending vacations together, and they also vary as to the terms they use to describe those with whom they have connected, from "acquaintance" to "friend" to "family."

1. Donor-Conceived Families: Half-Siblings and Their Parents

The donor world is filled with anecdotes of the different connections created by use of the same donor. The genetic ties among their children cause many women to feel various types of family-like connections to one other. One woman explained, "'We refer to one another as sister-moms. . . . We are close friends who care about one another's children.'"[159] Another woman explained that the other mothers who have used the same donor are "'part of my extended family, along with their children.'"[160] Often, parents may feel related to the donor-conceived children in other families. As Sherry Forsberg acknowledged, "'It's kind of weird, but the kids we find seem to be kind of like my own. . . . I worry about them just like I do mine and am proud of their own accomplishments . . . that connection we have through the kids having some of the same DNA makes us all "related."'"[161]

Gwenyth Jackaway, according to a story in O Magazine, searched for genetic relatives for her son, Dylan, because she wanted him to be "part of a larger community," and refers to the other children she found as "Dylan's siblings."[162] One mother explained the attachment that her daughter feels to her donor siblings: "'There are special bonds that she is forming with them that look[] like nothing else I've seen with friends of hers. . . . The fact he is her sibling draws them together like bees to honey. . . . I think she feels very full and good about herself as her experience of "family" grows and deepens.'"[163]

Then there's the "66 Club," the subject of an award-winning documentary. All members of the club share sperm from Donor 66, and they have get-togethers several times each year, including for Christmas. Suzanne Senk, whose son, Justin, is a member of the club, explained her feelings at finding his half-siblings: "'Justin had been an only child but overnight he had become one of a family of five siblings. It was unbelievable to see how alike they all looked. They even shared mannerisms.'"[164]

There is a self-consciousness in many of these stories that acknowledges how those involved are creating new family forms, even as these new families are shaped by shared genes. The connections result in feelings of contentment and belonging, of coming home. The parents often feel that they are filling in a gap in their children's communities, completing their families by finding genetically related siblings.

2. The Donors

Even anonymous donors often change their minds and want some kind of relationship with their offspring. They may want only nonidentifying information, or they may ultimately view their relationships with donor offspring whom they have met as akin to that with their own children.[165] They may agree to meet with all of their donor offspring, or only with one.[166] They may discover similarities in appearances and interests, and they may refer to their offspring as "donor kids" or even, simply, as "daughter" or "son."[167]

Mike Rubino was Donor 929 at California Cryobank.[168] He was inspired to find out what happened to the sperm he had provided to the Cryobank, and, through the DSR, discovered that Rachael McGhee had written a thank-you message to Donor 929. McGhee had given birth to two children using sperm from Donor 929, and, on Father's Day, she would remind the children to think about their donor and send him hugs. Rubino and McGhee, along with her two children, ultimately spent a week together, getting to know one another.

Or consider

> the remarkable story of Todd Whitehurst, now a 44-year-old physician in New York City, who donated sperm to a California sperm bank while a graduate student at Stanford University.
>
> One of the children conceived with his sperm tracked him down in 2007, using MySpace. Whitehurst soon met with that girl, who is now 17, and two half brothers, now 12 and 15, all three of them raised separately by single mothers who'd used the same sperm bank.
>
> This suddenly connected clan has gotten along so well that they keep in steady contact and have even taken vacations together, to a Pennsylvania resort, to Tennessee, and to Disney World.
>
> "It's been much better than I ever imagined," Whitehurst said. . . .
>
> One of the mothers, Cheryl Shuler of Butler, Pa., said meeting Whitehurst has been a wonderful experience for her 15-year-old son.
>
> Among the bonuses, Shuler wrote, was that Gavin now can observe a second source of his identity, reflecting the pronounced personality differences of his two biological parents.[169]

One Australian egg donor, who contributed to the birth of nineteen children and is known as "'mummy and daddy's special friend,'" remains in touch with several of the resulting families through emails, photo sharing, and dinner invitations, but has found it "easy to keep herself at arm's length."[170] Three of the families were at her wedding.

Even as they form larger communities of extended kinship, donor-conceived families may not always have the intimacy and ease that we typically associate with family members. Occasional visits or vacations do not necessarily become transformed into shared caretaking or secrets.[171] Indeed, face-to-face meetings are comparatively rare. Instead, donors and offspring are more likely to be in touch by email and to exchange photos.[172] And attitudes range from feeling that there is only a genetic relationship to feelings of a "special relationship" to feeling like the offspring really is the donor's own child.[173]

This chapter has surveyed some of the developments in research on the significance of donor-based relationships, although, as these families come together, there is much uncharted territory on how to define their new connections. Individuals connected through the same donor, but who do not share dependencies or a home, are searching for one another for numerous reasons. Once they find each other, they may develop emotional intimacies that resemble those of other familial structures. As the number of families that owe their existence to reproductive technology increases, those families are transcending the boundaries of the nuclear family and voluntarily creating larger kin networks. So far, the law has provided little support, and the next section of the book addresses how the law might approach these newly developing donor-created kin networks.

PART III

The Law and Donor Families

5

The Laws of the Donor World

Parents and Children

Numerous areas of the law converge in the donor world. Family law provides legal definitions of parenthood, determining when a donor is, or is not, a parent. It considers biology, intent, and function to identify the parents. Law also establishes the rights of children, determining whether children have interests distinct from their parents and it has the potential to answer questions such as whether half-siblings have any rights to access information about, and establish a relationship with, their donors. Health law issues concern the safety and testing of gametes, informed consent, medical information and history, and counseling. Privacy law, health law, and family law each address anonymity, and whether children should have rights to access information about their donors. And constitutional law issues on the meaning of autonomy, intimacy, family, and kinship provide the framework for considering all of these legal questions.

Most states have some laws that address who is defined as a parent in the donor world, and this chapter first explores those definitions and the legal protections accorded to that status. On the other hand, there are relatively few laws addressing any other aspect of donor family relationships; family and constitutional law from outside of the donor context provide potential analogies. Consequently, the chapter next examines more general laws affecting children, focusing first on concepts of children's rights and then turning to sibling rights. It then suggests how this body of law might apply to donor sibling relationships. Throughout this chapter, the theme underlying the detailed discussion of cases and of policy arguments is that there is relatively minimal regulation of donor family relationships, just as there is relatively minimal regulation of other aspects of reproductive technology.

I. Identifying the Parents

Each state has its own distinct approach to the issue of identifying the legal parents of donor-conceived children; the United States does not have a national parentage law that applies to every donor-conceived child. The law has multiple potential bases for determining parenthood, including contract, intent, marriage, or biology, or a standard that considers only the child's best interests. The most significant background for parenthood determinations, however, is the marital presumption. Historically, a married husband and wife were presumed to be the father and mother of children born into the marriage. Lord Mansfield's Rule, as explained in a 1777 British case, stated that "it is a rule, founded in decency, morality, and policy, that [the spouses] . . . shall not be permitted to say after marriage, that they have had no connection, and therefore that the offspring is spurious."[1] The rule effectively barred either spouse from testifying that the husband was not the child's father. Marriage guaranteed parental rights to the husband, and his paternity was virtually irrebuttable. Before the development of reliable blood and, now, DNA testing, the only way to rebut the marital presumption involved testimony as to the husband's absence or impotence or the wife's infidelity. Not only did the marital presumption bar testimony as to infidelity, which would also have established grounds for divorce, but it also established paternity, regardless of biological fact.

The marital presumption continues to exist in some form in virtually all states today. It applies to both heterosexual and same-sex marriages (in states that recognize them), and states with extensive civil-union or domestic-partnership statutes extend the marital presumption to couples in those relationships. Nonetheless, the spouses and the biological parent have the opportunity to rebut the presumption in most states both during the marriage and particularly at divorce.[2] States may provide great latitude in allowing rebuttals, or they may limit the circumstances in which it can be rebutted.

In an era in which biology can be determined with certainty, courts explain that the strong state interest in upholding the sanctity of marriage together with a preference for functional stability for a child over biological connections justify the ongoing use of the presumption.

Historically, when the biological parents were not married to each other, the law differed with respect to the bundle of rights that accompanied parenthood, and to the individuals who were accorded parental status. In English common law and in colonial America, nonmarital children had no legally recognized relationship with either biological parent, and the parents had no recognized familial relationship with the child. Not until the end of the nineteenth century did most states enact laws recognizing that "illegitimate" children were part of their mothers' families.

Until 1972, when the Supreme Court decided *Stanley v. Illinois*, most states granted fathers of nonmarital children few rights with respect to custody or consent to adoption (although they did have support obligations). Nonmarital fathers could not exercise parental powers and, in effect, were defined as nonparents. The Supreme Court's jurisprudence on the rights of nonmarital fathers together with a nonmarital birth rate that is over 40 percent has prompted dramatic change in the laws governing the establishment of paternity. The laws on motherhood have, historically, been straightforward: the woman who gives birth to a child has been presumed to be the mother. But the legal issues involved in establishing maternity have become more complex due to advances in technology and due to changing cultural norms as same-sex partners engage in mothering functions together.

Notwithstanding the changing social context, no single, comprehensive system has arisen to supplement, or even replace, the marital presumption. There have been several attempts at developing a uniform law so that the parentage designation would not vary depending on where the child is born. The Uniform Parentage Act (UPA), which first appeared in 1973, tried to deal with the parenthood of donor-conceived children. If a couple was married when the woman was inseminated, then the husband became the legal father of any resulting child, but only if (1) the husband's consent was given in writing, and (2) the insemination was done under the supervision of a licensed physician. The actual language, which has a somewhat antiquated tone to it (although it remains law in many states today), provides,

> If, under the supervision of a licensed physician and with the consent of her husband, a wife is inseminated artificially with semen donated by a man not her husband, the husband is treated in law as if he were the

natural father of a child thereby conceived. The husband's consent must be in writing and signed by him and his wife. The physician shall certify their signatures and the date of the insemination, and file the husband's consent with the [State Department of Health], where it shall be kept confidential and in a sealed file. However, the physician's failure to do so does not affect the father and child relationship. All papers and records pertaining to the insemination, whether part of the permanent record of a court or of a file held by the supervising physician or elsewhere, are subject to inspection only upon an order of the court for good cause shown.[3]

Although much was left out, the model act did clarify that the donor had no legal rights and that the husband, not the donor, was definitively the father. The UPA, however, said nothing about the parentage of children conceived through artificial insemination when the woman was not married. Consequently, although the UPA neither prevented single women and lesbians from using artificial insemination nor prevented women from using a turkey baster rather than a doctor, it left the parental status of the sperm provider unclear when either the woman was not married or, if married, she had not used a physician for the insemination process. Moreover, the UPA dealt only with artificial insemination. Most other assisted reproductive technologies were at extremely early stages: Louise Brown, the first baby conceived through in vitro fertilization, was not born until five years after the model act. The UPA was, however, revolutionary in setting the stage for "normalizing" children not born through traditional, marital intercourse.

The Uniform Parentage Act was adopted by eighteen states between 1975 and 1985,[4] and other states either developed their own laws or made decisions on a case-by-case basis. Because of changes in the family, including increases in the nonmarital birth rate, and changes in technology, a new Uniform Parentage Act was drafted early in the twenty-first century. Although the 1973 act had dealt only with artificial insemination using donated sperm, in recognition of the changes in technology, the new act addressed a variety of legal parentage problems that might result from egg or sperm donation as well as from the freezing of embryos.[5] The UPA now provides that a donor is not a father unless he signs a consent to paternity or, during the child's first two years of life, lives with the child and holds out the child as his offspring.[6] According to the final act, an egg or sperm donor is not a parent when a child is conceived through "assisted reproduction," meaning reproduction not involving sexual intercourse.[7] Indeed, the 2002 UPA comments clarify that "[i]n sum, donors are eliminated from the parental equation."[8] As the comments to the revised UPA explain, it governs the parentage issues in all cases in which the birth mother is also the woman who intends to parent the child. . . . [T]his section shields all donors, whether of sperm or eggs, (§ 102 (8), *supra*), from parenthood in all situations in which either a married woman or a single woman conceives a child through ART with the intent to be the child's parent, either by herself or with a man.[9]

Almost thirty years after the original act, a second Uniform Parentage Act finally addressed the relational rights established outside of marriage. Nonetheless, while the act applies to unmarried couples and covers donor eggs, it still does not explicitly address issues focusing on same-sex couples and the new reproductive technologies.

The UPA is now law in a minority of states.[10] Most other states terminate the potential parental rights of unknown sperm donors, and some terminate the rights of unknown eggs donors.

When a known donor is used, the situation changes. Jurisdictions' approaches to parenthood reflect their approaches to whether biology, intent, marriage, and contract might constitute the appropriate source of family identity. For example, a child in the District of Columbia could have three legal parents. A lesbian couple might agree that one of them will use donor sperm, and that both of them will be the parents of any child. In addition, if they use a known donor, they might also sign an agreement with him that recognizes him as a parent. The resulting child will have three parents because the law "conclusively establishes the partner as a parent. The agreement with the donor means that he, too, is a parent. The statute does not contain a means to choose one person over the other as the child's only other parent."[11]

The donor and recipient may make various types of agreements, ranging from one that precludes entirely the donor's involvement to one that allows for quasi-parental status. Or there may not be a formal agreement. Consider the relationship between George Russell and Carol Einhorn. He was a year ahead of her at Wesleyan; many years later, he contributed sperm "as a favor to a friend," and she became pregnant. Their son, Griffin, calls Russell "Uncle George," while his partner is "David." Although Russell spends four nights a week in the same apartment as Griffin, he explains, "'I don't feel paternal toward him. Yet it's odd when I look at him and I see me.'"[12]

The legal parameters of this relationship are fuzzy. Einhorn could sue Russell for child support, and he could sue her to establish custodial rights. Both would probably win. Even if they had a formal agreement, its enforceability depends on state laws concerning how artificial insemination must be

performed and whether there is explicit statutory recognition of these contracts. A few states do explicitly permit the recipient and the donor to enter
into an agreement concerning the donor's rights. New Hampshire, among
others, allows the sperm donor to agree to paternal responsibilities, including child support liability.[13] In Texas, a sperm donor can sign up to serve as
the father if he provides the sperm to a physician.[14] By contrast, in an Ohio
case, a known sperm donor who did relinquish his rights but then established a relationship with the child was able to claim paternal status.[15] Known
donors, then, may come back and assert parental rights to the child despite
an agreement not to do so. Indeed, if known sperm donors claim paternity,
then the men are often successful, regardless of the existence of a written
agreement providing otherwise. While the "laboratory of states" allows for
a multiplicity of approaches[16] to parenthood, the resulting patchwork results
in uncertainty for parents, children, and donors and fosters an incoherent
approach to fundamental issues of intimacy and identity. Many states have
simply not addressed the complex issues of parenthood involving nonmarital reproduction, egg donation, lack of physician involvement, or known
donors who do, or do not, seek rights.

The parentage statutes that are on the books generally attempt to erase
unknown donors by identifying the legal parents (although they are somewhat confused, and confusing, when it comes to known donors).[17] Donors
are similarly absent in other areas of the law. Apart from what is required for
safety regulation, there are no laws (apart from one statute enacted in Washington State in 2011 that is discussed later) that require any records from
donors or mandate that clinics or banks to maintain records, nor are there
any legal terms regarding confidentiality and disclosure.[18]

II. Half-Siblings?

Parents have firmly grounded rights in the custody, care, and control of their
children. The state also has well-established "*parens patriae*" interests in protecting children's welfare. The doctrine of *parens patriae* denotes the state's
responsibility to protect people under a legal disability, including minors.
The doctrine has justified state intervention in the family to protect a child's
welfare. Consequently, children can be difficult to situate as autonomous
beings within the legal system. Although they have clearly recognized rights
in some contexts, their rights are not identical to those of adults.

As a way to frame children's rights, the constitutional role of parents is
critical. Parents, who have the right to the "care, custody, and control" of
their children, can ordinarily be expected to act in their children's interests.

Parents are constitutionally entitled to raise a child in the manner that they choose. In *Meyer v. Nebraska* (1923), the Court held that the right of liberty "denotes not merely freedom from bodily restraint but also the right of the individual to contract, to engage in any of the common occupations of life . . . to marry, establish a home and bring up children." In the 1925 case of *Pierce v. Society of Sisters*, the Supreme Court stated, "The child is not the mere creature of the state; those who nurture him and direct his destiny have the right, coupled with the high duty, to recognize and prepare him for additional obligations." Seventy-five years later, in *Troxel v. Granville*, the Supreme Court reiterated that parents have a basic right to raise their children, and that the decisions of fit parents should receive great deference. Each of these decisions occurred within the context of a nuclear family, and the Court has repeatedly celebrated the intact nuclear family by, for example, permitting a state to accord no rights whatsoever to a biological father when the mother was married to another man. While children are recognized as capable of holding and exercising constitutional rights, such rights are most practically asserted where parents and children agree or where the child seeks to exercise rights in criminal or administrative proceedings. Asserting a separate right on behalf of the minor child, such as the right to know a donor or to contact a half-sibling, realistically requires the willingness to recognize tensions with established parental decision-making rights. In a few, limited contexts, such as reproductive rights, states have confronted this tension directly by, for example, allowing some girls to access contraceptives and abortions in the absence of parental permission.[19]

Constitutional decision making has overwhelmingly focused on parents' rights: Do unmarried fathers have the right to veto the adoption of their newborn children? Do custodial parents have the right to determine the terms of grandparent visitation? Do women who have relinquished their children for adoption have protections against disclosure of information? Such rights nonetheless involve a measure of reciprocity with children's interests. Family law decision making for younger children generally involves a triad of parties: either mother-father-child or parent-child-state. The assertion of a right by one almost inevitably involves restricting the rights of the others. If, for example, the parents have a thick constitutional right to decide what is in their children's best interests, then the child lacks a corresponding right to compel parents to act in accordance with that best interest standard. Thus, for example, unmarried parents who take certain steps do have constitutionally protected rights with respect to the adoption of their children, custodial parents are owed special deference in their decision making with respect to visitation with third parties, and, unless there is good cause, women have been protected against court-ordered disclosure of their identities in the adoption context.

The absence of a right, on the other hand, does not necessarily dictate a particular outcome. Instead, it may leave the issue open to public policy balancing. If, for example, a parent does not have a constitutional right to veto an abortion favored by the child, then a state may still choose to permit the parent some involvement, short of a veto, in his daughter's decision. In such a setting, the formal recognition of children's rights may be less critical than the question of what public policies influence the child's ability to exercise that right.

III. Sibling Rights

Donor family communities are based on the shared genetic material between "half-siblings," and members of the donor community are often interested in meeting both donors and siblings. Indeed, one large study found that donor-conceived offspring express the same degree of interest in the opportunity to establish a relationship with their donor as they express with respect to other half-siblings; 63 percent expressed interest in a relationship with their donor, while 62 percent expressed a similar interest in a relationship with their half-siblings.[20]

Yet donor siblings are, of course, different from siblings who have grown up together. They have no shared family history, no shared residence, and no common legal parent,[21] even though they share genes (and a lack of knowledge about their donor). Their relationships are based only on shared biological material, rather than on any other bases for claiming kinship.[22] The mother in the tween book *My So-Called Family* poignantly points out the difference between Leah's donor sibling and Charlie, the brother with whom she shares a house:

> "She's not your sister," Mom said. "All you share is a donor."
> "Then Charlie's not my brother," I told her. "All we share is a mother."
> "You don't really believe that," Mom said. "That all you share is me? You've been so much to each other. You're like another mother to him, and he needs you so much. You've grown up together. That's what being a brother or a sister is."[23]

Nonetheless, although many observations concerning siblings do not apply to donor-conceived children, they may offer analogies for thinking about connections between donor-conceived half-siblings. An initial, and foundational, question is what the word "sibling" actually means. The dictionary tells us that siblings have at least one parent in common and are brothers or sisters. California law grants certain rights for someone "to assert a relationship as a sibling related by blood, adoption, or affinity through a common legal or biological parent,"[24] which phrasing, if interpreted broadly, would seem to include donor-conceived siblings who are related by "blood" through a common biological parent.

The status of legal protections for sibling relationships under American law is unclear, even when nondonor siblings have grown up together. First, children's rights—aside from some protections in the contexts of reproduction, criminal law, and a few other limited situations—are generally subordinate to those of their parents. Second, siblings do not have definitive, constitutionally protected association rights regardless of the strength, and length, of their relationships. The U.S. Supreme Court has not recognized the right of siblings to stay together after divorce, foster care, adoption proceedings, or the dissolution of blended families. Moreover, the lower federal courts are far from uniform on the issue, with some recognizing sibling associational rights and others dismissing them entirely. However, Congress has accorded siblings some minimal rights in the foster care system, and some state courts and laws require similar recognition. Possible bases for legally protecting sibling relationships include constitutionally based claims focused on due process under the Fourteenth Amendment and the right of association under the First Amendment, as well as policy-based and pragmatic considerations that emphasize the social and psychological benefits of maintaining sibling relationships. All of these arguments (discussed below) have limited utility in the donor world, where the argument is not that *established* relationships must be protected but that protections should be accorded to *establishing* relationships. Moreover, to the extent that these rights have been protected in any way, this has occurred in the child abuse and neglect system, where the state is intervening in the family and often separates siblings. By contrast, in the donor world, the traditional doctrines of family privacy, which prevent state intervention in an ongoing family, may actually serve as a bar. Nonetheless, the current status of rights accorded existing sibling relationships merits exploration for the possibility of developing analogies. Siblings might obtain rights on the basis of either federal or state law.

1. Federal Laws

The strongest basis for protecting siblings' rights is the U.S. Constitution. But federal law is somewhat negative when it comes to the question of whether siblings have constitutional rights to remain in touch with one another if they have been separated because their parents have abused or neglected them.

Although the U.S. Supreme Court has discussed familial association rights, it has yet to explicitly recognize those rights in the context of sibling relationships. For instance, in the 1984 case of *Roberts v. United States Jaycees*, a nonprofit organization for young men challenged the application of a state statute that banned gender discrimination.[25] The organization claimed that the state had infringed on its male members' freedom of association.[26] Although *Roberts* did not specifically discuss sibling association rights, the decision provided a basis to recognize family association rights in certain contexts because the opinion noted that "[a]s a general matter, only relationships with [familial] sorts of qualities are likely to reflect the considerations that have led to an understanding of freedom of association as an intrinsic element of personal liberty."[27]

Although *Roberts* could provide support for recognizing familial association rights, the Supreme Court has implied that it is the parents who have the strongest rights in the family and can control who visits their children. If so, then this would override sibling interests.[28] In the 2000 case of *Troxel v. Granville*, two grandparents (one of whom was a member of the hit singing group, the Fleetwoods) petitioned for visitation with the children of their deceased son. They relied on Washington law, which—at that point—generously allowed "[a]ny person" to go to court to request "visitation rights at any time including, but not limited to, custody proceedings."[29] In denying the grandparents visitation, the Court worried that a broad application of the statute could lead to situations in which "a parent's decision that visitation would not be in the child's best interest [would be] accorded no deference."[30] The Court "recognized the fundamental right of parents to make decisions concerning the care, custody, and control of their children."[31] As a result of the heavy emphasis placed on parents' right to control who can see their children, a parent (or adoptive parent) arguably can deny a sibling who lives elsewhere the right to see the child. Therefore, the Court's decision in *Troxel* suggests that there is no federal constitutionally protected right for siblings to visit each other, at least when a parent, adoptive parent, or foster parent desires to prevent such contact. It should also be noted that the year before *Troxel* was decided, the Court denied certiorari and declined in *Hugo P. v. George P.* to decide whether or not siblings have constitutionally protected association rights.[32]

The circuit courts, the intermediate federal courts, have occasionally considered whether siblings have a constitutional right to associate.[33] Their views are far from uniform. Some have suggested that sibling associational rights might be protected, while some have not.[34] The lower, federal trial courts are similarly divided. For instance, in an attempt to establish that siblings have a constitutionally protected association right, one court eloquently stated that "[t]he relationship between two family members is the paradigm of such intimate human relationship [as discussed in the *Roberts* case]."[35] In another case, however, nine siblings sued New York State, claiming that the state failed to keep their family intact because four siblings who were voluntarily placed in foster care were prevented from being reunited with them.[36] The court rejected their argument that the "state [is required] to provide services . . . to keep their large family together."[37] Given the lack of uniformity, it appears uncertain whether siblings can establish in the near future a definitive, federally protected right to associate.

2. Siblings and State Law

Although the federal constitution may not give protection to siblings' associational rights, in some states, legislation or courts offer some hope for sibling relationships. The broad array of state statutes illustrates the diverse interpretation of sibling association rights.

Many state statutes have addressed the visitation rights for siblings, although there is enormous variation.[38] California and approximately nine other states give children the right to seek visitation with a sibling in the context of a dependency action.[39] Some states do not explicitly grant siblings the right to petition for visitation with each other, but instead require that sibling visitation rights be considered when children are involved with the abuse and neglect system.[40] For example, seven states and the District of Columbia[41] address sibling visitation only to the extent that it must be resolved when the state takes custody of a child.[42] Therefore, given the wide array of state statutes that address sibling visitation rights directly, indirectly, or not at all, the concept of general sibling association rights varies among states as well.

A number of state statutes also allude to sibling rights in custody disputes. Some state statutes take into account the child's relationship with his/her siblings, and a number of "legislatures and courts have even created a legal presumption against split custody as awareness has grown of the great importance that sibling bonds can have for children, particularly in the midst of marital dissolution."[43] At the same time, however, the rights of siblings during child protective proceedings are relatively weak. State agencies have great discretion as to where to place children who are in foster care, and "although the law in some states requires such agencies to attempt to keep siblings together in the same residence, in most states the law does not require them to keep siblings together when that would be best for them."[44] A number of states statutes, including those in Connecticut,[45] Massachusetts,[46] and New York,[47] similarly instruct state adoption agencies to try to place siblings with the same adoptive parents; however, these statutes do not require the agencies to actually place them together if doing so would not be in the children's best interests.[48] Therefore, while legislators appear to favor keeping siblings together, the statutes they produce also reveal a hesitation to grant absolute association rights among brothers and sisters.

Similar to statutes in the realms of custody and visitation, court cases reveal a divide among states as to whether or not siblings have association rights. Case law can be instructive with regard to the legal rights of donor families, so it is useful to explore how courts handle these issues. State courts will sometimes grant siblings the right to see or visit each other in the absence of or to supplement a state statute, particularly when sibling contact is found to be in the best interests of the subject child.[49] For instance, in *In re Tamara R.*, a father refused to allow his daughter, Tamara R., to see her siblings after she alleged that he sexually abused her and she was placed in the state's custody.[50] The court held that Tamara R. had a right to visit with her siblings and that the "state's interest in the protection of a minor child who has been removed from her parent's care is sufficiently compelling to justify over-riding her parent's opposition to visitation with her sibling, if there is evidence that denial of sibling visitation would harm the minor child."[51] Similarly, the Supreme Court of New Jersey has emphasized that "'[a] sibling relationship can be an independent emotionally supportive factor for children in ways quite distinctive from other relationships.'"[52] These state court decisions illustrate a view that sibling association rights should be protected when their families fragment.

However, not all state courts provide sibling rights with such strong protection. In 2002, the California Second District Court of Appeal, rejected a plaintiff's claim for visitation with her minor half-brother under a state statute that read, "If either parent of an unemancipated minor child is deceased . . . siblings may be granted reasonable visitation with the child during the child's minority upon a finding that the visitation would be in the best interest of the minor child."[53] Instead, the court ruled that the statute "unconstitutionally infringes" upon the "fundamental liberty interest of a fit [surviving] parent to select with whom the child should associate."[54] The court's ruling echoed the Supreme Court's holding in *Troxel* that parents should be afforded some control over who visits their children.

When it comes to siblings who have never lived together, as is the case for donor-conceived half-siblings, such state-provided rights are even weaker. In a Utah case, a woman who had custody of her youngest child wished to obtain custody of her oldest child.[55] The court rejected the mother's argument that she should have custody of the oldest child in order to keep the siblings together because "[e]xcept for brief periods of visitation, the brothers have never lived together. . . . No bonding between them occurred prior to their parents' divorce."[56] These cases suggest that a relationship purely based on biology, without the existence of any other connection, may not be protected. There usually needs to be a preexisting relationship, based on living together or visiting with each other, in order to establish and preserve sibling association rights.

Even where the siblings themselves make a case to stay together, courts reject their claims. Damon and Alleah had lived with their adoptive family for almost three years before their sister, Meridian, was born. Tiffani and Isaiah were the biological parents of all three children. When she was a few months old, Meridian was placed with a foster family who ultimately sought to adopt her. Damon and Alleah's parents objected, arguing that the children had a constitutional right to have Meridian live with them. The court reasoned that because Tiffani was no longer the parent of any of the three children, "we are not persuaded that it would be logical or prudent to conclude that a constitutionally protected sibling relationship somehow rises from the ashes of a lawfully terminated or relinquished parent-child relationship."[57] While the court conceded that the sibling relationship was one factor to be considered, it was not determinative, and it allowed the separation of the siblings.

Thus, state statutes and case law afford only limited protection to sibling association rights in some circumstances. However, especially in cases where the siblings have never met, such protection is far from universal and is often explicitly deemed nonexistent. The biological connection, without anything further, such as having lived together, does not give rise to a protected interest.

3. Siblings' Rights?

Although existing law is somewhat confused, and not entirely supportive, there are some promising arguments that provide a basis for grounding siblings' rights. The Fourteenth Amendment has been used as the basis for a substantive due process argument in favor of sibling association rights. For instance, the Supreme Court does protect familial relationships, and sibling associational rights fit within this jurisprudence.[58]

The First Amendment has also been used as a constitutional basis to protect the rights of siblings to associate with each other. The Supreme Court has recognized that "choices to enter into and maintain certain intimate human relationships must be secured against undue intrusion by the State because of the role of such relationships in safeguarding the individual freedom that is central to our constitutional scheme."[59] There are multiple cases in which, "[u]nder this theory, siblings who have been separated by the sate [sic] have successfully argued . . . that the State has deprived them of a constitutionally protected right to associate with each other."[60] However, despite the Court's acknowledgment of familial association rights, the Court may be hesitant to grant children any rights at the expense of their parents' wishes.

Some policy reasons in favor of sibling association rights are grounded in the social importance of sibling relationships. A multitude of law review articles and cases provide policy arguments in favor of keeping siblings together as much as possible. Proponents argue that preserving the bond between siblings provides many psychological and social benefits,[61] particularly in families that are in turmoil.[62] As one legal commentator has observed,

> The sibling relationship is unique—different from the relationships between husband and wife, parent and child, or friend and friend. It is an important part of a child's social development. Siblings act as socialization agents through long-term contacts; moreover, social skills and foundations for subsequent learning and personality developments are established. They learn how to share and compromise, resolve their differences, and work together.[63]

Indeed, courts have relied in part on the social and psychological benefits siblings provide each other to protect sibling association rights. In fact, one court observed that sibling visitation should be allowed "if there is evidence that denial of sibling visitation would harm the minor child who is separated from her family."[64] The Appellate Division of the New York Supreme Court decided in *Lyons v. Lyons* to grant custody of four children to a father in part because "there is a strong policy in maintaining close sibling relationships wherever possible."[65] Therefore, while courts most heavily rely on constitutional or statutory grounds to allow siblings to visit or see each other, they sometimes cite general policy reasons to keep sibling relations intact as well.

Although various arguments exist in favor of sibling association rights, the law remains largely unsettled. The U.S. Supreme Court has not recognized a federal constitutionally protected right for siblings to stay together after divorce, foster care, or adoption proceedings. Some federal cases, state decisions, and state statutes, however, do protect sibling relationships. The wide array of cases and state statutes regarding the issue illustrate that sibling association rights are not uniformly recognized. In thinking about different concepts of the state's role in this potential morass of conflicting interests, however, it is useful to note that there is certainly the option for law to acknowledge and protect sibling connections. For donor families, this means that space exists for half-siblings to develop relationships, and for legal regulation to provide the opportunity for this to occur. In turn, this suggests that the appropriate state role is supporting the development of new relationships with others who share the same donor, rather than adhering to a strict model of the nuclear family that forecloses the possibility of "half-siblings." Indeed, the need for such an approach is one of the core themes of this book: recognizing connections among donor-conceived kin is as much about the meaning of family as it is about how to regulate families. If donor-conceived families are, like traditional families, relational entities, then the law can protect and foster donor families. Accordingly, this means a focus on the meaning of family, not the technology and medicine that create the family members.

6

Law, Adoption, and Family Secrets

Disclosure and Incest

The pervasiveness and visibility of families in which children and one (or more) parent(s) do not share a biological tie is comparatively recent. While adoption has been practiced throughout history, its contemporary form—in which the adoptive family serves as a legally complete substitute for the biological family—is less than two centuries old. Adoption and ART have many parallels; most significant, of course, is that both enable people to become parents outside of the paradigm of heterosexual reproduction. Similarly, adoption and ART law, policy, and practice must balance the sometimes-competing rights and interests of the parties involved, whether they are gamete providers, recipients and donor-conceived offspring, or birth parents, adoptive parents, and adopted persons. Moreover, the adoption world has experienced issues of secrecy and disclosure that are comparable to those in the donor world, and both have also had to confront issues relating to the meaning of incest.

Indeed, while adoption and ART are different in many ways, practices in the adoption world provide some models for the donor world. After detailing

the similarities and differences between adoption and ART, this chapter
next discusses legal and cultural aspects of secrecy in both the adoption
and donor context. Finally, it turns to another family "secret": incest. Incest
has proven to be problematic in adoption law; in donor-conceived families,
incest is even more complicated, given the existence not only of secret biological connections but also of the possibility of dozens of related half-siblings. Consequently, exploring the similarities and dissimilarities between
adoption and the donor-conceived world provides a basis for the final part of
this book, which addresses the topic of regulation: adoption offers larger lessons on issues like the difficulty of adapting existing practices to include new
family forms. More specifically, it shows the importance of allowing children
to learn more about their biological identity and of preventing intimate relationships between family members.

I. Questioning the Adoption/ART Analogy

To be sure, the analogies between adoption and reproductive technology are
only that: analogies. There are numerous differences between them, beginning with the regulatory structure and continuing with the relational context. First, adoption has historically (since the mid-nineteenth century) been
subject to state oversight, and there is even an international treaty in the area;
and the child abuse and neglect/foster care system, which is closely related to
adoption, is highly regulated by both state and federal laws. State adoption
laws explicitly focus on decision making that is in the best interest of the
child and that considers the fitness of the parents, and there are laws that
clearly specify the rights and obligations of biological and adoptive parents.

States have well-established regulatory systems to protect the integrity of
the adoption process, including information about all parties to the adoption. An adoption can only be finalized pursuant to a court order; the rights
of the biological parents must be terminated (either voluntarily or involun-
tarily) before the child becomes available for adoption; adoption agencies
must be state-licensed; and, although agencies may charge fees for certain
expenses, including those related to the biological mother, there is a clear
prohibition on the sale of babies. Surrogacy presents a special situation, and
it is highly regulated; indeed, while it is permitted in many states and may
be treated comparably to adoptions, some states simply ban it as too close to
baby selling.

On the other hand, the regulation of reproductive technology is far less
unified and coherent. While adoption requires a judicial recognition of each
new parent-child relationship and provides clearly defined legal rights for all

parties, there need be no public aspect of any part of assisted reproduction. Donors' interests are protected by contracts and by laws that directly address parenthood through assisted reproduction, although the coverage and scope of these laws vary from state to state. Gametes are obtained through a private market with little oversight. Over the past twenty years, the federal government has become involved in regulating the safety of gamete handling and in preventing deceptive practices by clinics concerning the success of their procedures.[1] The Centers for Disease Control and Prevention (CDC) publishes an annual report summarizing success rates; the report does not include statistics on sperm donation, and there are no legal sanctions on clinics for failing to report their data.[2] While other countries limit the numbers of times one person can donate sperm or eggs, or the numbers of embryos that can be implanted in one woman, or the payments that can be made for gametes, there are no comparable binding federal limits on these issues in the United States (although a few states have provided some limits in these areas). While the industry's own self-regulatory organizations, such as the American Society for Reproductive Medicine (ASRM) and the American Association of Tissue Banks, do offer guidance on many of these issues, their recommendations are influential, but they are not mandatory.[3] Through their own initiative, individual clinics have also developed and implemented their own standards.

Second, the interests of the family members involved in reproductive technology and in adoption are overlapping, but not identical. Children conceived through donor gametes (aside from those conceived through donor embryos) typically live with one biologically related parent and perhaps even with related siblings, while the typical adoptee (outside of the significant number of children adopted by family members or those adopted from foster care) does not live with—or have contact with—anyone to whom he or she has any genetic connection. Consequently, while adoptees may wonder why their biological parents could not keep them, donor offspring do not have to face this particular set of issues.[4] Adoptees typically learn at a young age that they are adopted, but donor offspring are far less likely to learn of their status, and many parents do not disclose this information to them. The names of the biological parents of adoptees exist on an original birth certificate; donors are known by their numbers, and the permanence of any record about them is questionable. Moreover, while there is an increasing amount of research on biological parents who have relinquished their children for adoption, there is far less research on gamete donors.[5]

Nonetheless, both donor-conceived children and adoptees experience the same lack of connection with at least one-half of their genetic heritages. Writer A. M. Homes, who is adopted, describes what it was like to learn that she and her biological mother shared certain habits as "this indescribable subtlety of biology."[6] It is this lack of knowledge about their biological progenitors and the emotional needs for this knowledge, which many adoptees and donor offspring articulate, that has motivated advocates within each movement to push for disclosure, and that motivates calls for a national, mandatory databank. Based on a new regulatory paradigm that respects family, the law can respond to the voices of the donor conceived.

II. Secrecy and Disclosure

In the worlds of adoption and of donor conception, multiple layers of secrecy exist. First, in both types of families, the existence of a nonbiological parent-child relationship may be hidden from view. Indeed, adoption professionals historically tried to "match" babies to new parents, and the biological mother was encouraged to move on with her life as though she had never been pregnant. This layer of secrecy has dissipated more quickly in the adoption world than in the donor world as the stigma of nonmarital sexuality has almost disappeared, as birth parents have become more involved in the adoption process, as social workers have changed their practices, and as increasing numbers of different kind of families seek to adopt.

A second layer of secrecy relates to information about the biological parents. Like the reproductive technology field, adoption law has faced numerous issues concerning children's access to information about their biological progenitors,[7] even though each field has a different history of protecting confidentiality. It was not until the early twentieth century that adoption records began to become legally sealed from a prying public.[8] States allowed members of the adoption triad access to these records until the latter half of the twentieth century.

While this secret, closed system is a relatively recent phenomenon in adoption, the secrecy of donor sperm dates to its earliest known uses.[9] The history of secrecy in the donor eggs' context, as with adoption, is also fairly recent (indeed, the use of donor eggs has only been possible since the successful development of IVF thirty years ago). Donor eggs initially involved known donors, although today, egg providers are more likely to be unknown and promised confidentiality. Unlike adoption, where secrecy is preserved through state law, in the donor world, secrecy is highly dependent on private agreements between the donor and the sperm bank or egg agency. While the 1973 Uniform Parentage Act did direct that "[a]ll papers and records pertaining to the insemination, whether part of the permanent record of a court or of a file held by the supervising physician or elsewhere, are subject to inspection only upon an order of the court for good cause shown," this was not the law of many states; moreover, in context, it refers to the physician's medical procedures rather than records about the donor.[10] Indeed, today, the physician who performs the insemination may have no information about the donor that could be inspected.

The pressure for allowing donor-conceived children access to identifying information about their gamete providers is analogous to that in the adoption context, although responses to this pressure are less legally well developed in the latter context than in the former.[11] The private Donor Sibling Registry has taken the lead in helping families formed through donor gametes voluntarily find each other, but the registry's success has occurred without supporting laws.

The history of secrecy in adoption stems from a variety of sources that are comparable to those in the donor gamete situation. Keeping donor sperm or adoption secret has facilitated a couple's appearance of fertility and may have helped with the acceptance of the resulting children, who were not "strangers" within their new families.[12] Unlike adoption, which, although surrounded by secrecy, involves legal procedures and multiple parties outside the newly formed family, using donor sperm simulated the expected familial relationships because it requires no public involvement. In his 1964 book, Dr. Wilfred Finegold, the head of the Division of Sterility at the Planned Parenthood Center in Pittsburgh, explained the advantages of artificial insemination (AI): "The husband's infertility is a secret in A.I. To his friends, the husband has finally impregnated his wife. . . . In A.I., the child is never told."[13] The donor's characteristics should be, he observed, similar to those of the husband's and the two men must be of the same religion.[14] Further, Dr. Finegold explained that "all" physicians require an anonymous donor, and he listed a series of precautions for preserving the sperm provider's anonymity.[15] These mechanisms provided "cover" for the recipient family so that only the doctor would know for sure: they create "the family that would have been (absent infertility)." Returning to one of the book's guiding themes—the meaning of family—these practices maintained the appearance of a traditional family even as they began to provide the basis for forming alternative families. And, as discussed in earlier chapters, while parents may no longer seek to create the family that would have been, they have numerous other motivations in selecting specific donors.

1. Confidentiality and Adoption

Until the past several decades, many social workers and other professionals involved in adoption have reinforced the belief that a biological connection has no role to play once an adoption has occurred. The process was closed from the beginning. This approach viewed adoption as a complete substitute for any blood ties, and was thus generally against allowing any type of tie between adoptive and biological families, whether it be in the context of open adoptions, through which a biological parent retains some contact with the adoptee, or open records, such that an adoptee has access to her original birth certificate. In an effort to "overcome" any connections engendered by the biological relationship, experts attempted to deny it completely. Accordingly, biological mothers were frequently assured that, following the birth, they would be able to move on with their lives as though nothing had happened. Adoption records were sealed so that the adoptive family became "the same" as the biological family (and legally, this was true). The biological tie was considered erased for both the birth mother and the adoptee. When the first "modern" adoption statutes were enacted around the middle part of the nineteenth century, they focused on legitimizing the practice of adoption and protecting the welfare of the child.[16] These statutes did not address secrecy or confidentiality. Adoption evolved over the next century, becoming more bureaucratic and professionalized and, ultimately, more confidential in an effort to protect birth mothers and the newly formed family.

During the 1930s and 1940s, states began issuing new birth certificates to adopted children. The purpose of these new birth certificates was *not* to prevent adoptees from accessing their original birth certificates. Instead, this was an effort to improve the collection of children's vital statistics as well as to reduce the stigma of illegitimacy. As these children became adults during the 1970s, they brought lawsuits seeking access to their original birth records, and in the 1990s, their efforts resulted in some successful court cases and referenda. For donor-conceived people, who have similar interests in learning about genetic connections, the advocacy in the adoption movement provides useful lessons.

Two states—Kansas and Alaska—never sealed their records, and, over the past dozen years, another set of states has opened their adoption records and made them available, including Alabama, Delaware, Maine, New Hampshire, Oregon, and Tennessee.[17] In a group of additional states, there is limited access to this information: adult adoptees born during specific time periods do not have the right to access their birth certificates, while those who were born either before or after that time period are able to access their records.[18]

Other states have developed different approaches when it comes to the determination of whether adoptees should have access to identifying information, and some have enacted legislation establishing mutual voluntary registries or confidential intermediary systems.[19] Mutual voluntary (or passive) registries require the existence of consent for disclosure of the relevant information from both the adoptee and the biological parent before any information can be released. States have not adopted a uniform approach to the procedures for mutual consent registries. Most systems require consent from at least one biological parent and the adult adoptee (adoptive parents may be able to consent if the adopted person is still a minor), before the disclosure of any identifying information. The Donor Sibling Registry is an example of a mutual-consent registry in the gamete world that is already in existence and that works in a similar way—the key is voluntary registration by the two (or more) parties that produces the matches.

Another group of states has established a mechanism for a confidential intermediary system, which authorizes a third party to help find the biological family members to determine whether they will consent to the release of information.[20] Confidential intermediary systems are more active than the mutual consent registries because an adoptee can initiate the process, which might result in contact, and need not wait for the biological parent to indicate a willingness to be identified.[21] While, in a large group of states, adoptees do not have access to their original birth certificates or to records from their adoptions, they can nonetheless petition a court for the release of their original birth certificates and, for good cause shown, a court may grant this access.[22] Moreover, the number of adoptions in which the families have some kind of relationship from the beginning (pre-birth) has grown substantially, with the majority of adoptive and birth parents meeting in advance of an infant adoption.[23]

2. Confidentiality and Donor Gametes

Confidentiality protections in the donor gamete context come from various sources: statutes, private contracts, case law—and many participants' expectations. The Uniform Parentage Act (UPA) of 1973, in a section dealing with parentage in the context of donor insemination and echoing language from the adoption world, provides, "All papers and records pertaining to the insemination, whether part of the permanent record of a court or of a file held by the supervising physician or elsewhere, *are subject to inspection only upon an order of the court for good cause shown*."[24]

The UPA was enacted in eighteen states; although it remains on the books in numerous states, it has now (as discussed in chapter 5) been superseded by the 2002 UPA, which contains no such language in the provisions governing assisted reproduction using donor gametes.[25] Few other states have established even minimal record-keeping requirements.[26]

Accordingly, few cases involving donor identity disclosure have reached the United States courts. One of the first cases, *Johnson v. Superior Court*,[27] began in the mid-1990s when parents sued a clinic that had allegedly provided them with defective sperm from a donor who had a family history of kidney disease; issues involving the disclosure of the genetic parent's identity were incidental to the underlying tort claims. In order to gather evidence, the parents wanted to ask questions of the donor, who had been promised anonymity by the bank. The court considered the UPA to determine whether the contract between the recipient parents and the bank protecting confidentiality of the donor controlled the issue of whether the donor could be compelled to appear at a deposition. The court noted that there were no reported decisions concerning the UPA's "good cause" standard, and ultimately held that "insemination records, including a sperm donor's identity and related information contained in those records, may be disclosed under certain circumstances."[28] This was not a case where donor offspring sought access to information; consequently, the court was not called upon to decide the circumstances under which a court would disclose such information to a child pursuant to the UPA. Nonetheless, the court did not foreclose such a possibility, opining,

> And enforcement under all circumstances of a confidentiality provision such as the one in Cryobank's contract with the Johnsons conflicts with California's compelling interest in the health and welfare of children, including those conceived by artificial insemination. There may be instances under which a child conceived by artificial insemination may need his or her family's genetic and medical history for important medical decisions.[29]

No other court has interpreted this provision, although the term "good cause" has a long history in the adoption context when it comes to courts' allowing the disclosure of birth records.[30]

In another context, Minor J sued his mother, Diane J, to find out the identity of his biological father.[31] Minor J was born in 1989 to Ms. and Mr. J. His parents were divorced in 1995. Although both Minor J and Mr. J had assumed that Mr. J was the biological father, DNA tests after the divorce indicated that there was no biological connection between the two. Minor J sued his mother in 2006, seeking to require her to reveal the identity of his biological father. Both the trial and appellate courts refused to allow the case to proceed because of the marital presumption: the strong assumption that a child born into a marriage is the legal child of the husband and wife.[32]

In yet another sperm identity case, again not involving a child's effort to determine identifying information about a sperm donor, "Michael Hayes" sued an Oregon fertility clinic to determine whether his sperm was mistakenly used to inseminate a stranger rather than, as he had intended, his fiancée. M.H., as he is known in the court papers, wanted to establish a relationship with the child who might have been born. The woman who received the sperm—who had not revealed whether she gave birth to a child—wanted to be left alone, without revealing her identity (in the court papers, she is known only as "Jane Doe").[33] She alleges that she was forced to take a morning-after pill, and even offered a free abortion. The judge prevented M.H. from finding out whether he is a biological father, again using the marital presumption to shield the woman and her husband from further scrutiny.[34]

In Canada, by contrast, a donor-conceived offspring, Olivia Pratten, courageously sued the province of British Columbia in 2008, hoping to end anonymity. This lawsuit is a landmark in providing lessons for the donor-conceived advocacy movement. Ms. Pratten's mother, Shirley Pratten, went to a Vancouver fertility clinic seeking donor sperm, and her physician told her he would find a donor who resembled her husband. The physician also warned her not to tell her child about her origins.[35] (Subsequently, the only information that the family was able to learn about the donor was that he was apparently a healthy blue-eyed medical student with type A blood.)[36] A few years after her daughter's birth, Shirley Pratten helped found the first support group in Canada for parents of children who had been donor conceived.

Shirley Pratten did not follow her physician's advice about nondisclosure and, when her daughter was five, Ms. Pratten told her that she was donor conceived. Her mother, explained Olivia Pratten, "told me a simple story of the seed and the egg and how 'daddy didn't have enough so a nice man gave us extra.' I was told in a way that made me feel very special, wanted and loved. I remember asking sometimes to be told again and again, I thought it was so cool."[37] Before filing the lawsuit, she had contacted the doctor who performed the insemination, but he refused to reveal the donor's identity; as he later explained, not only was he not required to keep records for longer than six years, but also both Ms. Pratten's mother and the donor had filed statements protecting the donor's anonymity.[38] Indeed, in opposing the lawsuit, the lawyer representing British Columbia argued that the privacy rights of anonymous sperm donors should trump any potential constitutional rights that a donor offspring might assert.

Three years after the lawsuit began, Ms. Pratten's efforts were successful, at least for future donor-conceived offspring. A judge on the British Columbia Supreme Court issued a 123-page opinion finding that British Columbia should no longer allow anonymous donation of gametes.[39] The opinion was grounded in the Canadian Charter (equivalent to the U.S. Constitution) and in the law of British Columbia, which was amended in 1996 to allow adopted children, but not ART children, the right to gain information about their genetic parents. Indeed, British Columbia adoption law requires the retention of records concerning the medical and social history of the biological parents for at least nineteen years. The core issues surrounded whether donor-conceived people should have the same rights as adopted people.

As a prelude to its analysis of the legal arguments, the court reviewed the evidence presented at the trial, which included personal stories of donor-conceived offspring as well as expert testimony on the impact of anonymity. Based on this evidence, the court concluded that "assisted reproduction using an anonymous gamete donor is harmful to the child, and it is not in the best interests of donor offspring." With respect to the claim of discrimination between the donor conceived and adoptees, the court decided that the province impermissibly distinguished between those who are "disassociated from their biological parents" based on whether they were adopted or donor conceived. "The circumstances of adoptees and those of donor offspring with regard to the need to know and have connection with one's roots," the court observed, "are closely comparable."[40] While the court refused to find an affirmative obligation on the government to ensure that, both prospectively and retroactively, the donor conceived could access information, that was irrelevant to the claimed discrimination. The court gave the government fifteen months to change British Columbia law to protect the rights of donor-conceived offspring. Regardless of whether British Columbia ever changes its law, the case is significant for its recognition of the similarities of the needs of the donor-conceived and adoptees. It provides encouragement for other donor-conceived people who want to use the legal system to advocate for disclosure.

While donor offspring in the United States have not yet begun to bring lawsuits on their own behalf nor organized in the same manner concerning the need for disclosure as have adoptees (or Olivia Pratten in Canada), the donor movement is beginning to place pressure on the gamete industry for more disclosure. The Donor Sibling Registry has operated a voluntary, mutual, Internet-based registry for matching, but there are no comparable state-mandated procedures. The donor movement could learn from adoption rights advocates about the reasons for requiring disclosure. Particularly given the growing number of states that allow adoptees access to their original birth certificates, this may provide support for comparable legal claims to better records and disclosure for the donor conceived.

In addition, given that one man is capable of providing sperm for numerous children (in 2011, the *New York Times* reported on one man whose sperm had created 150 offspring),[41] information release would provide two additional services in the donor world that are unnecessary in the adoption world: first, it may prevent half-siblings from marrying each other; and second, it may allow for limits on the numbers of children created through one person's donation. In England, for example, there is a limit of no more than ten families per gamete donor, although the potential number of children per family is unlimited.[42] The ASRM has suggested guidelines for limitations on donations; they are not, however, binding.[43]

III. Incest? One Hundred Half-Siblings Is Too Many

The lack of limits on the number of children provides a focal point for regulation. Its dangers—infringing on the identity of children (discussed above) and creating an increased risk of incest (discussed below)—provide a clear illustration of the dangers of letting the market have unfettered control over the fertility industry. The potential for incest could be a way to create, change, or impose laws that regulate the fertility industry. Sweeping legal change often begins with something specific, and incest provides an excellent example or case study to use in pushing for wider regulation of the industry. Indeed, incest is an increasing concern in the brave new world of test tube families. In 1980, Martin Curie-Cohen raised the possibility of "inadvertent inbreeding" from donor sperm. Others have called this "accidental incest, where the offspring of donated sperm or ova meet and are unknowingly attracted."[44] The groundbreaking Warnock Commission report in 1984 mentioned the possibility of incestuous matings between donor-conceived offspring.[45]

Incest is one of the key, driving issues for disclosure. Indeed, parents may want to disclose as much as they can. A mother of a teenager conceived through sperm donation explained, "'My daughter knows her donor's number for this very reason. . . . She's been in school with numerous kids who were born through donors. She's had crushes on boys who are donor children. It's become part of sex education' for her."[46] It helps provide a justification for imposing limits on the number of children born from any individual donor. Nonetheless, no laws directly address the possibility of accidental incest in the donor world. Instead, existing incest laws must be applied to prevent half-siblings, or donors and their offspring, from marrying.

The incest prohibition that prevents relatives from marrying each other is deeply rooted in American law, and it is derived from British ecclesiastical laws on prohibited marriages. By the beginning of the twentieth century, all states banned some types of incestuous marriages.[47] Incestuous relationships may subject both parties to criminal prosecution and may result in voided marriages.[48] That is, incest is a double wrong against the public, with both a criminal and a civil component. States prosecute people who have become involved in prohibited sexual relationships with family members. Incest lies at the intersection of family law and criminal law: the crime depends on the definition of family; it criminalizes what would otherwise be legal, consensual acts because of the family relationship between the parties.

Nonetheless, states have differing parameters for which relationships qualify as incestuous, with a significant minority of states allowing, for example, first cousins to marry. Some states explicitly mention half-siblings, those who share one, but not another parent; some states explicitly mention adoptees. Moreover, when it comes to donor-conceived offspring, coverage is similarly unclear: the ban may not cover siblings who grow up in different families, nor those who are related by a half, rather than a full, genetic tie. Consequently, not all states might bar relationships between donors and their children, nor between donor-related siblings.

Consider the following cases. In 1986, an Indiana court overturned the incest conviction of a man who had intercourse with his biological daughter who had been adopted by another family at the age of four. The court reasoned that the adoption completely severed the biological relationship; the child's parents were her adoptive parents.[49] In overruling this decision three years later, however, the Indiana Supreme Court observed that "the link of consanguinity cannot be erased by enactment" of the adoption statute that confers legal parenthood.[50] Similarly, a Delaware court allowed an incest prosecution to proceed against a half-brother and half-sister who had the same mother.[51] The sister had been adopted when she was ten days old, and her brother had been raised as a ward of the state. Although the adoption statute eliminated any ties between the biological parents and the children, the blood relationship continued.

But perhaps the incest bar should not apply in the donor world, where the only tie is biological and the people are adults with no preexisting emotional relationships, power imbalances, or even domestic living arrangements. More generally, the incest ban has come under increasing attack as violating a right to privacy, and it may simply be that we don't need to ban incest between donor-conceived siblings. As William Saletan wrote in *Slate* a decade ago, "Morally, I think incest is bad because it confuses relationships. But legally, I don't see why a sexual right to privacy, if it exists, shouldn't cover consensual incest."[52] The traditional justifications for incest bans have centered on religion, genetics, and anthropology.[53] Newer accounts have relied on insight from evolutionary biology to support "kinship avoidance" behavior.[54] Freud opined that incest was natural, that girls inevitably felt sexual desire for their fathers.[55] Although the veracity of this analysis has been repeatedly questioned,[56] it does show the complexity of the issues involved in discussing incest, and the potential problems in using accidental incest as the basis for future regulation. Nonetheless, numerous reasons exist for applying the incest ban to donor-conceived family members.

1. Genetics

In any given nonconsanguineous relationship, the rate of severe abnormalities in offspring is estimated to be between 2 and 3 percent.[57] Between first cousins, the risk increases to between 4 and 7 percent, while children of siblings or a parent-child coupling have a risk between 32 and 44 percent.[58] While it is difficult to study the impact on humans over numerous generations, studies of other animals show the genetic and survival costs of inbreeding.[59] When sibling birds are paired over successive generations, the offspring line dies out because "some damaging genes are more likely to be expressed in inbred animals. Some potentially harmful genes are recessive and therefore harmless when they are paired with a dissimilar gene, but they become damaging in their effects when combined with an identical gene."[60]

The higher rate of genetic abnormalities in consanguineous relationships provides a partial justification for the incest prohibition. Yet it does not entirely explain the strength of the prohibition, given that the overwhelming number of children born to these relationships will not have abnormalities, and that we do not require genetic testing "even when there is a strong likelihood that each parent carries a recessive trait, as in the case of Tay-Sachs disease in the Ashkenazi Jewish community."[61] Moreover, the incest ban, which has existed for centuries, arose prior to our contemporary understanding of the relationship between genes and consanguinity. On the other hand, early incest bans may have resulted from the anecdotal observations of abnormal children who resulted from sexual relationships between closely related family members.[62]

Given our knowledge about genetics, we might decide that it is appropriate, given the potential harm, to police certain relationships because of the statistically significant increased risk of genetic abnormalities. The risk of harm to future offspring is palpable and certain (although most such offspring will not experience these abnormalities).[63] Modern understandings of genetics documented in the studies discussed above provide a strong basis for making such an assessment.

2. Evolutionary Biology

In his 1891 book, Edward Westermarck suggested that sexual aversion develops between family members who are raised together.[64] Subsequent studies have confirmed and refined his initial hypothesis, suggesting a strong psychological mechanism against sexual relationships with intimate family members that does not necessarily depend on shared genes, but rather on behaviors most likely to detect shared genes: while it is difficult to perform a controlled experiment on the Westermarck hypothesis, evidence from Israeli kibbutzim and Taiwanese marriages provides support for evolutionarily based incest avoidance behavior.[65]

3. Morality

Moral repugnance and disgust have served as traditional bases for the incest ban.[66] Many states legislate against activities such as incest "just because those activities are wrong."[67] Disgust is a cluster of approaches based in human emotional reactions to various acts, involving extreme aversion typically based on a fear of contamination.[68] It is inherently connected with underlying cultural values, although some behaviors appear to elicit disgust across cultures.[69] Disgust can provide a useful basis for judging the legality of certain acts: for example, disgust might help in distinguishing various kinds of murders, with more disgusting ones more deserving of harsher sanctions.[70] It might be possible to develop appropriately structured disgust responses within the law "so that we come to value what is *genuinely* high and to despise what is *genuinely* low."[71]

On the other hand, disgust is an emotion that has, as the Supreme Court's landmark opinion in *Lawrence v. Texas* shows, typically been used as a way to ostracize and discriminate against acts that are culturally unpopular.[72] Disgust establishes a hierarchy of appropriate behavior that attempts to limit not just public, but also intimate, actions.[73] While the acts themselves may not be harmful, culturally conditioned responses result in strong feelings of aversion that, without any other basis, are converted into law. The long history of anti-miscegenation laws provides an example of how one group's feelings of disgust resulted in discriminatory legislation. As Martha Nussbaum claims, not all incestuous relationships inspire the same amount of disgust: "if we want to find reasons to make [brother-sister or adult-first-cousin] incest illegal, disgust will not help us, and arguments about health issues are perhaps exactly what we need."[74] The emotion of disgust is, on this view, an unstable basis for making legal decisions.

Ultimately, the initial reaction of disgust may serve as a useful guide for establishing a legal framework for incest, so long as this reaction is subjected to a more rigorous analysis that explores its bases. Within the donor world, however, these feelings toward potential matings between offspring conceived with the same gametes can be quite intense.

4. Feminist Approaches

Numerous feminist scholars argue for relaxing the incest ban on consensual sexual relationships between adults. Such bans cannot, as law professors Jennifer Collins, Ethan Lieb, and Dan Markel observe, be maintained given the Supreme Court's recognition of a liberty right in consensual sexual relationships: "[A] respect for autonomy and limited government permits consenting adults to engage in the sexual relations they deem appropriate."[75] Although she does not advocate overturning incest laws, Professor Courtney Cahill urges "that the law reappraise the extent to which [it is motivated by] disgust."[76] The Supreme Court has never opined directly on the constitutionality of the incest ban, so states can experiment in developing their own laws on incest in the donor world and articulating the reasons for these laws. Indeed, it is possible to distinguish incest from other consensual sexual relationships that have elicited moral revulsion, using rationales other than disgust, such as abuse of trust or abuse of power.

While many of the traditional explanations for the incest prohibition do not apply in the donor world context when it comes to restrictions on gamete provision, it is useful to recognize that recipients of gametes from the same donor often do feel connection and kinship based on biology. Finding ten half-siblings is very different from learning about 150, or even 50. Responding to the concerns of donor-conceived families provides an important basis for seeking additional regulation. The examination in this chapter of incest from biological, ethical, feminist, and other perspectives shows the complexity of further regulation in the donor world by clarifying how donor-conceived families and their communities are both similar to, and different from, other kinds of families. Like the other issues discussed in this chapter relating to disclosure, incest serves as a dramatic illustration of the special nature of donor kinship.

PART IV

To Regulate or Not?

7

Reasons to Regulate

The future of regulation for assisted reproduction technologies depends on societal interests as well as the voices of the donor-conceived community. The looming question is whether these families *should* be further regulated by the law. Past regulation has protected the integrity and profitability of the fertility business and has also facilitated the use of donor gametes—and it has helped create many happy new families. On the other hand, as explored below, it has not adequately considered the interests of all members of these new, complex families. This chapter underscores the importance of developing a new framework that focuses on family and personhood in the ART world; these foundational issues are currently muffled by laws devoted to medicine and technology.

As more people use donor technology, the pressure has increased for supervision and oversight from two different constituencies. First, members of the donor world want more protection of their interests. Second, morality-based arguments have proliferated, with advocates calling for reforms that limit donor technology to comply with religious doctrine and beliefs on human dignity and reproduction. Indeed, regulating reproductive technology involves issues of procreative autonomy, which invariably return, politically, to the national debate over abortion.[1] Indeed, advances in reproductive technology have overtaken any cultural consensus on procreative rights. Beyond the visible culture clash over abortion, there are social, bioethical, and legal debates over egg donation, prenatal sex selection, and gestational surrogacy.[2] The ability to control reproduction has created new choices, choices that are generally welcomed by those able to take advantage of them but that also expose a regulatory vacuum.

While this book advocates further regulation to protect the interests of the donor world, it is nonetheless also important to consider what might be lost in legal regulation, particularly at this early stage when not only are donor kin networks a relatively new phenomenon but also the law itself is still adjusting to assisted reproductive technology. Issues include whether the law should intervene now or allow some social consensus to develop, whether imposing law would short-circuit a social experiment, and whether regulation would stifle, rather than promote, innovative forms of family. Chapter 10 discusses these objections to regulation.

The next two chapters return to the themes discussed in the introduction concerning how best to nurture families, and whether to treat donor-conceived families comparably to other kinds of families. The first theme explores how the law might begin to nurture relationships rather than intervene once the relationship becomes unraveled. Based on constitutional concepts of family privacy, the law engages in relatively limited direct intervention;[3] it generally focuses on relationships that are falling apart, as in divorce, or that are dysfunctional or abusive, as in child abuse and neglect and domestic violence cases. This theme, of how the law might foster healthy emotional connections and recognize the multiple forms of intrafamily relationships for any particular individual, proves important for donor families who exist without any legal support whatsoever.

A second theme focuses on equality of treatment, which has been a dominant theme in family law, most recently and prominently when it comes to the recognition of gay marriage. Equality has historically been significant with respect to a variety of other issues, including the rights of nonmarital/marital children and those of adoptees and biological children, the treatment of interracial/same-race marriage, common law/ceremonial marriages, cohabiting and marital relationships, and custody standards for fathers and mothers. Equality can sometimes be problematic, as numerous theorists have noted, when it attempts to treat differently situated families the same, or when it requires that all families look the same in order to achieve the same benefits. Past decisions must be carefully limited according to their sets of sufficiently dissimilar facts. If the law defines families as two parents (one man and one woman) with their child(ren), then legal actors will try to change the new families to fit into this image. If families are defined as intimate arrangements for the protection of adult intimacy and/or nurturing of children, then there is an obvious need for protecting and promoting such arrangements.

Equality does, however, provide some useful parameters with respect to donor-conceived families. For example, incest between donor-conceived family members should be treated the same as incest in biological and adoptive families. But when it comes to other issues, such as inheritance or criminal laws that provide special benefits or burdens based on family membership, then equality does not provide the most appropriate paradigm for treatment of donor family communities. These communities do not have the same emotional ties that have justified special treatment of family members in these contexts. This chapter suggests that lines could be drawn based on respectful, but not equal, treatment and based on voluntary, rather than genetic, association.

The chapter first explains why the law should step in, arguing for the promotion of two distinct goals: (1) to support the creation of connections among donor-conceived family communities; and (2) to promote safety and improved medical testing, including to protect against accidental incest. It then discusses how the law can play a significant role in changing the donor world before articulating the outlines of a new paradigm.

I. Reasons to Regulate

One could easily decide that the current system is working well enough, and does not need to be fixed. Fertility clinics are required to be truthful, people are forming families through donor gametes, donors are being paid fairly and are all legally required to undergo some testing, laws define the legal parents of any child, and donor-conceived people are developing just fine socially and psychologically.

The problem with doing nothing and maintaining the status quo, however, is that parts of the system are broken and do need to be fixed. Offspring of a donor who has made hundreds of donations might easily meet and fall in love with one another. Known donors assert rights that were not contemplated at the time of conception. Parents want and need updated medical information about their donors. Half-siblings seek contact with one another, and have no way of knowing how many family members they might have.

Many donor-conceived offspring want to know more about their genetic origins. Reproductive technology is creating more options to build families, outpacing current efforts at legislative control.

Consequently, numerous reasons exist to resolve problems with the current system. First, think about the various donor-conceived family members who post information on the Donor Sibling Registry, searching for guidance on how to proceed to find connections with others and then what to do once they are found. The law might, for example, provide parameters to foster and nurture donor-conceived family communities while also protecting against unwanted contact. Developing solutions need not mandate conformity, such as requiring contact between siblings, but can instead provide opportunities that do not currently exist. New solutions also offer recognition for the interests of those neglected under the current system. A second reason to regulate is to provide certainty and predictability, ensuring that all involved understand and appreciate the possibilities for connection. Under the current system, donors and other participants in donor-conceived families may be surprised when they are found through extrajudicial means of connection, for example, as a result of an Internet search. Moreover, pressure for reform is coming from within the donor-conceived world. As the donor conceived begin advocacy efforts through the legislative process and court systems,[4] and as other countries implement radically different frameworks,[5] the existing system confronts increasing tensions to allow the transmission of more information. Olivia Pratten's successful suit in British Columbia, although based on the Canadian Charter rather than the United States Constitution, provides a potential model for litigation with its arguments that the donor conceived are treated differently than, and unequally from, other people.

Finally, regulation that explicitly helps develop donor-conceived family communities can help families, and family law, constructively realize their goals of promoting intimacy and protection for emotional connections. The law's silence about these families provides space for limited contact, reflecting a normative view that these are medicalized interactions rather than familial connections. According to this perspective, it is sperm banks, egg agencies, and individuals interested in contact who establish the parameters of these communities, using frameworks established by contracts and health law. Indeed, as the former president of one of the leading fertility clinic trade associations explained, "'when these decisions are made by donor and a parent, the child doesn't have a say.'"[6] If this is a considered, society-wide choice to make decisions without accounting for the child's interest, then it is useful to acknowledge such a perspective so that members of the donor world understand that the law will not discourage them from developing connections but will not provide explicit support for this effort. Such a premise continues the focus on curing infertility, on helping patients, and on maintaining the existing free market.

Nonetheless, a focus only on patients ignores the very different presumptions in adoption,[7] the nascent development of pressure from advocates for the donor conceived, the very different regulatory framework established in other countries, and the early stirrings of lawsuits putting pressure on the existing system, all of which challenge the normative framework pursuant to which these communities are best left to regulation by health law and contracts. Existing regulations of reproductive technology, focused on gamete safety or truth in advertising, cater only to the parents as patients, not to the families they are creating.

1. Identity Interests

Recognizing the development of donor-conceived family networks and children's interests in identity, members of the donor community should be able to find out the identity of their donors and their biologically related "siblings." A first step is ensuring that offspring know they are donor conceived. As discussed later, this might be done through setting up special birth certificates for the donor conceived (although this may not be the optimal method). Moreover, all those involved in the donor world should encourage parents to disclose to their children (as the ASRM already does), changing to a culture of openness rather than one that accepts that parents may want the shades drawn in a clinic to ensure that no one sees them. But this is not enough: social and cultural attitudes toward infertility also must change, an enormous task that involves challenging deeply embedded norms about masculinity and femininity.

A second step involves acknowledging the potential connection among gamete providers and the recipients and their children; federal and state law could provide for identity disclosure once a child turns eighteen.[8] Laws guaranteeing the release of such information to mature adults would preempt private agreements (such as between the gamete provider and the intending parents or between the gamete provider and a gamete bank) to the contrary. Although all states have addressed this issue for adoptees, albeit without necessarily accepting open records,[9] few states have considered legislation on disclosure of the identity of gamete providers.

This step, involving information disclosure, not only respects potential relational interests but also recognizes the autonomy claims of offspring who are no longer children, subject to parental authority. While parental decision making results in the creation of donor-conceived children, children have their own separate rights and interests, and, as they mature, they assume adult rights and obligations. Moreover, donor-conceived offspring have claimed that they are the objects of discrimination because they do not have access to the identities of their biological parents.[10]

Even under a system of full disclosure, there certainly remains a critical distinction between "parenting" a child and contributing gametes to the creation of the child.[11] The parents have strong rights to make their own decisions concerning the control, care, and custody of their children.[12] Gamete providers, having sold genetic material to create the child, are not, of course, the parents, and thus (in the absence of an agreement otherwise) do not have enforceable rights in courts. (Consequently, donor-conceived children are not in the same position as children of divorce with various parents able to go into court to fight about visitation). Allowing information disclosure to adult offspring values parental rights to raise children as they see fit while the children are minors, but respects the "children's" rights once they are mature.[13]

While the rights and interests of biological parents and gamete providers should be accorded respect, they have created a new family and a child. Regulation should take account of these new entities by allowing the child to receive information about the people who helped to create her. Such a right should be established both retroactively and prospectively, such that adult offspring who today want information about their biological backgrounds should be able to obtain it, and prospective gamete provision arrangements should proceed in a legal context in which it is understood that offspring will have access to information once they become adults. Barbara Bennett Woodhouse has suggested, in the context of transracial adoption, the need for a child to be able to "claim her 'identity of origin,' defined as a right to know and explore, commensurate with her evolving capacity for autonomy, her identity as a member of the family and group into which she was born."[14] Applying this notion more generally in the gamete provision context, mature offspring in these families similarly need access to the ability to explore their biological families of origin.

The new paradigm suggests that donor-conceived offspring be able to obtain information about others conceived through the same gametes. In the United Kingdom, New South Wales (Australia), and New Zealand, offspring are entitled to information about whether any other individuals share the same donor gametes and, based on mutual consent, to identifying information about each other.[15]

Respecting donor-gamete-created families requires improving the regulatory framework and developing additional, as well as new, systems to promote connection and health.

2. The Complex Role of Law

New laws (or the lack thereof) will affect people's perceptions of donor-conceived family relationships and their actual experiences with them. If, for example, there are laws that accord these relationships some legal significance, this may encourage more people to find their donor-conceived families. Consider a law granting offspring the right to know their donors; this makes donation less secretive because no one is able to choose anonymous donation. The legal parent may also find it more difficult to conceal the donation from the child in this new environment. If the parent does not disclose the fact of donor conception, then the child will be all the more angry if and when he finds out because the law accords him a right to know the actual donor, and yet his parent kept the existence of the donation a secret. Legal regulation can transform beliefs about appropriate behavior, change the underlying behavior, and create new norms that establish informal social and cultural expectations with which people feel they must comply.[16]

Two responses to the risks of legal regulations show the importance of developing new approaches: first, even in the absence of explicit regulation, the law still defines the space for flourishing.[17] That is, the current system allows for voluntary connections and updating of medical histories, but creates neither expectations nor legally enforceable rights that these will occur. Second, the benefits from the normative vision articulated may justify the costs of the regulation. A normative vision of promoting affective ties, fairness, and other public goods[18] associated with respect for the dignity of donor-conceived families and for improved safety supports one type of regulation, while a normative vision associated with protecting patient autonomy, privacy, and the domesticated family supports different regulations. This book aspires to provide a basis for regulation based on recognition of the dignity of connection between donor families.

II. Reasons for Disclosure

Allowing for connections means addressing issues involving donor identity disclosure. (Note that the term "disclosure" does not mean making public but rather providing for release of information only to people conceived as a result of the donor's gametes.) Indeed, one of the reasons for regulation is ensuring the appropriate release of information.

In the comparable context of adoption, advocates have typically made five distinct, albeit interrelated, legal arguments for disclosure:

- Adult adopted persons have a fundamental "right to know" personal information about themselves.
- States do not have a legitimate role in withholding birth and/or adoption information from adopted persons once they are adults.
- Withholding birth and/or adoption information from adult adopted persons violates legal equal protection guarantees by denying them the same rights as other persons.
- Placing the decision on release of this information in the hands of courts has resulted in inequitable decision making.
- Adopted persons should not be bound by decisions on anonymity made by birth parents and adoptive parents at the time of the adoption.[19]

Each of these resonates in the donor-conceived world. Courts in the United States have not yet decided these issues in the ART context, so it is difficult to predict which set of arguments will be more successful within the legal system. As the number of donor-conceived people increases and as people become more likely to know of their origins, they are just beginning to develop more organized advocacy, while adoptees have a very different history. Basing their decisions on the adoption analogy, however, courts are likely to uphold as constitutional laws enacted by states that require the disclosure of information;[20] what is less clear is courts' receptivity to arguments from members of donor-conceived family communities compelling the release of information.

Beyond consideration of these legal rights—and regardless of the outcome of court cases—however, there are additional reasons to require limited disclosure that respects the interests of donor-conceived offspring,[21] the recipient parents, and the donors themselves. Even though banks increasingly allow their clients to choose either identified or anonymous donors, there is no obligation on donors to provide accurate information to banks and no obligation for one donor not to donate repeatedly. Limited disclosure might help with the veracity of information because donors would know that they may be accountable not only to the bank but also to future offspring.

Given the importance to many parents of having a genetic connection to their child, it should be unremarkable that children are themselves interested in learning about those to whom they have a genetic connection. In the case of gamete provision, where couples establish a genetic attachment between one of them and a child, it should not be surprising that children would want to know about other aspects of their genetic heritage. Professor Mary Lyndon Shanley explores multiple ironies:

> At the same time, however, secrecy and anonymity suggested that the identity of the donor involved in begetting the child *was* important: if the genetic tie had no significance whatsoever, it would not need to be hidden. . . .
>
> But many people who used donated sperm or eggs to conceive a child who was genetically related to one parent attributed a different kind of significance to their genetic link to the child. Having a child genetically related to one member of the couple gave a sense of continuity both to the genetically related parent and to the spouse who would see his or her partner reflected in their child.[22]

That is, if the genetic link is unimportant, then so too is the donor, and there is no reason to hide the donor's identity; and the child's genetic connection to one parent should be equally insignificant. Of course, the genetic link *is* important. Donor families bring biology back into the discussion of "family." Regardless of whether biology/genes are somehow hardwired, or whether needing that connection is socially constructed due to the importance placed on biology, this kind of continuity, with both the future and the past, is, understandably, crucial to many donor offspring.

III. Changing Our Approach

The most fundamental change requires a paradigm shift towards donor-conceived families: they must take their place in the jurisprudence of family law and constitutional law, not solely in the administrative jurisprudence of technology, health, and safety regulation. They have been medicalized[23] rather than humanized. In the context of technology regulation, the law has focused on gametes and the fertility industry by, for example, developing standards that test gametes for various health risks.[24] The focus of the health context is protecting patients.[25] Legal scholars have discussed the utility of breach of warranty concepts in the donor gamete context. These interventions are important but they are technical, focused on the product itself, and not on what the product creates.

Future regulation must develop from the perspective of family law, which focuses on the interests of all involved as individuals, rather than as patients or producers or products. This grounding provides a more coherent and cohesive justification for moving forward toward recognition of these new relationships. Importantly, family law cannot be imported, full-scale, onto these new family networks. There remain critical distinctions between donor kin networks and other families. But the basic insight, that the focus must be on relationships and potentially differing interests as well as on products, points toward more human, and humane, legal approaches. Legal treatment of the donor relationships in reproductive technology might draw on legal treatment of adoptive relationships, with its focus on children and other relational interests.[26] Given a state goal to foster institutions that sustain family,[27] various guiding principles help structure the framework for these new policies. First, the state must give explicit recognition to donor-conceived family communities, acknowledging the emotional and biological connections. And, beyond this recognition, the state must adopt a position that is either neutral toward, or that affirmatively facilitates, these communities. Second, the state must ensure the safety of gamete donors, of gametes, and of donor-conceived offspring through better record keeping, testing, and the incest ban.

This guidance provides the basis for the recommendations developed in the next two chapters, which focus on additional regulation of the fertility industry and further facilitation of the integrity of the family networks. Specific recommendations include requiring the entire fertility industry to engage in better record keeping and allowing donor-conceived offspring to learn their origins, the identity of the donor, and the existence of any siblings; setting limits on the number of children born from any gamete provider; and developing a new familial-type status that donor-conceived families might choose to assume. What is clear is that family law and health scholars/advocates should begin considering how to nurture these newly developing families.

Accordingly, in recognition of the possibility of emotional connection,[28] the state should provide some protections for donor-conceived family communities. Conceptualizing these potential networks as relational entities with emotional interconnections provides a basis for developing a new legal framework. Even within traditional family law, there is a growing appreciation that relationships continue even after a family dissolves.[29] The increasing number of challenges to the binary nature of family law—parent/nonparent, spouse/nonspouse, sibling/nonsibling[30]—indicates the need for a more nuanced approach that recognizes and allows various levels of connection. Focusing not on individual rights but on potential relationships and emotions among people might provide a space for fostering donor family networks. Families are inevitably embedded in larger structures of care and support,[31] and allowing one donor-conceived family to connect with another is consistent with this realization.

The law should respond at two critical points: first, it should clarify the legal relationships among donors, recipients, and offspring; and second, it should facilitate connections among donor-conceived families who share the same genetic heritage. While most states have laws on the relationship between sperm donors and recipients, fewer states have enacted laws on egg donors, and even fewer on embryo donation. And, of course, the laws that do exist do not cover all contingencies. Donors must be assured that they will have no parental rights or obligations unless they have arranged otherwise.[32] This certainty facilitates contact based on the knowledge of all involved that donors will not become responsible for child support or able to assert custody and visitation with respect to any of their donor-conceived offspring.

Second, once these families are created, laws can facilitate and regulate these connections. A few areas for legal intervention show that donor-conceived families are different but nonetheless entitled to some form of legal recognition and protection. Legal decision makers should take affirmative steps to facilitate the recognition of these families, according them privileges based simply on status. For example, the state accords multiple benefits to couples based on marriage, ranging from tax treatment to surrogate decision-making authority in the case of illness to intestacy preferences.[33] The state might accord similar benefits to donor-conceived families, such as mandatory disclosure of identifying information or delegation of surrogate authority for health care decision making or inclusion in Family and Medical Leave Act protections.[34]

Several of the proposed reforms require that the fertility industry take affirmative steps to foster connections and to improve safety, including by mandating better record keeping that would ultimately allow for limited disclosure of the identity of donors to their offspring. It is the fertility clinics and egg brokers and surrogacy agencies who will be responsible for collecting these records, even if it is a government agency that is then responsible for maintaining them securely. These records would include identifying information about the donor, as well as the number of offspring.

The future of regulation for assisted reproduction technologies must consider the interests of all members of these new families. Regulation must be grounded more firmly in the importance of family: donor-conceived people are created to expand or create families, which consist of people (not genes), and accordingly, the law needs to shift its dominant focus on medicine and technology (and commodification) and rely on family and constitutional law as well. The industry, because it is ultimately about creating families, needs to be subjected to laws that regulate people, not things.

8

Regulating for Connection

Regardless of family type, most donor-conceived people are interested in learning more about the donor and any half-siblings who were conceived through use of the same donor. There are numerous issues—and potential approaches—to the question of how to promote these connections. This chapter discusses two different types of solutions: one set of proposals facilitates donor-conceived families finding each other; and a second concerns legal links, or the possibility of more formal legal recognition, between families through, for example, expansion of coverage of family and medical leave laws. These new forms of regulation are part of the paradigm shift away from viewing donor-conceived families and their communities as scientific and medical constructs and instead viewing them as relational entities.

I. Finding Families

Once the decision is made to help families find one another, the question is how to do so. The most realistic solution involves some form of a databank. A databank might be placed on two intersecting axes: mandatory or voluntary, private or public. The term "voluntary," in turn, has two different aspects: clinics can participate voluntarily and choose whether to provide information; and/or donors/offspring can participate voluntarily, so that matches occur only when there is a mutual desire for contact, without any required disclosure of identity when, for example, the offspring reaches a certain age.

These can, in turn, be expanded to four specific options on how to proceed:

- do nothing, and continue with the private system that we have (recognizing the possibilities and limits of registries like the Donor Sibling Registry or the ones established by members of the industry);
- establish a national voluntary databank with standards, and with an administrative board composed of stakeholders, including donor offspring, donors, recipients, and the fertility industry, with private funding;[1]
- develop a state-based voluntary or mandatory databank; or
- develop a national mandatory or voluntary databank.

The optimal outcome, for numerous reasons, is the final one, the development of a *national* mandatory databank, where offspring over the age of eighteen can obtain access to information, and to which gamete banks and fertility clinics must contribute information, including data about live births.

While the fertility industry has a strong stake in ensuring the effectiveness of such a registry[2] and an interest in administering it, there are numerous other stakeholders who must be involved. Private solutions depend on voluntary compliance, so an industry-based registry could not ensure universal reporting and record keeping. Consider that less than 20 percent of fertility clinics comply with the voluntary industry-established guidelines designed to establish parameters for the number of embryos transferred into women under the age of thirty-five.[3] Moreover, if the industry insisted on maintaining control of the registry, parents, donors, and offspring could be shut out of decision making. Wendy Kramer, somewhat more cynically, suggests that "[a] national registry that is set up, run, and governed by the sperm banking industry is only a fearful reaction to the possibility of the FDA imposing its own regulations and will only serve to protect this industry's own best interests."[4]

To begin the national process, Congress needs to enact legislation requiring that fertility clinics, sperm and egg banks, and physicians' offices maintain records for each child born through donor gametes—egg, sperm, and embryos—and guaranteeing that gamete offspring have the right to access those records. Governmental mandates can ensure widespread participation and can effectively impose sanctions on entities that do not report. Such a registry could fit within the oversight system already operated by the federal government over the fertility industry. The Centers for Disease Control and Prevention (CDC) collects and publishes information annually on the pregnancy rate of individual fertility clinics pursuant to the Fertility Clinic Success Rate and Certification Act of 1992;[5] the most recent report weighed in at 574 pages.[6] The federal Food and Drug Administration (FDA) has issued extensive regulations governing the testing and safety of gametes.[7]

One alternative to either the fertility industry or the federal government operating the registry might be state implementation.[8] Indeed, Washington State has taken the first step. Under a 2011 law, anyone who provides sperm or eggs to a fertility clinic in the state must also provide identifying information and a medical history.[9] While that is, in fact, a customary practice for most fertility clinics, another part of the law allows children born from donated gametes to return to the fertility clinic when they reach the age of eighteen to request the identifying information and the medical history. Although the donor can file a disclosure veto that prevents the clinic from revealing the identifying information, the donor offspring will still be entitled to the medical information.

The Washington state legislation is a start at recognizing the need for a gamete registry, but it is flawed. First, it appears to apply only to donors in Washington state, so Washington state residents who use donors in other states are not subject to the law. While there is an argument that any child who is donor conceived—regardless of whether the gametes were provided to a clinic in Washington—can request information, there is a strong argument that the law would not cover those children. On the other hand, if the donation occurred in Washington, there does not seem to be a limit on where the offspring must live. Second, the donors can sign an affidavit of nondisclosure that forbids the release of any identifying information (although that affidavit does not apply to nonidentifying medical information).

The Washington law helps to show the problems with a piecemeal approach, rather than a uniform, one in which all states would have the same laws. There are four specific problems with the state-by-state approach. First, even if uniform legislation is developed, states might modify the legislation prior to enactment, so the registration and disclosure requirements could vary dramatically. Second, children might not know the state in which their parents obtained gametic material and underwent fertility treatment, and so might need to engage in searches of multiple state registries. Third, even if states attempted to coordinate their databank systems, this would require yet another oversight body to ensure the necessary cooperation. Finally, rather than establishing one system for information collection and retention, all fifty states would have to set up their own systems, causing a potentially overwhelming amount of duplicative work. A federal-level structure could more efficiently and effectively implement any large-scale collection of information and oversight of the process.[10]

1. Models

There are different models for a federal registry. One set of options assumes that the decision has been made to guarantee limited disclosure in the future, while a second set of options provides only for voluntary registration. Within the first set of options, depicted in figure 8.1, the most desirable outcome mandates the collection of information on future gamete donations, as well as any information, including donors' identity, that exists on past donations. A second option would mandate the collection of similar information moving forward, but would not require the identities of past donors. A final option would mandate the collection of identifying and other information prospectively, but would not require information on past donations, although it could be provided voluntarily.

The second, and less desirable, set of options would not require prospective identity disclosure. This would satisfy the fertility industry; the American Society for Reproductive Medicine is decidedly against mandated disclosure.[11] Some have suggested model legislation that would require the state or fertility clinics to maintain records concerning the identity of gamete donors and recipients, but would permit donors to choose to remain anonymous[12] or would require only the release of medical and genetic information, not identifying information.[13] This differs only slightly from the status quo, under which consumers can choose identity-release donors, and clinics make medical information available.

Advocates argue that people prefer anonymous donation, and this set of proposals preserves freedom of choice for consumer-parents, protects donor privacy, and prevents against too much heavy-handed government regulation. Nonetheless, it does not go far enough. Any proposal that continues to permit donor anonymity under any circumstance is inadequate because it does not recognize the offspring's needs for information, nor the donors' and recipients' needs for closure and connection.

Actual implementation of the registry might be modeled on the Human Fertilisation & Embryology Authority (HFEA), which operates pursuant to an enactment of the British Parliament.[14] While the HFEA is administered by the government, a U.S. national databank could be operated with federal

Figure 8.1

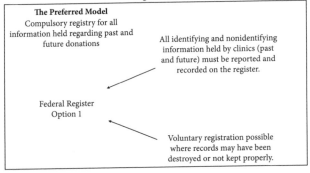

The Preferred Model
Compulsory registry for all information held regarding past and future donations

All identifying and nonidentifying information held by clinics (past and future) must be reported and recorded on the register.

Federal Register
Option 1

Voluntary registration possible where records may have been destroyed or not kept properly.

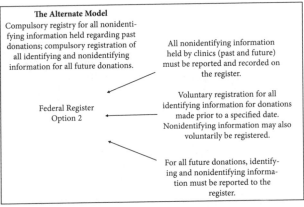

The Alternate Model
Compulsory registry for all nonidentifying information held regarding past donations; compulsory registration of all identifying and nonidentifying information for all future donations.

All nonidentifying information held by clinics (past and future) must be reported and recorded on the register.

Federal Register
Option 2

Voluntary registration for all identifying information for donations made prior to a specified date. Nonidentifying information may also voluntarily be registered.

For all future donations, identifying and nonidentifying information must be reported to the register.

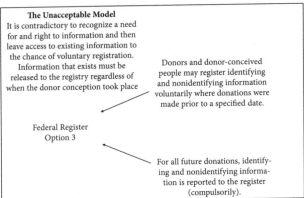

The Unacceptable Model
It is contradictory to recognize a need for and right to information and then leave access to existing information to the chance of voluntary registration. Information that exists must be released to the registry regardless of when the donor conception took place

Donors and donor-conceived people may register identifying and nonidentifying information voluntarily where donations were made prior to a specified date.

Federal Register
Option 3

For all future donations, identifying and nonidentifying information is reported to the register (compulsorily).

Dr. Sonia Allan, Submission to the Senate Legal and Constitutional Affairs Committee Inquiry into Donor Conception, Access to Genetic Information and Donor Identification (2010), pp. 18-19 (Submission 30, http://www.aph.gov.au/senate/committee/legcon_ctte/donor_conception/submissions.htm at 15 July 2011). Used by permission of Dr. Allan.

funding and a congressional mandate. The board for the databank could be composed of stakeholders from the donor-conceived community, including parents, children, and donors, the fertility industry, and regulators. Information would remain private, except to the donor, the offspring, and the gamete recipients. The HFEA system allows children to check whether they result from donor gametes. Donors might also be required to update their information when the child turns eighteen. And, when donor-conceived people reach the age of majority, they should be able to receive identifying information about their donors. A "no contact" statement would be helpful as donor-conceived people considered what to do with the information.

Allowing for the release of a donor's identity recognizes that biology is not everything, but that a child's identity develops through multiple sources. Releasing this information does not change the identity of the child's parents, because the law must guarantee that donors cannot assert parental rights based on their status as donor; in the case of known donors, if the donor signs a contract providing for contact with the child, or if there is some other basis—such as functional parenthood—then, of course, the donor may be able to use these other legal mechanisms for establishing rights.[15] Legal certainty concerning the rights—or lack thereof—of donors must accompany the establishment of a registry in order to protect the interests of the recipient parents in the stability of their new family and to clarify the donor's responsibilities to any resulting child.

2. Forward and Backward

A final issue concerns the retroactive/prospective nature of a registry. It is important to acknowledge that permitting access may disrupt the expectations of some donors and recipients who have relied on continued secrecy; it appears to negate past choices by the donors and the recipients. And, it limits future choice: neither recipients nor donors will be able to choose anonymity. Other jurisdictions that have abandoned anonymity have not required retrospective application of the new laws due to fears of infringing settled expectations even with the benefit of granting rights to offspring.

Mandating the release of identifying information might be contrary to agreements between donors and sperm banks or fertility clinics.[16] Nonetheless, in other contexts, courts and legislatures have reformed or struck down agreements that are deemed to be contrary to public policy or in violation of constitutionally protected rights.[17] In the adoption context, several states have provided that regardless of private agreements, adopted adults will receive access to information about their birth parents.[18] Indeed, as in other areas of family law, the interests of adults and their settled expectations are subject to override based on public policy concerns, including a child's best interests or other reasons underlying the change in controlling law.[19] When states have allowed adoptees access to their original birth certificates, they have done so retroactively. Even beyond the best interests of the child, other societal interests justify mandatory disclosure, including removing the stigma of infertility and fostering the acceptance of alternative families.

Nonetheless, difficult issues remain. Retroactivity in the donor world differs from the abolition of anonymity in adoptions; the state has always been involved in establishing the parameters of adoption, while it has had much less involvement when it comes to donating gametes, which have typically involved private contracts between a donor and a bank. Respecting donors means respecting their rights to retain the anonymity under which they agreed to donate. Respecting donor-conceived offspring, however, means ensuring their rights to access information about their biological heritage. Moreover, while contractual interests are subject to strong protections, donor familial rights are based on a state-created status. As in the adoption cases, the state may justifiably, carefully, and under certain circumstances change this status.

While I advocate retrospective application, I recognize that this may be politically even more difficult than prospective disclosure. An alternative, albeit second-best, solution involves establishing a national voluntary database that might collect information on past donor conception practices based on donor identification numbers as well as registrants' DNA (see figure 8.1). When donors and offspring mutually consent to disclosure, the database would facilitate the contact. Donor siblings could use the same national voluntary database to find one another, or a separate one focused only on siblings could be established. Both the Netherlands and the United Kingdom have implemented donor-sibling registries.[20] The UK DonorLink, which began with government funding, acts as an intermediary once a match is made through the site, contacting all parties to ensure that there is mutual consent to the release of information.[21]

Prospectively, the issues are easier: a new system could guarantee that all involved in the donor process are made aware through mandated counseling of the changing aspect of disclosure. All donor records would still remain sealed, except in the limited circumstance of allowing an offspring access to information.

For multiple reasons, the United States should move toward a mandatory databank that would collect information on donor gametes. All clinics and sperm banks should be required to report certain data. Sperm banks should provide information on each donor, including number of "donations," as well as identity. Clinics should provide comparable data on egg and embryo donors, just as they already do on the number of pregnancies and births. There may be no need to include egg and embryo banks or recruiters because use of eggs or embryos requires a clinic's involvement.

To ensure the security of this information and heightened protection against hacking, the registry would be required to establish sophisticated encryption protocols. Second, donors could keep their identities secret, but only until any future offspring reached the age of eighteen, at which time the offspring could be granted access to the identifying information. In recognition of the donors' interests, donors could file a no-contact preference form, indicating their desire not to be contacted; in recognition of the off-spring's interests, the identifying information would nonetheless be disclosed (together with the existence of the no-contact form). Some countries permit disclosure at an earlier age, and some Australian states allow disclosure of some information upon consent of the donor and the parents.[22]

In addition, the government should establish a national, federal voluntary registry that would allow for connections among family members prior to off-spring reaching the age of eighteen.[23] States that have developed such a system for adoptees typically require a consent from at least one biological parent and the adult adoptee (adoptive parents may be able to consent if the adopted person is still a minor) before the disclosure of any identifying information. The Donor Sibling Registry is an example of a mutual-consent registry in the gamete world that is already in existence and that works in a similar way—the key is voluntary registration by the two (or more) parties that produces the matches. Finally, the United States should mandate limits on the number of offspring produced by any one donor's gametic contributions.

Ultimately, the next steps must focus on regulation to protect the best interests of the future and existing donor-conceived offspring. The needs of existing donor-conceived offspring, their family members, and donors must also be respected by, for example, supporting ongoing efforts to facilitate mutual-consent contact.

Taking those next steps will require the involvement, participation, and cooperation of multiple stakeholders both within and outside of the donor world, in recognition that donor-conceived families and their communities are relational entities.

II. Knowing about Donor Conception

A national databank would help offspring who choose to learn the identity of their donors, but there is a second, interrelated part to the right to know:

the right to know that one has been conceived through donor gametes in the first place.[24] The very real possibility, even today, exists that the offspring may not know they had been donor conceived. Parents have the right not to tell their children about their origins, so if laws develop that will allow children to learn of their origins despite their parents' decision not to disclose, then this affects parents' constitutionally protected interest (at least when the children are under the age of eighteen). In light of parental autonomy and the corresponding assumption that not all parents will tell their children, then how might law support their interests in learning about and/or connecting with their biological community?

As discussed earlier, one big step—that does not involve conflicting rights and interests—concerns changing the culture inside and outside of fertility clinics to promote openness. A critical issue involves ensuring that offspring know they are donor conceived. Given parental autonomy, some offspring might never learn they were donor conceived, so it is important to think about how the law might support their interests in learning about and/or connecting with their biological community. Even countries that allow offspring access to identifying information neither require parents to tell their children of their donor conceptions nor mandate any other way of providing notice;[25] if children are not told, then it is only through inadvertent discoveries, such as via otherwise hidden documents or genetic tests that are typically undertaken for a different reason. While I don't recommend requiring that parents inform their children, there are other methods that allow individuals to find out if they are donor conceived. For example, they could be officially notified upon the age of majority so they could then pursue information or waive their interest in obtaining it (think of Hagrid's telling Harry Potter that he is a wizard!). Of course, mandating disclosure or somehow *requiring* that parents tell their children of their donor-conceived status is highly problematic; not only is it difficult to enforce, but it is highly intrusive of intrafamilial relationships. Even in the world of adoption, there is no mandate that parents tell their children. Instead, adoption professionals provide strong encouragement to parents to do so. The adoption narrative historically emphasized the "chosen child" to help children cope with the sometimes negative perception that adoption was an inadequate substitute for a "real" (biologically linked) family. While the "chosen child" narrative is problematic—a child might wonder whether she could be returned, the story denies any role to the biological parents—it has served to reassure adoptive parents that it is safe to tell their children about their origins. In the donor-conceived world (as discussed earlier), there are numerous potential narratives to help parents explain their children's creation.

There are, however, other possibilities for ensuring that children know that their biological and legal parents are different people without genetic testing. One option is for birth certificates of children conceived with donor gametes to be stamped with "by donation" next to the mother and/or father's name.[26] This ensures that the legal parent is identified on the official birth record, but it also provides a clear indication that the child was conceived through the use of donor gametes, facilitating offspring's knowledge and access to this information. On the other hand, this option has several drawbacks; first, not only does it place pressure on parents to inform their children of their biological origins but it also makes this information part of an easily available public record. Or, a second possibility is that babies could receive two birth certificates, one that becomes part of the public record and does not include any notation regarding the child's donor-conceived status, and a second one, which would only be available once the child turns eighteen and which would include identifying information about the donor.[27] The second certificate would be available on the basis of specific state criteria. Adopted individuals are issued two birth certificates, so there is precedent for this concept.

A comparable system was proposed in Britain, which considered legislation that would require special notations on birth certificates for the donor-conceived.[28] In late 2007, some members of the British Parliament suggested that birth certificates indicate the donor status of a child with a special stamp or by including the words "from donor," although this never became law.[29] Children born after 1990 can already petition the British Human Fertilisation and Embryology Authority (HFEA) to disclose whether they are donor conceived.[30] The state of Victoria, in Australia, has launched a "Time to Tell" campaign, encouraging parents to tell their children of their origins in an effort to ensure honesty as well as to prevent consanguineous unions, and the state itself is taking other actions to help individuals who are donor conceived learn their status.[31]

A combination of media campaigns with the ability of the donor conceived to determine their status provides a system that accounts for family privacy while also changing cultural norms to dissolve the "unnatural" status of the donor conceived. To be sure, some offspring will never know their status, but this system provides a voluntary option that allows people to determine whether they are donor conceived and that encourages openness, disclosure, and acceptance. Parents might, of course, object that the government should not provide this form of private information to their children without their consent, an issue that echoes the basic problem of the potential conflicts between parents' and children's interests in this area.

Ultimately, however, for the mental and physical health of donor-conceived people, to prevent accidental incest, and to encourage a more open approach to all of these issues, offspring's interests should control here.

Changing current law will be difficult. A variety of interests—clinics, some recipients, some children, and many past, present, and future donors—are opposed to at least some aspects of a mandatory donor gamete databank. The culture of gamete use has come to value secrecy or, at least, the *choice* of identity release. In the analogous context of open records for adoption, advocates have laboriously proceeded state by state, using lawsuits, lobbying, and referenda in an ongoing effort to change the existing closed-records situation. On the other hand, as technology enables the donor world to obtain more information through genetic tests and Internet registries, existing practices are clearly being challenged.

III. Intent to Create Connections

Two different sets of issues intersect when it comes to moving forward with connection: relationships between donors and offspring, and relationships among donor-conceived families. In both contexts, however, intent is critical in opening up the possibilities for connection. The choice of whether to contact and meet other members of the donor network provides the basis for establishing any bonds.

1. Donors

First, given the uncertainty and confusion in existing parentage laws, states need to clarify the relationship between donors and the families they help create. The legal status of parenthood should be definitively separated from the certainty of biology, even while acknowledging that the right to know the truth of biological parenthood belongs to the child. The lack of legal clarity in the donor world is frightening: donors might fear child support obligations, recipient parents might fear that donors will seek some form of child custody or visitation, and people who have used the same donor might fear the imposition of responsibilities toward one another. Accordingly, in the absence of an agreement otherwise, donors should have no rights and no obligations to donor-conceived offspring. The release of identifying information requires legal clarity on the relationship between donors and the families they help create. In the absence of a written agreement, a donor is not a parent.

For donors to feel comfortable in moving forward with connections, they must be reassured that they will have no legal obligations to their offspring.

Otherwise, contact between donors and offspring becomes highly problematic, raising potential issues of financial liability, as well as emotional complexities. The default rules would ensure that a donor is not a parent, but would respect donor intent to opt in through a written agreement.

2. Relationships among Families

Second, and similarly, in the absence of an agreement, donor-conceived families should have no rights and obligations to one another. Like donors, however, members of the donor world should be able to opt in to connections. Donor families could sign up to contact others with the same donor, or they could sign up for other recognition of their connections.

As behavioral economists know, people's choices are structured and influenced by the background architecture, and people are more likely to choose the default rules than opt into different ones.[32] If the choice is between signing up for organ donation or opting out of organ donation, then people are more likely to go with the option that does not require further action, regardless of how important they consider the disposition of their bodies.[33] An opt-in choice to join donor kin networks ensures that people intentionally form these relationships when they are interested in doing so.

Similarly, the default rules would ensure that a donor is not a parent, but would allow for opting in through a written agreement. Similarly, families who have used the same donor would not have any responsibilities to one another, in the absence of an agreement to the contrary. Donor families could sign up to contact others with the same donor, or they could sign up for other recognition of their connections.

Indeed, once connections have been made, the newly formed donor-conceived communities may want more formal respect of their relationship. This does not mean according parental status or providing all of the affirmative legal protections accorded to families under American law. This might mean, for example, that donor-conceived families could opt into a quasi-familial status. Their biological connections could give rise to some limited rights that depend on context and on choice. As family law increasingly moves toward privatization, toward customizing the meaning of family through mechanisms ranging from open adoption agreements to premarital contracts,[34] donor-conceived family communities might be able to choose a weak form of legal recognition.

While my goal is to suggest a paradigm change rather than a specific laundry list of policy prescriptions, this new status could provide various privileges and obligations. Connected families might, for example, be eligible to

take family and medical leave for one another,[35] to inherit, to act as a surrogate decision maker in cases of illness, or to serve as a legal guardian in
cases where the parents are incapacitated or have died.[36] It might also involve
some form of statutory recognition for sibling associational rights, a step that
would have a much broader impact on child welfare.[37] To provide administrative ease, the default rule would remain that these rights are unavailable
in the absence of explicit agreements otherwise. Under the existing system,
donor-conceived families can already designate other community members
as agents for health care and financial decision making. New laws, could,
however, expand the rights available even in the absence of these specific
designations. One option might be allowing donor-conceived family communities to enter into a status comparable to designated beneficiaries under
some state laws. For example, Colorado provides for a "designated benefi-
ciary" agreement.[38] The Colorado legislation is limited to same-sex couples,
as well as other couples legally prohibited from marrying one another, but,
once registered, the couples are eligible for such benefits as health insurance, inheritance rights, and retirement benefits. It is notable for the ease
with which couples can enter and exit the legal status, and the freedom parties have to define the scope of the relationship and rights conferred to their
partners; partners are free to choose which rights and protections they want
to extend to one another, and there is no requirement of reciprocity.

The purpose is not to create a new legal status that is identical or substantially similar to that of domestic partners or spouses, or even all of the rights
and privileges accorded to family members.[39] The state and federal govern-
ments should not accord legal recognition in a way that is even remotely
comparable to the government's recognition of the family, such as the auto-
matic conferral of a series of rights, duties, and obligations. Instead, the goal
is to allow members of donor-conceived family communities to opt in to
these rights and duties through voluntary designation of a specified legal
status.

Moreover, advocacy to expand benefits might cause the underlying laws to
change. For example, the federal FMLA is limited in scope and application;
its grudging support for families reflects a compromise in which employers
had a significant voice. It only covers employers with fifty or more workers,
and employees only become eligible after one year of work. They are then
entitled to take up to twelve weeks of unpaid leave from work for medical
reasons related to a *spouse, child, or parent*. It does not allow siblings to take
leave (so would not, on its own current terms, apply to half-siblings).

To date, efforts to expand it by, for example, allowing paid leave have been
unsuccessful. Nonetheless, advocates within the donor world might join

with others to encourage expanded coverage to include care for siblings and half-siblings (donor-conceived families might be required to opt into this coverage).

The system outlined above preserves choice but provides legal certainty. Consider, instead, a system of general application that does not allow any exceptions. Thus, even if a donor and recipient tried to set the terms of their own agreement—for example, guaranteeing limited visitation rights—they could not do so. The state would simply mandate the role of a sperm donor, with no possible deviation. This alternative, however, is problematic: with its fixed rules, it prevents people from working out their own arrangements for connection, and it renders intent irrelevant.

Given the problems with other approaches, intent—imperfect as it is— should become the deciding factor. Signing an agreement indicates consent and status. The solution to the current uncertainty of parentage laws, and to the lack of any laws facilitating connection, requires that states recognize written agreements between donors and recipients and other families.

9

Regulating for Health and Safety

Setting Limits in the Gamete World

Donors are helping to create new families, yet their gametes are subject to minimal testing requirements, they are not required to update their medical information, and there is no limit on the number of children born from their gametes. Applying a new paradigm means that the fertility industry, including clinics, sperm banks, and egg donor brokers, needs further incentives to ensure the best interests of donor-conceived family communities. This principle leads to a reconsideration of existing approaches to ensure that relational interests are a significant factor in the formulation of law and policy. Legislatures must require improved record keeping, limits on the numbers of children born per donor, and more thorough counseling and disclosure to parents and donors.

Congress has served as the primary regulator for gamete donation. Similarly, a federal structure could more efficiently and effectively implement any large-scale collection of information and oversight of the process.[1] Indeed, the basic structure for improving health and safety outcomes is in place at the national level. Two divisions within the federal Department of Health and

Human Services already exercise oversight over ART: the FDA has issued human tissue safety regulations, and the CDC collects data on ART. The FDA could expand the existing regulations to require that clinics and gamete banks and agencies collect additional information and perform additional testing, and the two agencies could work together to provide safeguards. This could lead to better tracking of donor gametes, improved testing and counseling, and data protection.

While the ASRM recommends counseling, there are no requirements that clinics actually offer, much less engage in, this counseling. The informed-consent procedures are relatively minimal. This chapter explores the second set of critical regulations in the donor world, those that ensure the safety and health of providers, recipients, and donor-conceived individuals. These regulations range from informed consent to new medical testing to limiting the number of offspring created by any individual donor.

I. Protecting Donors

Many gamete donors experience psychological consequences after they have donated, even if they were quite casual at the time. They realize that their eggs or sperm have created a child, a living person rather than an inanimate object,[2] or they may feel and express regrets, believing that they have engaged in an exploitative process—by providing eggs or sperm they are commodifying body products, giving away their potential children.[3] When it comes to informed consent, safe medical practice, and limiting the number of donations, these psychological consequences must be considered along with additional issues that are gender specific. (Issues involved in limiting donations to protect offspring against inheriting health risks and to prevent inadvertent consanguinity are addressed later in this chapter.)

For egg donors (in contrast to sperm donors), additional intervention is much easier to justify on the basis of health risks, and the feminist health community has mobilized to document the effects of fertility drugs on women. For example, Judy Norsigian, the executive director of Our Bodies, Ourselves, has written about the "substantial risks to women's health" from multiple egg extraction.[4] There is also a potential problem with medical disclosure—egg donors are often not provided with sufficient information concerning potential risks.[5]

Aside from emotional and psychological concerns,[6] egg donation poses both short- and long-term health risks for the woman donor. The first set of health risks results from the impact of the hormones. The most common short-term complication for oocyte donors is ovarian hyperstimulation syndrome (OHSS).[7] Indeed, the donation procedure itself is actually controlled oocyte hyperstimulation, designed to produce the maximum number of mature eggs, and a mild form of OHSS is considered almost inevitable.[8] Severe OHSS is rare but can be fatal, with symptoms that include kidney and liver dysfunction, and respiratory distress.[9] Some studies have shown that severe OHSS may be less common in outside donors than in women undergoing IVF, partially because outside donors stop hormone treatment after the eggs have been retrieved, while IVF patients continue with additional procedures and hormones in their attempts to conceive.[10] However, the risk increases according to the number of donations.[11] To minimize OHSS, researchers are studying new drug protocols and possible genetic markers, although the risks remain.[12]

Finally, the long-term risks of the hormones involved in oocyte donation remain understudied, although they may include various gynecological cancers, such as breast, ovarian, and uterine.[13] Several medical studies have shown that women who repeatedly undergo treatment with fertility drugs, as do repeat oocyte donors, have an increased risk for these cancers.[14] However, the evidence is based largely on infertile women undergoing IVF, and several causes of infertility may be related to cancer as well.[15] Disentangling the data is difficult, but initial analysis suggests that healthy donors do not necessarily share the same increased risk for breast and ovarian cancer, although the extent to which fertility treatments do affect those cancers for healthy donors is uncertain.[16] The data on the risk of uterine cancer for healthy donors is sparse but of more concern.[17] Moreover, researchers are uncertain about whether repeated donations can affect the donor's future fertility, and they are still unsure about the psychological consequences.

A second set of risks, beyond those associated with taking hormones, concerns the oocyte retrieval process itself. This is a surgical procedure that requires repeated punctures of the vaginal wall and ovarian follicles.[18] As with any other surgery, complications are possible, including vaginal bleeding and infection.[19] While the procedure is generally done on an outpatient basis, physicians usually use some form of sedation.[20] Thus, the risks inherent in anesthesia, such as stroke and respiratory failure, are also present.

The short- and long-term health risks involved in oocyte donation are numerous and potentially serious, and most researchers and policymakers believe that these risks require further research.[21] Nonetheless, the ASRM concluded that "there are no clearly documented long-term risks" for egg donors, although, "because of the possible health risks . . . it would seem prudent to consider limiting the number of stimulated cycles for a given oocyte donor to approximately six."[22] Although numerous eggs can be retrieved in each cycle, many of them will not be fertilized and develop into children. The ASRM recommendation thus could provide a potential limit on the number of children who might be born from the gametes of any individual oocyte donor. Indeed, many fertility clinics do limit donation cycles per donor to six and some to as few as three.[23] These limits are entirely self-imposed, however, and a donor with proven fecundity is valuable to these clinics. There are well-publicized stories of women who have donated at double the recommended limit.[24]

II. Promoting Health and Safety

The regulations that do exist for the fertility industry focus on gamete safety and protecting consumers. These are important. Patients absolutely need assurances that gametes have been tested for various diseases, and that fertility clinics are not engaging in false advertising. Regulations that are primarily concerned with informing patients, however, are limited in scope. They do not address any other aspect of the donor world, including record keeping or inadvertent consanguinity.

More specifically, as a fundamental first step, clinics and banks must keep track of the children who result from any particular egg or sperm donor, and report this information to a central registry. Parents who had used gametes could be required to report to the fertility clinic or to the birthing hospital details about the gamete provider and any resulting births, and the sperm banks and medical care providers could be responsible for ensuring accurate reporting. Only with improved data collection and retention can meaningful changes result. Additional information, such as genetic data, could also be collected about donors to support potential regulation on repetitious donations.[25]

The federal government already requires tracking from the donor to the recipient and from the recipient to the donor along with a distinct, nonidentifying coding system, and mandates that these records be preserved for at least ten years.[26] The basic system for retaining information is in place. Additional requirements should include not just (as discussed above) tracking the donor to any children who are ultimately born but also keeping the records for at least twenty-five years, setting up a system to match the nonidentifying code with the donor's identity, and mandating that donors update their data by providing information about serious illnesses that are associated with genetic abnormalities. This allows for donor-conceived people to access health, medical, and identifying information; it also ensures a tracking system so that donor families are aware of potential genetic disorders. A subsequent step would include collecting information from donor-conceived

families about genetically associated diseases to enable enhanced information sharing that could help with both treatment and prevention.[27]

Importantly, these steps are possible; the industry itself has, for example,
recommended voluntary limits on the number of offspring per donor.[28] Limits already exist in numerous other countries, and the ASRM's limits may
be the most appropriate basis for legislation in the United States. Although
parents are not required to report the birth of a child using donor gametes,
the Centers for Disease Control already collect information on the success
of ART procedures involving eggs and embryos; this could be expanded to
include information about sperm as well as the number of children born.
Other countries have required the specific regulatory body responsible for
ART or an independent agency to maintain this information;[29] the precise
form of entity, its means for protecting confidentiality, and the length of time
during which records must be kept will depend on political factors as well as
other responsibilities that such an organization might acquire. Even those
opposed to any further regulation or disclosure of identifying information
should recognize the importance of ensuring that one donor does not populate the world and that genetically related offspring do not marry each other.

While each of these steps could be justified on the basis of health and
safety concerns involved in using ART,[30] they gain additional strength
because of their interrelationship with a standard that focuses on the best
interests of offspring. Indeed, a family law framework would focus not only
on the offspring's interests but also on other public goods as well, such as
support for human capabilities.[31] Moreover, further regulation provides a
backdrop for additional means of recognizing both children's interests and
the familial relationships.

1. Improved Testing

Although the American Society for Reproductive Medicine has set standards
for what genetic tests should be performed on donors, these standards are
quite broad.[32] Indeed, clinics vary when it comes to the types of genetic testing they routinely perform. Charles Sims, the medical director and owner of
California Cryobank, together with a few colleagues, surveyed banks to find
out the types of genetic tests they administer. Almost all of the banks tested
for cystic fibrosis, three-quarters of the banks tested Jewish donors for Tay-
Sachs, and slightly more than half of the banks undertook a chromosomal
testing.[33] None of the banks, however, screened for spinal muscular atrophy
(SMA), which occurs in approximately one out of every ten thousand live
births, and which is carried by approximately 2 percent of the population.[34]

To guarantee the safety of ART procedures, additional guidelines must be developed for safe practices, testing, counseling, and considerations related to age or physical condition in accordance with the type of approach used for other medical treatments. Genetic testing has become an increasingly afford-able and more widely available technology. Although testing might increase the cost of gametes, presumably consumers would be willing to pay more for the safety and security of protection against health risks. In the absence of federally mandated testing, banks might offer a new status of donors to indi-cate which genetic tests they had undergone, or might provide a checklist of diseases so that consumers could request (and pay for) certain tests. States could also enact legislation. New Hampshire, for example, has a somewhat vague statute requiring medical evaluation of the sperm donor.[35]

2. Other Steps: Counseling and Updating Medical Histories

Improved safety and protection against genetic risks involves other steps beyond testing at the time of original donation: (1) counseling recipients and donors on genetic risks; (2) tracking where gametes are sent; (3) requiring updated health information from the donors; and (4) appropriately dissemi-nating that updated information. Relatively few banks have genetic special-ists on staff who can advise recipients about risks that take into account their medical histories. The specialists should also provide preconceptual counsel-ing about the limitations of donor screening and a discussion of the avail-ability (and costs) of additional tests both for the recipients and for the gam-etes. More complete genetic testing at the time of donation should also be accompanied by mandatory requirements that donors update their medical conditions every five years. And, when clinics learn of serious illnesses or genetic abnormalities in the donor or in any family that has used a particu-lar donor's gametes, that information must be provided to recipients of the same donor. Improving access to medical data can be critical for donor-con-ceived people. Rebecca Blackwell, a special education teacher who is a single mother, tried to contact her son's donor. She sent him a certified letter with a picture of Tyler, her son, but the donor never responded. The donor's sister found Blackwell through the website, Ancestry.com, and told her that the donor, along with several of his relatives, had a potentially fatal genetic heart defect, as well as Asperger's syndrome. The defect can be cured through cor-rective surgery, and Tyler underwent the surgery after his biological aunt told him about his risk.[36] With records on children born through the use of one donor's gametes and a requirement to update medical information, the process will become more streamlined: no longer will recipient parents need to post on voluntary websites in the hopes that they will be found.

A final aspect of counseling focuses on ensuring that the intending parents understand not just the questions their children will ask about their origins but also their own attitudes toward the use of donor gametes. While both men and women are more negative about using donor sperm than donor eggs, they still believe that donor eggs are problematic.[37] Helping the parents acknowledge these attitudes before conception may result in improved communication after conception. Two states in Australia mandate that all participants receive counseling. For intending parents, the recommended counseling includes the legal, social, and psychological implications of using a donor as well as the impact on the parents' relationship to each other.[38]

Even if the United States requires more stringent testing and counseling, fertility is international. The paradox of fertility tourism is that the very thing motivating people to seek treatment abroad (the ability to take advantage of different international laws regulating reproductive technologies) also opens the door to many health risks and legal concerns. Inconsistent laws from country to country mean that standards of treatment vary, opening patients up to health risks. For example, while Britain and Scandinavian countries permit the implantation of only one or two embryos after IVF treatment, other countries have higher limits or none at all; this increases the risk of multiple pregnancies, which can pose health risks for the mother and babies.[39] The International Federation of Fertility Societies has called for international standards to be set in order to minimize cross-border treatments and potential health hazards.[40] While the variation among countries should not preclude the United States from acting and joining other countries that have established safeguards, it may call for international advocacy and for domestic efforts to place more controls on fertility tourism.

III. Expanding Access

While donor sperm is relatively affordable, any other means of gaining access to the donor world is more expensive. Rather than limit these services to wealthier individuals who can afford their own treatments without any form of financial aid, assisted reproductive technologies should be available more widely. Greater public funding for fertility services through health care reform can also provide more treatment for the diseases that contribute to infertility. Infertility is not caused by age alone; other factors, such as inadequate health care, contribute. For those with access to health care, coverage makes a difference. Approximately one-quarter of states mandate that private insurance cover infertility treatment;[41] this number should be expanded. Reproductive autonomy is most readily available for the affluent and the sophisticated because they can afford the high costs without subsidy; it is increasingly beyond the reach of the middle class and most economically vulnerable people.

Part of the problem is that infertility is not necessarily seen as a medical condition but as involving a choice of life patterns. Given the high incidence of unexplained infertility along with the correlation of infertility with age,[42] there is a reluctance to classify infertility as a disease. Moreover, infertility is intertwined with the complicated politics of reproductive choice in the United States. If, however, the federal government is willing to require that insurance plans cover contraceptives, breast pumps and other critical components of reproductive control, then infertility could become part of the standard package.

IV. Regulating to Prevent Incest

Many other countries have imposed limits on the numbers of offspring produced by an individual donor. In its landmark report in 1984, England's Warnock Commission recommended that no more than ten children be born from any one individual donor.[43] The commission explained its concern about "the remote possibility of unwitting incest between children of the same donor, and because of risks of transmission of inherited disease" but also noted that "there was no conclusive argument for any particular figure."[44] The British Human Fertilisation & Embryology Authority responded to this recommendation by enacting a similar policy—instead of limiting the number of *children* born with any particular donor's gametes, the authority limited the number of *families* who could use any one donor's gametes to ten (each family could have more than ten children, of course).[45] Similarly, Austria allows donors to provide gametes to only one clinic, where no more than three couples may use them.[46] Other countries have focused on the number of children born from a single donor. For example, in Hong Kong, legislation was enacted in 2007 to limit the number of children born from a single donor to three.[47] Spain limits the number of children born from any one donor's gametes to six.[48]

This section explores the reasons for limiting the number of children born through any individual donor's gametes. A preliminary issue, however, is whether a ban on incest itself can be justified.

1. Incest Is Different?

A justification for continuing the incest ban in any context must satisfy three tests to be coherent: (1) it must be segregable from the ban on incest's possible uses as a legal and cultural reinforcement of the marital family; (2) it must carefully craft an approach toward moral repugnance so that disgust is not determinative of our ban on incestuous relationships; and (3) it must not call into question the growing acceptance of same-sex relationships.

Consider the California Supreme Court's invocation of incest in its decision requiring the state to recognize same-sex marriage. The court carefully distinguished its rationale on the equality of same-sex relationships from the rationales supporting other sexual matings, noting,

> We emphasize that our conclusion that the constitutional right to marry properly must be interpreted to apply to gay individuals and gay couples does not mean that this constitutional right similarly must be understood to extend to polygamous or incestuous relationships . . . *because of their potentially detrimental effect on a sound family environment.*[49]

Constitutionally, there are several methods for upholding the incest ban depending on the level of scrutiny applied. First, even if consensual sexual relationships are part of a protected fundamental right and subjected to strict scrutiny, the state may have a compelling interest in banning them.[50] Compelling interests may range from protecting children from abuse to protecting the future offspring of incestuous relationships from increased risk of genetic disorders.[51] If the level of scrutiny is either intermediate or rational basis, then the state's compelling interest certainly justifies the ban.[52]

Second, there is a more fundamental question (as it were) that relates to what types of consensual sexual relationships are included within the right to sexual privacy. If the right is defined to include only partners in noncaretaking, dependency relationships,[53] for example, then the level of scrutiny is irrelevant, and certain incestuous relationships fall outside the scope of the right. The right to sexual privacy could be defined to include relationships between: (1) adults who were never part of a caretaking relationship—this would exclude not just parent-child incest, but also stepparent-child incest, even in the absence of a legally recognized bond between the parent and the child (a stepparent who has not adopted a child is not a legal parent); and (2) adults who are related through affinity or blood as second cousins or further removed—this would exclude uncle/aunt–niece/nephew incest.[54]

Third, even if some incest laws—such as those between comparatively distantly related relatives—might be suspect under a privacy analysis,[55] a nuanced application of constitutional law could help in drawing the right lines both inside and outside of the reproductive technology world. While *Lawrence* may call into question some forms of consensual intrafamilial relationships, it still allows for carefully crafted laws banning some forms of incest.[56]

Establishing the standard for measuring the constitutionality of an incest ban or the parameters of a right to sexual privacy depends on the question of what justifications exist for the prohibition. The risk of birth defects may provide a rationale for the ban on incest in itself, though gay and lesbian sex does not result in such palpable harms. This rationale is strongest between immediate family members and becomes more attenuated with cousins, as discussed earlier. Once the ban is recognized as requiring a compelling state interest, it does not necessarily follow that every type of incest ban is subject to strict scrutiny, but the dividing line among different forms of incest bans may be arbitrary.

2. Setting Limits

For donors, the primary issue—aside from commodification—is not the donor's health or future fertility but how many related children should be allowed to result from one donor. A limit on the number of offspring can be justified on the basis of fears about incest as well as fears about the widespread transmission of disease. Any form of donation, either egg or sperm, involves the potential for "inadvertent consanguinity," where a donor has provided gametes to different families and the resulting children do not know of their shared genetic heritage.[57] As one former donor explained his unease at having produced sperm that might have resulted in hundreds of offspring, "If you do the math again, there may be 100 young women out there that are basically my son's age that are his half siblings. I have to tell him that's how it is."[58]

Some sperm banks impose a limit on the number of children who can be born from one person's donated sperm.[59] The ASRM recommends taking into account the geographical area and population base for a particular donor, suggesting a limit of twenty-five births per donor per every population of eight hundred thousand people.[60] Assuming a need to set limits, then this number provides a good starting point—albeit in a mobile country the entire country's population should be taken into account. I am not certain of the correct number but believe that multiple stakeholders, including donor-conceived offspring, the industry, the FDA, donors, and recipients, should be involved in discussions of the appropriate limit. As an example of the types of issues that must be addressed, some members of the British Fertility Society have expressed concern that the abolition of donor anonymity may have contributed to a sperm shortage in the United Kingdom and have suggested increasing the current limit of ten families per donor.[61] Particularly in an age of easy travel, donor secrecy, and newly developing understandings of genetics, reducing the number of children that can be born from each donor reduces the possibility of inadvertent consanguinity.

Federally imposed limits would also prevent the widespread dissemination of disease. For example, five donor-conceived offspring in Michigan—products of the same donor—all share the same extremely rare disease of congenital neutropenia.[62] In 2011, a Danish sperm bank warned that at least nine children, born from the same donor sperm, had inherited the genetic disorder neurofibromatosis.[63] As these examples show, donation allows an individual to have multiple offspring before the full potential of disease transmission is realized. Setting limits cannot prevent against disease transmission, but it can help minimize the number of people affected.

Institutions, clinics, and sperm banks should maintain sufficient records to allow a limit to be set for the number of pregnancies for which a given donor is responsible. It is difficult to provide a precise number of times that a given donor can be used because one must take into consideration the population base from which the donor is selected and the geographic area that may be served by a given donor. The ASRM Practice Committee has developed recommendations on the number of babies born with one donor's gametes.[64] These recommendations are explicitly based on concerns about genetically related donor offspring having children together (rather than, for example, risks of widespread transmission of genetic disease or health issues for donors).[65] Accordingly, its suggested limits deserve deference but do not necessarily provide the definitive standard.[66]

These standards are highly influential, but, as discussed earlier, there is no regulatory agency that oversees individual donors or that monitors gamete banks on a routine basis. Banks and clinics are not required to verify the personal information or much of the medical information that donors provide them, and there is no mechanism for monitoring limits on the number of times that one individual can provide gametic material to another individual.[67] Banks are also not required to monitor what happens to the gametic material once it leaves their offices, and there is no required tracking of donors' or their offspring's genetic diseases or other health problems.[68] The occasional "mix-ups" that make their way into court remind consumers and the public of the lack of oversight,[69] but these reminders have not been enough to rectify the existing, inadequate legal framework for preventing and remedying these "mix-ups."[70] Moreover, given the mobility of many Americans (and overseas gamete purchasers), the advisory limits based on an area population of eight hundred thousand may not be adequate.[71] Donors—those who use their gametic material—and donor-conceived off-spring are beginning to understand the limits of current oversight and to advocate for change.[72] Because the nonbinding industry standards do not adequately address all relevant issues and concerns, laws must mandate bet-ter practices rather than relying on industry-internal guidelines and volun-tary compliance.

In other countries, the fears of accidental incest have resulted in precau-tionary legislation that places limits on the number of offspring any given donor can produce. The Netherlands restricts the number of children from any individual donor to twenty-five.[73] As discussed earlier, in Austria, a donor can only provide sperm to one clinic, and no more than three couples can use that sperm.[74] In England, no more than ten families can use the same donor, although the number of children per family is unlimited.[75]

Even as the regulatory framework must shift toward a recognition of family connections, the donor world continues to need legal protections to ensure safety and health. These regulations range, as this chapter has shown, from new medical testing to limiting the number of offspring created by any individual donor, and provide a more sound basis for the larger paradigm shift.

10

Why Not to Regulate

Making changes to the existing system will not be easy. No consensus exists on the basic principles of supplementing a commercial model with a family-based, nurturant model, nor of further government involvement in the fertility markets. There is even less agreement on specific policy proposals. The fertility industry is protective of its ability to self-regulate, without outside intervention. Consider the vehemence with which Jamie Grifo, the program director of the New York University Fertility Center, defended the industry in the wake of disclosures about large numbers of children produced by the same sperm donor: "Too often in medicine, regulators and legislators feel forced to use legislation to make a knee-jerk response to what seems to be alarming information without knowing the full consequences of their action."[1] Strong legal arguments against various regulatory efforts, such as disclosure, include protection of the rights to familial and reproductive privacy, protection of the right to prevent disclosure of information, protection against a violation of adoptive parents' privacy, and protection of the right to equal protection.[2]

Even if the United States were ready to move toward more regulation of the fertility markets, the fundamental paradigm shift, along with the policies of facilitating connections and improving safety, would be subject to a series of objections that have been raised in related contexts. The first argument is that donor-conceived family networks differ so fundamentally from more traditional families that they deserve different legal treatment. The second is that disclosure of identifying information will decrease the supply of donors and restrict parental choice without any countervailing benefits. A third set of arguments notes the negative potential of regulation to allow for the imposition of particular political views that might prevent, for example, single people or gay and lesbian couples from using ART, and that might upset the balance of parents' and children's rights. A final set of concerns relates to the potential for imposition of unwanted relationships, for undermining the integrity of the donor-conceived family, and for invading the privacy rights of donors.

I. Family Networks Are Not Families

Connections among families, according to this argument, take a very different form from families. While shared genes may be important in each context, the similarities end there. Families involve adults related by emotional and sexual intimacy, and may include children related through biology or legally recognized adoption who share (or, in the case of divorce, have shared) lives together; donor-conceived family networks (those formed when families who have used the same donor find one another) typically do not involve any adult intimate relationships, do not include any past sharing of lives, and involve children unrelated to any parents in the second family. Finally, such families raise the danger of overemphasizing one's genetic identity at the expense of the functional family, or "genetic essentialism," the concept that a person is the sum of his genes. Particularly at a time when family law really is attempting to deemphasize biology, a more appropriate response to the rise of donor communities might entail making such connections more difficult to establish, rather than facilitating them.

This cluster of objections is useful in helping to craft the framework of rights to be accorded family networks and in thinking through the role of biology, but it is otherwise unpersuasive in its effort to deny any type of familial-type rights. First, the lack of a shared life among donor-conceived family communities does count for something. It suggests, for example, that the range of cohabitants' rights is inapplicable in this context.[3] There is no shared property that must be accounted for. Parents of one donor-conceived child would have no legal rights to custody of a child conceived through the same donor.

But second, even if the analogy is not perfect, it does provide a useful way of thinking about these networks. Some analogy is needed. Gametes form families. Given the need for administrable approaches, the family analogy may be the best one even if it does not account ideally for all of the possible ways in which donor-conceived kin networks are different. While critics might argue that the analogy should more appropriately be to the regulation of new technologies, this provides an incomplete response to the need for legal regulation because of its narrow focus.

Third, I am not convinced that technologically focused regulation always or even generally can account for the full range of needs displayed by these families. Changing the paradigm to family-focused regulation means that any new law must be analyzed not only on the basis of its scientific justifications but also according to its implications for the interests of gamete providers, recipients, and, most importantly, donor offspring. Explicit reliance on the basic family law principle of "best interests of the child" provides guidance in developing these new laws. This principle justifies regulations to ensure gamete safety, but it also justifies the broader regulations discussed below.

Part of the difficulty is that the argument that donor-conceived family networks are different employs a somewhat limited concept of what family law covers. Families once linked by shared interdependencies and living space are still subject to family law once they dissolve. Although the adult partners may no longer be interdependent emotionally or financially, and although family members may occupy different living spaces, child custody, visitation, and support law continue to regulate family relationships. The image of the traditional family with married parents and children living in the same home is deeply ingrained, but modern families have rendered this image somewhat outdated. Forty percent of children are born outside of a marital family, and the divorce rate hovers around 40 percent.[4] Contemporary families no longer look like traditional families and, as, discussed earlier, the different strands of the family-as-domesticity critique help point toward future applications of family law. As a result, basic principles of family law are of some utility here.

I do not mean to dismiss the concerns about the types of differences between family networks and families. These are very real concerns and should be taken very seriously in crafting new approaches. But donor-conceived family communities exhibit many of the bonds of affinity that have characterized family, and there are shared consanguineous bonds as well. Concerns about the total transfer of family law into family networks should help structure the determinations of which existing laws should be applicable.

The final issue concerns the importance of biology: perhaps we should try to overcome beliefs and interests about the importance of the genetic tie. As Professor Laura Kessler notes in a slightly different context, we might work to expose "heterosexuality and biology to be mere symbols of a privileged relationship,"[5] and then to undermine that privileging by celebrating not just the alternative forms of family made possible by donor gametes but also the non–biologically based connections between parent and child. The law matters here. We have the power to consciously shape human behavior through developing norms and law that deemphasize, rather than emphasize, biology.

One easy response is to observe that donor-conceived people themselves want this opportunity for connection, and we must listen to them. That is too pat: it accepts, without challenging, the message from the surrounding culture that biology is important. Like everyone else, donor-conceived people are certainly recipients of this message.

The more nuanced response recognizes that biology is important. We are not blank slates. Moreover, many people are searching to fill in missing parts of their identity, to learn more about potential health issues, and to help them integrate nature and nurture. They recognize that genes are not determinative of one's identity, or even of one's physical reality. Knowing that a parent has developed cancer, heart disease, or depression does not definitively indicate that the child will also. Genes do not tell us about a person's culture, family, friends, or moral beliefs. Acquiring genetic information does not allow an adoptee or a child of gamete provision to predict, or even to explain, all of her personal characteristics and traits. Knowing about one's genetic history does not, then, mean that every aspect of one's life will suddenly be explained. Nonetheless, a genetic history does contain useful information about potential medical conditions, and it may provide some grounding for those children who want to know, helping them shape future behavior.

And, even as donor-conceived families disrupt traditional notions of how families are formed, genes are critical to their creation, and it is biology and biology-based ties that create donor communities (even the affinities between parents are based on their children's shared genes). As family law today begins to deemphasize biology in favor of focusing on intent and function, one response to the rise of donor communities could entail making such connections more difficult to establish, rather than facilitating them. Notwithstanding the recognition that people care about biology, perhaps the role of law is to work to overcome such beliefs and interests. Yet treating donor-conceived family communities differently from other kinship networks continues to stigmatize them by treating them differently. The law respects extended families in numerous ways, ranging from kinship preferences in foster care to favoring relatives when someone dies intestate (without a will). Recognizing donor-created family communities simply acknowledges that connection can be—and is—created in numerous ways, including on the basis of genes.

Ultimately, the purpose of disclosing the identity of biological relatives is to aid offspring and the various parents in their personal and emotional development, not solely to provide genetic information (although this may be an important byproduct). Ultimately, the reasons why adoptees or gamete children seek information go far beyond genetically related rationales. The information provides additional background to their full identities—genetic, emotional, and even cultural.

II. But What about Supply and Parental Choice?

A second objection to the approach developed in this book is that it will affect the supply of donors, decreasing the options available to parents. Some have argued that, without a guarantee of anonymity, donor supply will decline dramatically, and the United States will be forced to recruit new donors internationally. As Charles Sims, the medical director of a large sperm bank warned, "In many European countries there are very few or no sperm donors because of government regulations."[6] This then also implicates procreative rights, which are, on this argument, constitutionally protected.[7] A related claim is that donors will place conditions on their donations, having the ability to specify who can receive their sperm or eggs.

These are risks that must be acknowledged. First, with respect to the supply of donors, some evidence exists that, when countries have required identity disclosure, some donors are less likely to come forward. If gamete providers know that they can be found, the argument goes, then they may be less likely to give gametic material out of fear that an unknown child will come knocking on their door twenty years later, while current practices appear to protect their ongoing anonymity. Legal scholar Gaia Bernstein eloquently connects disclosure to a decreasing supply of donor gametes.[8] Indeed, most observers agree that mandatory disclosure has at least some effect on supply, although disagreement arises on the precise impact.[9] Indeed, studies have repeatedly shown that about half of both egg and sperm donors would not participate if anonymity were removed—but that the other half would continue to provide gametes.[10] Early studies from countries that have moved toward mandatory donor identification similarly showed that donors were less willing to provide gametes if they knew their identity would be disclosed.[11] Even the future possibility that a law will require such disclosure may have a dampening effect.[12] Indeed, after Sweden enacted legislation in 1985 that required the release of information concerning gamete providers when the child reached the age of eighteen, there was some concern that the legislation had caused a severe decline in the number of sperm donors.[13]

A variety of countries, including Switzerland and the United Kingdom (in addition to Sweden), have abolished anonymity.[14] Not everyone agrees that the new donor-anonymity laws have had a direct causal impact on gamete shortages, thus forcing people to go abroad. Instead, many banks have developed new recruiting practices in order to increase their supplies. In Sweden, for example, the decline appears to have been a short-term one that was overcome by increased recruitment efforts. In the quarter-century since donor-anonymity rules were enacted, however, there appears to be an increase in the number of sperm providers, and fears that donor-identity release requirements would inhibit semen provision have been allayed.[15]

In England, commentators raised similar concern over decreasing numbers of donors once national law precluded anonymous donation in April 2005. British media declared a "fertility treatment crisis" following the implementation of the law banning donor anonymity in 2005.[16] But the actual situation is more complicated. First, in the ten years preceding implementation of the new law, the amount of donor sperm treatment declined substantially. While more than twenty-five thousand donor sperm treatments occurred in 1992-1993, that number fell to slightly over six thousand such treatments by 2002-2003; by contrast, the number of treatments involving micro-manipulation of sperm (ICSI or intra-cytoplasmic sperm injection), which was virtually nonexistent in 1992-1993, topped fifteen thousand in 2002-2003.[17]

Second, while the total number of gamete providers dipped during the few years after anonymity ended, it steadily increased after that.[18] As journalist Liza Mundy tartly documented, "there has not been a decline in registered sperm donors following the 2005 change, and it's arguable that there is not a shortage of donor sperm now. The number of sperm donors has risen in the UK since the identity-disclosure rule took effect."[19] (The decline in total number of donors was due to a decrease in egg donors.) One blog post on the Donor Sibling Registry noted that the number of sperm donors in the United Kingdom (480) in 2010 was higher than in any previous year on record, while the number of egg donors was the second highest on record.[20]

The London Sperm Bank has developed innovative marketing techniques such as a humorous logo and a responsive management system, and it has been successful in recruiting (during a one-year period, it had more than three thousand inquiries from potential sperm donors).[21] The real problem may not be a decline in the number of donors or donations, but rather an inefficient system of treating women with donor sperm, which can be corrected by improved record keeping and communication among clinics.[22] Thus, while requiring the release of information may have some initial impact on the number of donors, predictions of drastic long-term effects appear to be overblown and, indeed, to distort the actual effect. Moreover, such legislation may result in the development of new methods to recruit other donors; in Scotland, men were offered oats, and the British National Health Service has targeted sports fans.[23] When it adopted a new approach in 2012, including increased compensation for donors, the HFEA explained that it was tackling problems with donor recruitment that it had identified and seeking to improve "customer service."[24]

In addition, the publicity associated with new laws may encourage different types of donors to come forward.[25] By changing advertising techniques to emphasize helping others rather than the amount of payment, banks may be able to recruit donors who care less about money and more about facilitating the creation of families. As one physician at a fertility center in England explained, "we need to change our strategies to target older men in established relationships. Since it appears they are likely to offer help for altruistic purposes, we must . . . increase public knowledge of the need for donors up to the age of 40."[26] If open-identity programs are mandated, then this will more likely attract men who are older than the current pool of donors, who already have children, who believe that donating sperm is an altruistic act, and who assume that open-identity programs are appropriate.[27] Finally, payment seems an important component; when Canada outlawed payment for sperm donors, the sperm supply decreased dramatically.[28]

Even granting that there could be a potential impact on the number of donors as a result of increased regulation, this objection remains problematic. It fits nicely within a paradigm in which the donor world is regulated as a scientific or medical area with a focus on the rights of patients (parents) to make their own binding choices (anonymity for their children), but not within a family law paradigm. As I explained earlier, recognizing relationships in addition to medical needs should serve as the basis for moving the law forward. This objection provides critical insights into tensions in the ART field. Unlike adoption, which has explicitly focused on the child's best interests, ART has developed to serve (potential) parents' interests in producing a child.[29] And, as an industry has flourished in this environment, it too has strong interests in serving these potential parents. Donors supply a highly desirable commodity, and children are the highly desired outcome. While birth mothers have helped produce changes in the adoption world, including somewhat more control for them, there is little such advocacy in the donor world. On the other hand, allowing for the limited release of donor identity might result in the development of new methods to recruit donors, such as through appealing to altruism or expanding the age groups solicited.[30]

In the comparable context of adoption in the United States, leaving the original birth certificates unsealed has not compromised the integrity of the adoption process nor served as a harsh limit on the number of children adopted. Indeed, in the two states that never closed their records, there were higher than average rates of adoption.[31]

It appears, then, that the requirement that children receive access to donor information will not necessarily result in a dramatic decrease in donors. It is their interests and, in many cases, the interests of their parents that are respected through a disclosure regime.

III. The Slippery Slope

While the supply issues can be resolved by finding additional sources of recruiting, a more fundamental objection is to any potential regulation that would affect the market. On this argument, three potentially disastrous consequences might result. First, laws structuring the donation process would be part of a slippery slope toward regulating not just *what* gametes are available but *who* has access to those gametes. Particularly given the restrictions on the access of gay, lesbian, or single people to reproductive technology in some countries, this is certainly a rational fear. Indeed, legal support for these families is not an entirely positive good and, particularly in areas involving the intersection of sex, family, and intimacy, there is healthy skepticism of state regulation, even well-intentioned state regulation.[32]

Second, beyond concerns about restrictions on access, more law may not help donor-conceived families and their communities. These families simply may not be better off with a regulatory scheme and, indeed, may derive pleasure and benefit in being able to form relationships outside of the law. Families are finding each other and are developing affective ties, so there may be no need to put these ties into a legal framework and, indeed, there may be affirmative benefit to resist state regulation. Rather than "indulg[ing] in the misplaced view that, if something important is at stake, law should regulate it,"[33] we might instead create space by not regulating, thereby allowing these new networks to help destabilize existing conceptions of the traditional family. And finally, by changing the character of who might be willing to donate by requiring limited disclosure, we are tinkering with supply.

1. Politics

To be sure, the politics in the United States are quite complex, ranging from those who are against any kind of regulation to those who are for limited regulation to those who want to ban ART entirely.[34] And there are strange coalitions of anti-choice and pro-choice activists. The Institute for American Values (IAV) report discussed earlier, which compares adoptees and donor individuals, suggests that "adoption's legality should not justify other practices that intentionally separate children from their biological parents."[35] (One of the IAV's primary goals is, according to its website, "[t]o increase the proportion of children growing up with their two married parents.")[36] Indeed, Elizabeth Marquardt, one of the report's coauthors, testified that donor-conceived people may have problems because "'[t]here seems to be something else about knowing that the person who raised you also deliberately denied you your other parent before you were even born.'"[37]

New regulations might in fact open up the possibility of restricting access to any type of third-party gametes or, more specifically, restricting access by the LGBT community. And, they might provide an opening for restrictions more generally on procreative choices. In Italy, which restricts the use of IVF to heterosexual couples, no one can use donor sperm or eggs.[38] The mandates for insurance coverage of in vitro fertilization in some states already specify that the patient's eggs must be fertilized by her "spouse," thereby excluding all unmarried couples and individuals.[39] And some fertility clinics already conduct their own gatekeeping against LGBT and single patients.[40]

Nonetheless, additional restrictions are not an inevitable result of regulations based within a paradigm that respects family formation. England, where the fertility industry is highly regulated, extended equality of treatment to same-sex couples after it abolished anonymity.[41] Moreover, the California Supreme Court ruled that physicians could not treat lesbian patients differently from others seeking alternative insemination.[42] Enacting laws that protect and foster relationships within the donor world, laws that focus on identity, connection, and children, involves entirely separate interests and politics from enacting laws that restrict access to that world.

2. Stunting Development

It may be that donor-conceived family communities are better served without a regulatory scheme specifically focused on them. Being outside of the law allows families to find each other voluntarily and develop their own affective ties, without legal oversight. As Columbia law professor Katherine

Franke points out, the expansion of rights does not necessarily offer more power and more opportunity, but instead may involve the state in restrictively defining relationships.[43] While legal regulation and recognition may help solidify and recognize the ties among donor-conceived family communities, this may be inappropriate not only in actual cases where there are no affective ties but also as a more abstract goal. The assumption that creating a legal structure will simply help those who want to develop ties and allow those who do not to remain outside the system is, on this view, unwarranted: a new legal structure will affect everyone.

The argument that state involvement inherently changes the rules of the game is, of course, accurate. The more important issue, however, is whether these new rules are better than old rules (or none at all). The need to provide support for these new families provides the basis for state involvement. The absence of rules fostering connection inhibits the development of donor-conceived family communities, restricting their opportunities to find each other, and it also prevents donor-conceived people from finding out about their donors. Moreover, because the affective relationships remain voluntary, those who do not want any connection can effectuate their wishes and continue to exist "outside" of regulation.

3. Upsetting the Balance

Finally, the slippery slope argument suggests that regulation might have profound, and negative, effects on the existing balance between parents' and children's rights. We generally allow parents decision-making authority with respect to their children, and we defer to those choices, unless they lead to abuse or neglect.[44] According to this perspective, we should defer to the family's private choice; the government should not "dictate how and when families make intimate decisions."[45] Making disclosure into a government mandate ignores the very real, significant interests of parents in raising their children as they see fit. Moreover, when prospective parents decide to use anonymous donors, the parents are, according to this argument, not just looking after their own interests but also protecting their future child's interests. Parents, then, have the constitutionally protected right to make certain choices that affect their children, including agreeing to confidentiality of the donor. Indeed, there is an enormous amount of deference to parents, allowing them to make decisions that have significant psychological and other repercussions, ranging from whether to circumcise a child to where to live to whether to get a divorce. While the parent may make a decision that the child disagrees with, it was the parent's right to make that decision in the first place, as part of the decision to bring the child into existence. Even when the child turns eighteen and the parents are no longer legally responsible, she should remain bound by certain decisions.

A related argument suggests that banning anonymity leads to a change in the nature of donors, thereby restricting parents' options.[46] Harvard Law School Professor Glenn Cohen argues that any alteration of when, whether, or with whom we reproduce cannot necessarily be justified on the basis of a focus on any resulting child's best interests. As he explains,

> [W]henever the proposed intervention will itself determine whether a particular child will come into existence, best interest arguments premised on that child's welfare are problematic. So long as a child will not be provided a "life not worth living," the child cannot be said to be harmed when its counterfactual was not existing, or by having a different child (genetically speaking) substituted for it. Thus, any intervention that will alter whether, with whom, or even when individuals reproduce cannot be justified by concern for protecting the resulting child's welfare unless the child would have a life not worth living absent the intervention.
>
> Prohibitions on sperm-donor anonymity tend to alter whether and with whom individuals reproduce. Such regulation may cause some would-be donors not to donate, altering when and with whom they reproduce.[47]

Indeed, he argues that using this justification for regulations affecting anonymity is "deeply intellectually problematic."[48]

There are numerous responses to this philosophical concern. First, rather than focus solely on the interests of a child who only comes into being as a result of the use of donor gametes, we should consider the rights of a child who *actually* comes into existence.[49] At that point, the test should not be, Would this child have been better off not being born? Instead, as Amartya Sen and Martha Nussbaum have emphasized, there is a responsibility to maximize human capabilities.[50] The capabilities approach emphasizes the freedom of individuals to achieve the life that they would choose for themselves. As elaborated by Nussbaum, the capabilities include "being able to be treated as a dignified being whose worth is equal to that of others."[51] While that statement is quite broad, many donor-conceived offspring seek the same opportunity as others to know their biological heritage. Or, to put it more bluntly, here are the words of Elizabeth Marquardt, a researcher who is the director of the Center for Marriage and Families at the Institute for American Values:

To those who suggest donor offspring should shut up and be grateful because without this intervention they wouldn't "be here," I say this: Ever had an issue with your mom? Your dad? Whoops, sorry, you can't talk about that! Without them, after all, you wouldn't *exist.*

Sure, we should all be grateful to be alive. . . . But donor offspring do not more than any one else among us owe a lifelong debt of gratitude to their bio/legal/social/donor parents simply for the opportunity to be alive.[52]

Once the child comes into being, the issue is how to maximize the child's welfare. While we can still defer to parents' choices for their children at the time of conception, by the time the child reaches eighteen, she becomes legally independent, with her own constitutional interests. In *Pratten*, Justice Adair chastised those who adhered to the discriminatory stereotype about donor-conceived individuals "that, because they are 'wanted' children, it is acceptable to disregard their best interests in favour of the interests of their parents, who may have compelling reasons for preferring (or requiring) donor anonymity."[53] It is not, she observed.

Prospectively, at least, under a system that guarantees limited disclosure, any donor who provides gametes will be aware of responsibilities to children created from those gametes. Indeed, without anonymity, donors are more likely to confront and understand their roles in creating new families.[54]

As in other areas, it is entirely appropriate for society, through its lawmakers, to make policy based on judgments about how to maximize human happiness, and if the judgment is that kids will be happier with rights to access genetic information, then to regulate so they get that information—even if that reduces the total number of children (which is absurd, since other interests are at stake).

Indeed (and second), any argument for mandatory disclosure should focus not just on the child but also on the interests of donors, parents, the donor family network, or the larger community. Some parental interests would be *furthered* through these same regulations, interests such as making contact with genetically related offspring and even the donor, ensuring the integrity of their own families, and respecting their children's interests. These regulations also promote donors' interests in becoming known and possibly establishing a relationship with their offspring.[55]

Moreover, the culture of anonymity developed because of the stigma of infertility, the shame of not being able to produce biologically related offspring. With the increasing number of single and gay and lesbian parents who are obviously unable to create biologically related offspring, the stigma of using donor gametes may dissolve. Requiring disclosure can also help change the culture of secrecy by showing how "ordinary" (if not "natural") and common donor-conceived people actually are. Of course, it is entirely unclear what will actually cause a shift in norms surrounding infertility and reproduction; the long-term effects of donor regulation are impossible to predict. Nonetheless, the law can play an expressive role in promoting change. Laws embody and reflect certain values, and they can promote the development of attitudes that provide even more support to those values. For example, before the Massachusetts Supreme Court decision recognizing gay marriage in 2003, about two in five Americans supported gay marriage; as other states have permitted same-sex marriage, the number has increased, so that today, more than half of all Americans support gay marriage.[56] Similarly, a law on limited disclosure might prompt parents to tell their children of their donor-conceived status.

Finally, a child who does not yet exist is not harmed through its nonexistence.[57] That is, a nonexisting child has no rights—to be born or not.[58] We may believe that any barrier to the existence of a particular child is morally problematic, and that the barrier cannot be justified; at its extreme, this argument means that not only abortion but also birth control and male masturbation should be banned because each prevents the creation of certain children. More than 90 percent of United States women will use contraception at some point in their lives, and even the Catholic Church permits the rhythm method. We thus must allow for some barriers to the existence of a child, and the question then becomes which ones we, as a culture, will choose to impose and why—how we decide which regulations are appropriate. Abortion rights and the ability to use birth control are about empowering parental choice as to the circumstances under which they will conceive. While any regulation requiring the use of an anonymous donor affects parental choice, it is unrelated to the fundamental ability to become a parent.

As a constitutional matter, the parameters of a procreative right concerning assisted reproduction are, somewhat surprisingly, less than clear.[59] While there are rights to adult sexual intimacy and to bear and rear children, these may not include the ability to use assisted reproductive technology.[60] Even if they do, and the right to use reproductive technology is protected as fundamental, however, there may well be compelling state interests in promulgating certain narrowly tailored regulations. Consequently, the existence of a procreative right provides only the starting point for determining whether restrictions may be constitutional.

Taken together, these arguments show the importance of focusing on the interests of the resulting child and her web of relationships and support. Ensuring an adequate supply of donors is critical to a medical model of donor families, but that does not need to be sacrificed to the relational concerns of family law; they are not mutually exclusive. While it is important not to limit access to reproductive technology on the basis of the parents, it is critical to think about the impact of using particular technologies on all involved.

The second concern, that donors will have more control over selecting potential recipients, parallels some of the control that birth mothers have begun to assert over adoption. There has been a shift in power from adoptive to birth parents. As the competition among would-be adoptive parents has intensified in response to the sharp decline in adoptable infants, a more distinctive "seller's market" has emerged. Birth parents are not only choosing the persons who will parent their children but are often asking to remain a part of the new adoptive family's life. Popular culture has certainly utilized this theme. One subplot in the 2010 movie *Mother and Child* (starring Annette Bening, among others) involves a pregnant teen girl who initially decides to relinquish her child for adoption after several intense interviews with the prospective adoptive parents, and then, after giving birth, changes her mind. Similarly, in *Juno*, the pregnant teen spends a great deal of time with the prospective parents before following through on her placement agreement; in *Baby Mama* (2008), Tina Fey allows the surrogate mother she has chosen to live in her apartment throughout her pregnancy. In *The Complete Adoption Book*, the authors note that many birth mothers choose independent adoptions because of the control they experience in choosing the adoptive parents.[61]

This is, however, one of those areas where the donor and adoption worlds differ. Adoptions are subject to much more regulation than is realistic in ART. Each adoption must be court approved, for example. Second, one man can produce hundreds of vials of sperm, and a woman can produce dozens of eggs, so controlling who uses them could be a daunting task; birth parents are generally seeking to place only one child. Donors might seek to condition gamete usage on the recipients meeting certain criteria, such as ethnicity or sexual orientation or religion. Agencies and banks, however, generally conduct little screening of recipients and, given the added expense, time, and administrative resources required to comply with donor requests, are unlikely to do more. Third, even if donors are able to exercise more control over who used their gametes, the number of individuals involved should ensure preferences for a variety of potential recipients. Finally, if this concern becomes a reality, then antidiscrimination law could prevent clinics from allowing donors to make these choices; biological parents express preferences in the adoption world, but those preferences are not controlling when they are based on impermissible discrimination.

IV. Privacy and Unwanted Contact

One man, who has been donating anonymously since 2004, said he was not opposed to his thirteen offspring contacting him when they were adults but wanted "fair warning" before his phone number and address were handed out. "These people are strangers so of course I would be concerned if they were given my home number," he said. "What if my own child was to answer the phone to someone who said 'hello, I'm your sister.' I think the privacy of my fiancé and prospective children should be protected considering I did this anonymously."[62]

A final objection is that simply allowing for identifying information about the donor and other genetic offspring will then result in unwanted contacts and efforts to establish a relationship, violating the constitutionally protected privacy rights of all involved and perhaps even constituting criminal acts, such as harassment and stalking. The strongest version of this argument also suggests that this will disrupt relationships in the donor-conceived families as well as in the donor's family. This argument predicts that offspring or their parents will "force" themselves into other families where, for example, the offspring may not even know they were donor conceived, or the donor may never have told her family about the potential existence of these children. Donors may be reluctant to find out that they have helped conceive dozens of offspring, they may be concerned about legal liability, or they may be worried about offspring who are emotionally needy. As a corollary, contact may feel threatening to the parents as they wonder about "sharing" their child.[63]

The primary problem with this argument is that it conflates the right to identity with the obligation to form a relationship. It also suggests a deep-seated insecurity in the donor-conceived family between parent and child. Laws permitting contact recognize the legitimate interest in obtaining this information, but do not require contact or further interaction by anyone involved; there are no mandatory legally recognized relationships. Donor family networks depend on mutuality and reciprocity.[64] Of course, while many families and donors will welcome the contact, some may not want any kind of relationship. Claims about unwanted intrusions suggest that those interested in searching will be unable to set limits. Indeed, some donor-conceived people have told me of friends who, with the best of intentions, have attempted to contact their donors, and have been profoundly hurt when the contact has been rejected. Nonetheless, in the comparable context of adoption, when states have opened records, there have been few complaints about unwelcome contacts.[65] Some donors may be overwhelmed by the number of offspring they have helped create, and may respond to the first twenty but then stop. They are, of course, under no legal obligation to respond to the remaining eighty.

Parents who have created families with donor gametes may not welcome contact from half-siblings, and may feel threatened in their own parenting as their offspring search. For example, parents who do not disclose the fact of donation are often worried about the harm to their relationship to their children, particularly between the child and the nonbiological parent.[66] A nonbiological parent may fear rejection if a child finds the genetically related donor, or lesbian families may hesitate about reaching out to straight donors.

There are three responses. First, most contacts are positive;[67] donor-conceived people are typically curious about the donor but are not trying to find a new parent. Where contact is unwanted, donors (or offspring) can file civil damages suits, seek a domestic violence order prohibiting contact, or involve the criminal justice system in enforcing antiharassment and stalking laws. But second, given the rate of technological change in the ability of genetic tracing, practices of anonymity may simply collapse as science allows for increasingly accurate genetic identifications[68] and as the Internet becomes increasingly sophisticated (see chapter 3). Even though the federal government protects health information privacy, even if clinics promise to shred records, and even though any attorneys involved are subject to professional ethics of confidentiality, donors cannot be certain that they will never be found. Beyond potential DNA identification, donors provide basic information that may allow them to be traced via social media or other websites.[69] Pragmatically, donors can no longer rely on guaranteed, life-long anonymity regardless of written promises to the contrary.

While these practical realities do not answer jurisprudential concerns about privacy, they do show the urgency of addressing the jurisprudential issues. One solution, which would mirror the adoption world, permits the filing of contact preference forms, so that a donor or donor-conceived family could indicate no interest in contact.[70] While difficult to enforce outside of stalking laws, these forms would provide useful information about the willingness of the gamete provider to engage with offspring. Those requesting and receiving information might also be required to receive counseling, particularly important where a no-contact form is on file.

Finally, privacy is a relational concept that relates to our expectations. As we consider what will be disclosed, information must be considered in context, which means that "the relationships in which the information is transferred and the ways in which it is used become the central focus of inquiry."[71] Disclosure, then, is harmful when information is disseminated beyond its intended audience, but the mere act of disclosure is not intrinsically harmful.[72] Allowing only the donor-conceived person access to this information provides protection against widespread dissemination. In the adoption context, courts have rejected this argument, finding that "the disclosure of private information to adult adoptees . . . is not sufficiently analogous to fundamental familial and reproductive privacy rights."[73] The traditional conceptualizations and articulation of the constitutional right to privacy relates to different interests than those involved in the release of identifying information about a donor. While retroactive release of identifying information may raise privacy issues, future laws that establish parameters for identity release in the donation process do not trigger these concerns.[74] Prospectively, donors are on notice that their identities are subject to limited disclosure, and intending parents understand the parameters of their choice to use donor gametes.

The needs of infertile couples—regardless of whether the infertility is medical or social[75]—are complex, not simply based on the need for medical services or consumer protection. Many of them now search for donors willing to be identified in the future, many of them rue that they opted for anonymous donors, and many of them are aware that their children may want additional information about the donors.[76]

Conclusion

Challenging and Creating Kinship

As donor-conceived families come together, there is much uncharted territory on how to define their connections. While existing doctrine provides some useful analogies, they are incomplete models. This book has explored how we might begin to nurture relationships, foster emotional connection, promote children's interests, and recognize the multiple forms of intrafamily relationships. It has suggested a paradigm shift toward regulating donor-conceived families and their communities not just as scientific and medical constructs but also as relational entities. Families connected through the same donor, but who do not share dependencies or a home, may develop emotional intimacies that resemble those of other familial structures. These relationships transcend their origins, which may be rooted in commercial transactions and medical cures. Family law will need to adapt existing doctrines as it develops an approach to these families. The difficulty, as is the case whenever existing laws must evolve to cover new situations, is determining how to apply legal standards and institutions developed for other purposes.

The United States has exhibited a unique hesitation to regulate any aspect of the lucrative infertility industry. Individuals who have made use of, or who are products of, assisted reproduction have developed their own methods for living with the profound ways in which assisted reproduction has an impact on their lives. Instead, it is time for the law to foster connections among distinct family groups, not on the basis of a radical reconceptualization of what constitutes a family bond but in recognition of the second-degree genetic relationships connecting these families that in other circumstances would be known, encouraged, fostered, and nurtured.

This process of evolution must respect the particular characteristics of donor-conceived familial relationships. As shown throughout this book, assisted reproduction creates families that are both like and unlike others. Just as there are aspects of adoptive family relationships that reveal to us that not every facet of an adoptive family is congruent with what we find in biological families, third-party-gamete-donor families are also not the same. The book has suggested that the law adapt to these new families in two basic ways. First, these relationships must find a home within family law in addition to their current home within health law. Second, and relatedly, the traditional focus in family law on relationships and on a child's best interests should replace the existing medicalized focus on patients' interests in the donor world. While the simple biological relationship should not necessarily entitle members to privileges or state support of the relationships within traditional family law doctrine, it should entitle members to state regulation based on fairness and other important goods at stake.

The law already provides a background to the development of donor-conceived family communities; it does not provide adequate structure to answer the challenges raised by these networks. As the number of families that owe their existence to reproductive technology increases, the paradigm for regulation and respect must be based on family law, which has historically regulated comparable relationships and which has focused on a child's best interests.

The new framework places donor-conceived family communities within legal constructs recognizing and supporting relationships and emphasizing children's interests, while also continuing and expanding existing regulations rooted within health law. The paradigm shift in the donor world could prompt broader changes more generally, creating options beyond framing all families within the dyadic nuclear family model. Without diluting parental responsibility, a new model can acknowledge pluralism of family forms. The result would benefit those in all family forms, including heterosexual, biologically formed ones.

These principles can lead to changes in the way we approach numerous other aspects of families. The kinds of reforms with respect to gamete donation will reinforce the open-records-in-adoption movement, and should help in the recognition of the equality of collaboratively formed families of various kinds—adoptive families (both domestic and transnational), donor gamete families, and surrogacy families, regardless of their genetic relatedness. Ultimately, recognizing donor-conceived family communities will promote a more nuanced understanding of the meaning of family relationships. It can affirm the integrity and privacy of families, however they are formed, while also recognizing the significance of understanding and connecting to one's genetic origins (without undercutting the legal and social parents). Donor families show the importance of rethinking family bonds to acknowledge the numerous means by which we create connections, the ways that the state can foster those connections, and the development of alternative family forms. While donor family communities do not need treatment equal to that of other kinds of families, they do need special treatment to ensure their existence and continuation.

As we learn from donor-conceived families and their communities, people are embedded in several families simultaneously in their lifetimes, with wide ranges in the degree of connection. Consideration of donor families leads us to reconsider how we define, experience, and connect with our own families.

NOTES

INTRODUCTION

1. *See* Janet L. Dolgin, *Biological Evaluation: Blood, Genes, and Family*, 41 Akron L. Rev. 347, 349 (2008) (analyzing "the shifting uses of biology in the social construction of family").

2. *See* Laura Mamo, *Biomedicalizing Kinship: Sperm Banks and the Creation of Affinity-Ties*, 14 Science as Culture 237, 247 (2005).

3. *See* Janet Halley & Kerry Rittich, *Critical Directions in Comparative Family Law: Genealogies and Contemporary Studies of Family Law Exceptionalism*, 58 Am. J. Comp. L. 753, 761-62 (2010).

4. Judith Stacey, Unhitched: Love, Marriage, and Family Values from West Hollywood to Western China 4 (2011).

5. For representative writings, *see, e.g.*, Dan Markel, Jennifer M. Collins & Ethan J. Leib, Privilege or Punish: Criminal Justice and the Challenge of Family Ties (2009); Clare Huntington, *Repairing Family Law*, 57 Duke L.J. 1245, 1277 (2008).

6. *Donor Unknown: Adventures in the Sperm Trade* Press Packet 5 (2010), http://www.donorunknown.com/images/presspackupdatedagain.pdf.

7. Amy Harmon, *Hello, I'm Your Sister: Our Father Is Donor 150*, N.Y. Times, Nov. 20, 2005, http://www.nytimes.com/2006/01/20/national/20donor.html?pagewanted=all.

8. *Donor Unknown: Adventures in the Sperm Trade: Joellen* 5 (2010), http://www.donorunknown.com/meet-the-siblings.

9. *See, e.g.*, Robin L. Bennett, The Practical Guide to the Genetic Family History 245 (2d ed. 2010); Caroline Lorbach, Experiences of Donor Conception: Parents, Offspring, and Donors through the Years 168 (2003).

10. *See* Lawrie McFarlane, *Donor Case Strikes at Basic Family Foundations*, Times Colonist (British Columbia), July 15, 2011, http://www2.canada.com/victoriatimescolonist/news/comment/story.html?id=7074bc86-6d1a-41b5-b6e2-e3da99ec38d3&p=1 ("The contemporary fixation with searching for a 'biological parent' . . . gives the animal act of reproduction equal standing with human values like devotion and caring.").

11. *See, e.g.*, George Lakoff, Don't Think of an Elephant! Know Your Values and Frame the Debate xv (2004) ("Frames are mental structures that shape the way we *see* the world. As a result, they shape the goals we seek . . . and what counts as a good or bad outcome of our actions. In politics our frames shape our social policies and the institutions we form to carry out policies."); Amy Kapczynski, *The Access to Knowledge Mobilization and the New Politics of Intellectual Property*, 117 Yale L.J. 804, 814 (2008) ("Each frame is socially mediated, which is to say, each act of framing represents a process of interpretation that takes place between rather than strictly within individuals.").

12. *See, e.g.*, Martha Ertman, *What's Wrong with a Parenthood Market? A New and Improved Theory of Commodification*, 82 N.C. L. Rev. 1, 3-4 n.5 (2003).

13. *See* Michele Goodwin, Black Markets: The Supply and Demand of Body Parts 160–61 (2006). There is also a robust scholarly discussion of seller liability. *See, e.g.*, J. Brad Reich & Dawn Swink, *You Can't Put the Genie Back in the Bottle: Potential Rights and Obligations of Egg Donors in the Cyberprocreation Era*, 20 Alb. L.J. Sci. & Tech. 1, 43–64 (2010) (analyzing the applicability of contract and tort principles to the egg market).

14. *See* Ertman, *supra* note 12 at 11–12; Kimberly D. Krawiec, *Sunny Samaritans and Ego-maniacs: Price-Fixing in the Gamete Market*, Law & Contemp. Probs. 59, 84-85 (Summer 2009); Debora Spar & Anna M. Harrington, *Building a Better Baby Business*, 10 Minn. J.L. Sci. & Tech. 41, 60–62 (2009).

15. Sociologist Rene Almeling discusses how the language influences the perceptions of the donors themselves. Rene Almeling, Sex Cells: The Medical Market in Eggs and Sperm 110-41 (2011).

16. Stephanie Smith, *Dim Economy Drives Women to Donate Eggs for Profit*, CNN.com, Aug. 8, 2008, http:// www.cnn.com/2008/HEALTH/08/05/selling.eggs/index.html. For a discussion of donor motivation *see* Rene Almeling, *Selling Genes, Selling Gender: Egg Agencies, Sperm Banks, and the Medical Market in Genetic Material*, 72 Am. Soc. Rev. 319, 320 (2007) (comparing "how staff at commercial fertility agencies organize the process of egg and sperm donation," and concluding that "the market in genetic material is organized differently depending on the type of body being commodified"); Rene Almeling, *"Why Do You Want to Be a Donor?": Gender and the Production of Altruism in Egg and Sperm Donation*, 25 New Genetics & Soc'y 143, 155 (2006) ("Donor profiles are packaged representations, shaped by the donor's interest in being selected and the agency's interest in recruiting clients, and these interests are structured in part by gendered social norms.").

CHAPTER 1

1. Liza N. Burby, *A Fact of Life*, Newsday, Feb. 6, 2006, at B10.

2. Mark P. Connolly, Stijn Hoorens & Georgina M. Chambers, *The Costs and Consequences of Assisted Reproductive Technology: An Economic Perspective*, 16 Hum. Reprod. Update 603, 605, 607 (2010).

3. Centers for Disease Control and Prevention, *Assisted Reproductive Technology Success Rates: National Summary and Fertility Clinic Reports 2008* 3 (2010), http://www.cdc. gov/art/ART2008/PDF/ART_2008_Full.pdf; Ctrs. for Disease Control and Prevention & Nat'l Ctr. for Health Statistics, Vital and Health Statistics Ser. 23, No. 25, *Fertility, Family Planning, and Reproductive Health of U.S. Women: Data from the 2002 National Survey of Family Growth* 137, table 98 (Dec. 2005), http://www.cdc.gov/nchs/data/ series/sr_23_025.pdf.

4. Liza Mundy, Everything Conceivable: How Assisted Reproduction Is Changing Men, Women, and the World 73-79 (2007).

5. *See, e.g.*, David Plotz, The Genius Factory: The Curious History of the Nobel Prize Sperm Bank (2005) (discussing the development of increasingly sophisticated sperm banks); Debora L. Spar, The Baby Business: How Money, Science, and Politics Drive the Commerce of Conception 23-67 (2006) (discussing the historical development of various fertility techniques, ranging from hormones to egg donation).

6. Spar, *supra* note 5, at 21.

7. Spar, *supra* note 5, at 44-45.

8. *See* Gretchen Livingston & D'Vera Cohn, The New Demography of American Mother-hood 4 (2010), http://pewsocialtrends.org/files/2010/10/754-new-demography-of-motherhood.pdf.

9. Carolyn Butler, *Ovaries Have Not Adjusted to Many Women's Decision to Delay Having Children*, Wash. Post, Feb. 23, 2010, http://www.washingtonpost.com/wp-dyn/content/article/2010/02/22/AR2010022203639.html.

10. *See, e.g.*, Am. Soc'y for Reprod. Med., *Age-Related Fertility Decline: A Committee Opinion*, 90 Fertility & Sterility S154, S154 (2008).

11. Holly Finn, *My Fertility Crisis*, Wall Street Journal, July 23, 2011, http://online.wsj.com/article_email/SB10001424053111903461104576458134196248312-lMyQjAxMTAxMDIw-MjEyNDIyWj.html.

12. Naomi Cahn & June Carbone, Red Families v. Blue Families: Legal Polarization and the Creation of Culture (2010).

13. *See id.* The Red/Blue paradigm is an ideological construct that helps explain behavioral patterns.

14. *See* Ajay K. Nangia, Donald S. Likosky & Dongmei Wang, *Access to Assisted Reproductive Technology Centers in the United States*, 93 Fertility & Sterility 745 (2010).

15. Tarun Jain, *Socioeconomic and Racial Disparities among Infertility Patients Seeking Care*, 85 Fertility & Sterility 876, 878 (2006) ("[W]omen with and without a high school diploma had a higher prevalence of infertility than women with a bachelor's degree or higher (8.1%, 8.5% percent, and 5.6% percent, respectively).").

16. *See, e.g., id.*

17. *Id.*; Tarun Jain & Mark D. Hornstein, *Disparities in Access to Infertility Services in a State with Mandated Insurance Coverage*, 84 Fertility & Sterility 221 (2005); Molly Shanley & Adrienne Asch, *Involuntary Childlessness, Reproductive Technology, and Social Justice: The Medical Mask on Social Illness*, 34 Signs 851, 856-57 (2009); Mark P. Connolly, Stijn Hoorens & Georgina M. Chambers, *The Costs and Consequences of Assisted Reproductive Technology: An Economic Perspective*, 16 Hum. Reprod. Update 605, 607 (2010).

18. Ahmad O. Hammoud et al., *In Vitro Fertilization Availability and Utilization in the United States: A Study of Demographic, Social, and Economic Factors*, 91 Fertility & Sterility 1630 (2009).

19. Anjani Chandra & Elizabeth Hervey Stephen, *Infertility Service Use among U.S. Women: 1995 and 2002*, 93 Fertility and Sterility 725, 728 (2010).

20. J. Farley Ordovensky Staniec & Natalie J. Webb, *Utilization of Infertility Services: How Much Does Money Matter?* 42 Health Serv. Res. 971, 982-83 (2007); Connolly et al., *supra* note 17, at 607; *see generally* Judith F. Daar, *Accessing Reproductive Technologies: Invisible Barriers, Indelible Harms*, 23 Berkeley J. Gender L. & Just. 18, 36-38 (2008); Hammoud et al., *supra* note 18.

21. Staniec & Webb, *supra* note 20, at 983. ART was defined as intrauterine insemination, IVF, and similar medical interventions. *Id.* at 976.

22. Bradley J. Van Voorhis, *In Vitro Fertilization*, 356 New Engl. J. Med. 379 (2007).

23. *See* Staniec & Webb, *supra* note 20, at 981; Lynn White, Julia McQuillan & Arthur L Greil, *Explaining Disparities in Treatment Seeking: The Case of Infertility*, 85 Fertility & Sterility 853 (2006).

24. Tarun Jain, *Socioeconomic and Racial Disparities among Infertility Patients Seeking Care*, 85 Fertility & Sterility 876, 878 (2006).

25. Michael L. Eisenberg et al., *Perceived Negative Consequences of Donor Gametes from Male and Female Members of Infertile Couples*, 94 Fertility & Sterility 921, 921 (2010).
26. *Id.* at 924.
27. *Id.* at 925-26.
28. Gay Becker, The Elusive Embryo 136-37 (2000).
29. Charis Thompson, Making Parents: The Ontological Choreography of Reproductive Technologies 133 (2005) ("[T]he infertility stigma for men included compromised virility and was not simply a matter of the compromised ability to have children.").
30. *Id.* at 127.
31. *Id.* at 129.
32. Centers for Disease Control and Prevention, *Assisted Reproductive Technology Success Rates: National Summary Report; 2009 National Summary* (2011), http://apps.nccd.cdc.gov/art/Apps/NationalSummaryReport.aspx.
33. *Id.*
34. Centers for Disease Control and Prevention, ART 2008, *supra* note 3, at 18 (figs. 4, 46).
35. *Id.* at 61 (fig. 47).
36. Paul Taylor & Wendy Wang, *For Millienials, Parenthood Trumps Marriage* (2011), http://pewsocialtrends.org/2011/03/09/for-millennials-parenthood-trumps-marriage.
37. *See* Peter Conrad, The Medicalization of Society: On the Transformation of Human Conditions into Treatable Disorders (2007). While insemination by donor could be deemed to have been "demedicalized"—*see, e.g.,* Daniel Winkler & Norma J. Winkler, *Turkey-Baster Babies: The Demedicalization of Artificial Insemination*, 69 Milbank Q. 5 (1991)—and indeed, the Centers for Disease Control do not define this as part of "assisted reproductive technology," it still occurs within the larger context of medicalization.
38. Laura Mamo, *Negotiating Conception: Lesbians' Hybrid Technological Practices*, 32 Sci., Tech. & Hum. Values 369, 370 (2007).
39. *Id.* at 385.
40. Laura Mamo, Queering Reproduction: Achieving Pregnancy in the Age of Technoscience 25 (2008).
41. *See* Karey Harwood, The Infertility Treadmill: Feminist Ethics, Personal Choice, and the Use of Reproductive Technologies (2007).
42. Alfred Koerner, *Medicolegal Considerations in Artificial Insemination*, 8 La. L. Rev. 484, 490 (1948).
43. Mamo, *supra* note 40, at 29.
44. Karen M. Ginsberg, Note: *FDA Approved? A Critique of the Artificial Insemination Industry in the United States*, 30 U. Mich. J.L. Reform 823, 826 (1997) (noting that although the number of sperm banks used is not specified, "[b]y 1993, more than 80,000 women were undergoing AI each year, resulting in the conception of more than 30,000 babies").
45. *See* Office of Tech. Assessment, U.S. Congress, Artificial Insemination: Practice in the United States: Summary of a 1987 Survey 63 (1988).
46. *See* David Plotz, *Collected "Seed,"* Slate, June 7, 2005, http://www.slate.com/id/2119808.
47. *See* Mundy, *supra* note 4, at 112.
48. *See* Steve Dilbeck, *Sperm Donors Wanted, Only High-Caliber Jocks Need Apply*, Daily News of L.A., Aug. 26, 2008, at A1.
49. *See* Spar, *supra* note 5, at 48.

50. *See Golden Eggs; Drowning in Credit-Card Debt and Student Loans, Young Women Are Selling Their Eggs for Big Payoffs: But Can They Really Make the Right Medical and Moral Decisions When They're Tempted with $15,000?* Boston Globe, June 25, 2006, Magazine, at 18.

51. *See* Spar, *supra* note 5, at 42; Bonnie Steinbock, *Payment for Egg Donation and Surrogacy*, 7 Mt. Sinai J. Med. 255, 257-58 (2004) (explaining that close friends and relatives served as egg donors when egg donation was first introduced).

52. *See* Spar, *supra* note 5, at 44–46.

53. *See* Ethics Comm., ASRM, *Financial Compensation of Oocyte Donors*, 88 Fertility & Sterility 305, 305 (2007).

54. *See* Jeffrey Kluger, *Eggs on the Rocks: A New Procedure May Offer Women the Chance to Freeze Their Ova—and Stop Their Biological Clock*, Time, Oct. 27, 1997, at 105 (explaining that while sperm and fertilized eggs can remain viable when frozen, unfertilized eggs are fragile and are often damaged by freezing); *see also* Gina Kolata, *Successful Births Reported with Frozen Human Eggs*, N.Y. Times, Oct. 17, 1997, at A1 (reporting on the first successful pregnancy in the United States using an egg that had been frozen); Press Release, ASRM, *Highlights from the 63rd Annual Meeting of the American Society for Reproductive Medicine: ASRM Urges Caution, Strong Counseling for Women Seeking Egg Freezing* (Oct. 16, 2007), http://www.asrm.org/Media/Press/AM07urgecautioneggfreezing.html (emphasizing that egg freezing remains an experimental procedure and that the data available is too limited to allow egg freezing to be considered an established medical treatment).

55. *See* James W. Akin, Katrina A. Bell, Diana Thomas & Jeffrey Boldt, *Initial Experience with a Donor Egg Bank*, 88 Fertility & Sterility 497.e1, 497.e3 (2007).

56. Sara Elizabeth Richards, *Is Egg Freezing Unfairly Marginalized? Why the Experimental Label Should Be Removed from the Procedure*, Slate, March 15, 2010, http://www.slate.com/articles/double_x/doublex_health/2010/03/is_egg_freezing_unfairly_marginalized.html.

57. *See* Rene Almeling, *Selling Genes, Selling Gender: Egg Agencies, Sperm Banks, and the Medical Market in Genetic Material*, 72 Am. Soc. Rev. 319 (2007).

58. *See id.*

59. *See id.* at 329; ASRM, *Psychological Assessment of Gamete Donors and Recipients*, 77 Fertility & Sterility S11 (2002).

60. *California Cryobank: Reproductive Tissue Services*, http://www.cryobank.com/Donor-of-the-Month/2011/December (last visited Dec. 2, 2011).

61. This description draws on my own analysis of egg and sperm banks as well as that of Rene Almeling. *See* Almeling, *supra* note 57, at 329.

62. *See* Naomi Cahn, Test Tube Families: Why the Fertility Markets Need Legal Regulation, chapter 3 (2009).

63. The Fertility Success Rate and Certification Act of 1992, 42 U.S.C. § 263(a)(1) (2011) (requiring assisted reproductive technology programs to annually report pregnancy success rates).

64. Judith Daar, *ART and the Search for Perfectionism: On Selecting Gender, Genes, and Gametes*, 9 J. Gender Race & Just. 241, 254-55 (2005).

65. 42 U.S.C. § 263a-2(i) (2011) (restricting both the federal government and the states from establishing, as part of the certification program, "any regulation, standard, or requirement which has the effect of exercising supervision or control over the practice of

medicine in assisted reproduction technology programs"); *see also* Margaret Foster Riley & Richard A. Merrill, *Regulating Reproductive Genetics: A Review of American Bioethics Commissions and Comparison to the British Human Fertilization and Embryology Authority*, 6 Colum. Sci. & Tech. L. Rev. 1, 4 (2005).

66. Lori Andrews & Nanette Elster, *Regulating Reproductive Technologies*, 21 J. Leg. Med. 35 (2000); 64 Fed. Reg. 39374 (1999).

67. Implementation of the Fertility Clinic Success Rate and Certification Act of 1992: A Model Program for the Certification of Embryo Laboratories, *CDC*, 64 Fed. Reg. 39374 (July 21, 1999).

68. President's Council on Bioethics, Reproduction & Responsibility, *The Regulation of New Biotechnologies* 150 (2004), http://www.bioethics.gov/reports/reproductionandre-sponsibility/index.html.

69. 42 U.S.C. §263a-1 (2011).

70. CDC, *Commonly Asked Questions about the U.S. ART Reporting System* (2011), http://www.cdc.gov/art/ART2008/faq.htm#4.

71. There is one other possibility for ensuring that clinics' claims match their practices. The Federal Trade Commission, which has the authority to monitor marketing claims, has sporadically investigated fertility clinic advertisements.

72. 21 C.F.R. § 1271.1 et seq. (2011). The regulations provide that "[e]xamples of HCT/Ps include, but are not limited to . . . semen or other reproductive tissue." 21 C.F.R. § 1271.3(d) (2011).

73. 21 C.F.R. §1271.75 (2011).

74. 21 CFR § § 1271.75, 1271.80, 1271.85(a) and (c)(2011).

75. 21 C.F.R. § 1271.80(c)(2011).

76. 21 C.F.R. § 1271.85(d) (2011); 21 C.F.R § 1271.60(a) (2011).

77. 21 C.F.R. § 1271.60 (a) (2011).

78. 21 C.F.R. § 1271.90(a)(2) (2011).

79. 21 C.F.R. § 1271.75(e) (2011).

80. 21 C.F.R. § 1271.170 (2011).

81. 21 C.F.R. § 1271.160 (2011).

82. 21 C.F.R. § 1271.47 (2011).

83. 21 C.F.R. § 1271.47(c) (2011).

84. U.S. Food and Drug Administration, *Guidance for Industry: Eligibility Determination for Donors of Human Cells, Tissues, and Cellular and Tissue-Based Products (HCT/Ps)* (2007), http://www.fda.gov/BiologicsBloodVaccines/GuidanceComplianceRegulatory-Information/Guidances/Tissue/ucm073964.htm.

85. U.S. Food and Drug Admin., *HCT/P Inspection Information Inspections Performed in Fiscal Years 1998 to 2010* (2011), http://www.fda.gov/BiologicsBloodVaccines/GuidanceComplianceRegulatoryInforma-tion/ComplianceActivities/ucm136342.htm.

86. Jenna Marotta, *Do Egg Donors Lie?* Jezebel, Dec. 1, 2011, http://jezebel.com/5863529/do-egg-donors-lie.

87. FDA, *What You Should Know: Reproductive Tissue Donation* (2010), http://www.fda.gov/BiologicsBloodVaccines/SafetyAvailability/TissueSafety/ucm232876.htm.

88. While California law is now clear that clinics cannot discriminate on the basis of sexual orientation, *see N. Coast Women's Care Med. Group v. San Diego County Super. Ct.*, 189 P.3d 959 (ruling that the First Amendment right to free exercise does not grant

physicians the right to deny fertility treatments to lesbian patients), the law is far less settled in other states.

89. Steven Kotler, *The God of Sperm: In an Industry Veiled in Secrecy, a Powerful L.A. Sperm Peddler Shapes the Nation's Rules on Disease, Genetics—and Accidental Incest,* L.A. Weekly, Sept. 27, 2007.

90. *See SART, What Is SART?* http://www.sart.org/What_is_SART (last visited May 17, 2012) ("[M]embers of SART have worked diligently to protect our patients and the practice of ART from inappropriate external intrusion and regulation. We have worked successfully to mitigate many of the somewhat onerous requirements that had been initially proposed by the Food and Drug Administration, including the need to quarantine all embryos derived from donor eggs."); Bob Pool & Maria L. La Ganga, *Fooling Nature, and the Fertility Doctor,* L.A. Times, Jan. 30, 2007, at A1 (quoting one physician who worried that "'[a]s soon as you get into an area of zero tolerance, it's easy to find a case when regulation becomes wrong or harmful. . . . To go and try to interfere with someone's reproductive rights is a very touchy area'").

91. ASRM, *Oversight of Assisted Reproductive Technology* (2010), http://www.asrm.org/uploadedFiles/Content/About_Us/Media_and_Public_Affairs/OversiteOfART%20%282%29.pdf; *cf.* Spar, *supra* note 5, at 34. ("The threat of regulation hangs heavily over the industry, prodding suppliers to conform to a fairly rigorous regime of self-regulation and often to act as if they were anticipating a regulatory response.")

92. For example, more than 90 percent of American fertility clinics belong to SART, which has strict membership requirements, including that the clinic's embryology laboratories be accredited and that the clinic have appropriately trained staff. SART has a Validation, Registry, and Quality Assurance Committee that also helps with the CDC-regulated inspection of fertility clinics. *See* ASRM, *Oversight, supra* note 91, at 9.

93. *See generally* ASRM, *Ethics Committee Reports and Statements,* http://www.asrm.org/EthicsReports (last visited Nov. 25, 2011); ASRM, *Practice Committee Guidelines,* http://www.asrm.org/Guidelines (last visited Nov. 25, 2011).

94. Practice Comms. SART and ASRM, *Committee Opinion: Elective Single Embryo Transfer,* http://www.asrm.org/uploadedFiles/ASRM_Content/News_and_Publications/Practice_Guidelines/Committee_Opinions/eSET-printable.pdf (last visited Nov. 25, 2011).

95. Jeremy Laurance, *Study Highlights Dangers of IVF Treatment Overseas,* The Independent, Sept. 14, 2010, http://www.independent.co.uk/life-style/health-and-families/health-news/study-highlights-dangers-of-ivf-treatment-overseas-2078447.html.

96. Lisa C. Ikemoto, *Reproductive Tourism: Equality Concerns in the Global Market for Fertility Services,* 27 Law & Ineq. 277, 283 (2009).

97. Michelle Lang, *Quest for Baby Crosses Borders,* Calgary Herald, Feb. 16, 2009, http://www2.canada.com/calgaryherald/news/story.html?id=acc1bb50-bd19-44d5-8902-c7e55749bffa&p=2.

98. Ikemoto, *supra* note 96, at 286.

99. Gaia Bernstein, *Regulating Reproductive Technologies: Timing, Uncertainty, and Donor Anonymity,* 90 B.U. L. Rev. 1189, 1216 (2010).

100. Rene Almeling, Sex Cells: The Medical Market in Eggs and Sperm 15 (2011).

101. *Become an Egg Donor,* http://www.shadygrovefertility.com/become-egg-donor?gclid=CJH-w5CWi6kCFYJ75QodUxarrg (last visited May 28, 2011).

102. Jennifer Wolff, *The Egg (Donor) Market,* Women's Health, Jan./Feb. 2011, http://www.womenshealthmag.com/life/female-egg-donation; *see* Aaron D. Levine, *Self-Regulation, Compensation, and the Ethical Recruitment of Oocyte Donors,* 40 Hastings Center Report 25 (2010).

103. NW Cryobank, *Sperm Donation* (2010), https://www.nwcryobank.com/sperm-donation (last visited Dec. 5, 2011).

104. California Cryobank, *Become a Sperm Donor,* http://www.spermbank.com (last visited Dec. 5, 2011). The website does mention, at another tab, that sperm donors can provide hope to those who want to complete their families while also receiving compensation, and offers prizes such as movie tickets for the effort involved.

105. *E.g.,* Vasanti Jadva, Tabitha Freeman, Wendy Kramer & Susan Golombok, *Sperm and Oocyte Donors' Experiences of Anonymous Donation and Subsequent Contact with Their Donor Offspring,* 26 Hum. Reprod. 638 (2011).

106. *Id.*

107. Alan Mozes, *Egg Donors Happy They Helped Out: Study,* Oct. 27, 2010, http://www.usatoday.com/yourlife/health/medical/infertility/2010-10-31-egg-donors_N.htm?POE=click-refer.

108. Nancy J. Kenney & Michelle L. McGowan, *Looking Back: Egg Donors' Retrospective Evaluations of Their Motivations, Expectations, and Experiences during Their First Donation Cycle,* 93 Fertility & Sterility 455 (2010).

109. Aaron D. Levine, *The Oversight and Practice of Oocyte Donation in the United States, United Kingdom, and Canada,* 23 HEC Forum 15, 25, 27 (2011).

110. Jadva et al., *supra* note 105, at table VII.

111. Ruth Ragan, *Where Are My Eggs?* N.Y. Times, Motherlode, July 22, 2011, http://parenting.blogs.nytimes.com/2011/07/22/an-egg-donor-responds.

CHAPTER 2

1. David M. Schneider, American Kinship: A Cultural Account 30 (1968).

2. *Id.* at 33.

3. Pew Research Center, *The Decline of Marriage and Rise of New Families* 40 (2010), http://pewsocialtrends.org/files/2010/11/pew-social-trends-2010-families.pdf.

4. Pamela Haag, Marriage Confidential: The Post-Romantic Age of Workhorse Wives, Royal Children, Undersexed Spouses, and Rebel Couples Who Are Rewriting the Rules 119 (2011).

5. Sarah Franklin & Susan McKinnon, Introduction, in Relative Values: Reconfiguring Kinship Studies 1, 1 (Sarah Franklin & Susan McKinnon eds. 2001).

6. For further discussions of this, *see, e.g.,* Susan Moller Okin, Justice, Gender, and the Family (1989); Maxine Eichner, The Supportive State: Families, Government, and America's Political Ideals (2011).

7. Janet Dolgin, *Personhood, Discrimination, and the New Genetics,* 66 Brooklyn L. Rev. 755, 800 (2000-2001); *see* Schneider, *supra* note 1, at 25.

8. *See* Nancy E. Levine, *Alternative Kinship, Marriage, and Reproduction,* 37 Ann. Rev. Anthropology 375, 377, 381 (2008).

9. Marcia C. Inhorn & Daphna Birenbaum-Carmeli, *Assisted Reproductive Technologies and Culture Change,* 37 Ann. Rev. Anthropology 177, 182 (2008).
10. *See, e.g., id.* at 182-83.
11. Levine, *supra* note 8, at 382.
12. Marilyn Strathern, Kinship, Law, and the Unexpected: Relatives are Always a Surprise 25 (2005).
13. Susan Gary, Jerome Borison, Naomi Cahn & Susan Gary, Contemporary Approaches to Trusts and Estates, chapter 2 (2011).
14. Janet Halley & Kerry Rittich, *Critical Directions in Comparative Family Law: Genealogies and Contemporary Studies of Family Law Exceptionalism,* 58 Am. J. Comp. L. 753, 761-62 (2010).
15. *Schafer v. Astrue,* 641 F.3d 49 (4th Circ. 2011).
16. *See, e.g.,* Sasha Roseneil, Sociability, Sexuality, Self: Relationality and Individualization (2010); Sasha Roseneil, On Not Living with a Partner: Unpicking Coupledom and Cohabitation, 11 Soc. Res. Online (Sept. 30, 2006); Charles Q. Strohn et al., *"Living Apart Together" Relationships in the United States,* 21 Demographic Res. 177 (2009), http://www.demographic-research.org/volumes/vol21/7/21-7.pdf (Aug. 13, 2009).
17. Irene Levin, *Living Apart Together: A New Family Form,* 52 Current Soc. 223, 227 (2004).
18. Strohn et al., *supra* note 16, at 200.
19. *Id.* at 199.
20. *Id.* at 202.
21. *See, e.g.,* Neil Gross, *The Detraditionalization of Intimacy Reconsidered,* 25 Soc. Theory 286 (2005).
22. *See, e.g.,* Joan C. Williams, Reshaping the Work-Family Debate: Why Men and Class Matter 151-60 (2010); Annette Lareau, Unequal Childhoods: Class, Race, and Family Life 204-6 (2003).
23. Ray Pahl & Liz Spencer, *Personal Communities: Not Simply Families of "Fate" or "Choice,"* 52 Current Soc. 199, 215 (2004). Pahl and Spencer define "personal communities" as those "which represent people's significant personal relationships and include bonds which give both structure and meaning to their lives." Liz Spencer & Ray Pahl, Rethinking Friendship: Hidden Solidarities Today 45 (2006). They identify a continuum between simple and complex friendship, ranging from "useful contact" to "soulmate." *Id.* at 60. A soulmate need not be a romantic partner.
24. Ray Pahl & Liz Spencer, *Families, Friends, and Personal Communities: Changing Models-in-the-Mind,* 2 J. Fam. Theory & Rev. 197, 198-99, 203 (2010).
25. Sasha Roseneil & Shelley Bludgeon, *Cultures of Intimacy and Care Beyond "the Family": Personal Life and Social Change in the Early 21st Century,* 52 Current Soc. 135, 153 (2004).
26. *Id.* at 146-48.
27. *See* Graham Allen, *Flexibility, Friendship, and Family,* 15 Pers. Rel. 1, 7 (2008).
28. *See* Nancy Levit & Douglas O. Linder, The Happy Lawyer: Making a Good Life in the Law 90-91 (2010).
29. James H. Fowler & Nicholas A. Christakis, *Dynamic Spread of Happiness in a Large Social Network: Longitudinal Analysis over 20 Years in the Framingham Heart Study,* 337 Brit. Med. J. 2338 (2008).

30. *See* Simone Schnall et al., *Social Support and the Perception of Geographical Slant*, 44 J. Experimental Soc. Psychol. 1246 (2008). Breast cancer survival rates appear to be enhanced by the existence of a network of social support. *See* Candace H. Kroenke et al., *Social Networks, Social Support, and Survival after Breast Cancer Diagnosis*, 24 J. Clinical Oncology 1105 (2006).

31. *See* Julianne Holt-Lunstad, Timothy B. Smith & J. Bradley Layton, *Social Relationships and Mortality Risks: A Meta-Analytic Review*, PLOS Medicine (July 2010), http://www.plosmedicine.org/article/info%3Adoi%2F10.1371%2Fjournal.pmed.1000316;jsessionid=1 FEB1AAF83E79A31811CBCA854B74636.ambra02.

32. *See, e.g.*, Nicholas A. Christakis & James H. Fowler, *The Spread of Obesity in a Large Social Network over 32 Years*, 357 New Eng. J. Med. 370, 378 (2007).

33. James N. Rosenquist, James H. Fowler & Nicholas A. Christakis, *Social Network Determinants of Depression*, Molecular Psychiatry 1, 8 (2010), http://jhfowler.ucsd.edu/social_network_determinants_of_depression.pdf.

34. *See* Ethan J. Leib, *Contracts and Friendships*, 59 Emory L.J. 649, 703-5 (2010); Ethan J. Leib, *Friends as Fiduciaries*, 86 Wash. U. L. Rev. 665, 699 (2009); *see also* Ethan J. Leib, *Friendship and the Law*, 54 UCLA L. Rev. 631, 638-53 (2007) (exploring definitions of friends).

35. *See, e.g.*, Melissa Murray, *The Networked Family: Reframing the Legal Understanding of Caregiving and Caregivers*, 94 Va. L. Rev. 385, 426-27 (2008).

36. Laura A. Rosenbury, *Friends with Benefits?*, 106 Mich. L. Rev. 189, 240 (2007).

37. *See, e.g.*, Unif. Parentage Act § 204(a)(5) (amended 2002); Susan Frelich Appleton, *Presuming Women: Revisiting the Presumption of Legitimacy in the Same-Sex Couple Era*, 86 B.U. L. Rev. 227, 258 (2006); *see also* Unif. Parentage Act § 706 (amended 2002) (allowing for paternity presumption to be challenged where, among other elements, the putative father was not cohabiting with the mother when the child was conceived).

38. Ethics Committee of the American Society for Reproductive Medicine, *Financial Compensation of Oocyte Donors*, 88 Fertility & Sterility 305, 308 (2007).

39. Kim Krawiec, *When Sunny Samaritans Sue, Part III*, The Faculty Lounge (April 19, 2011), http://www.thefacultylounge.org/2011/04/when-sunny-samaritans-sue-part-iii.html.

40. Kim Krawiec, *Politics and Profits in The Egg Business (When Sunny Samaritans Sue, IV)*, The Faculty Lounge (April 21, 2011), http://www.thefacultylounge.org/2011/04/politics-and-profits-in-the-egg-business-when-sunny-samaritans-sue-iv.html.

41. John A. Robertson, *Is There an Ethical Problem Here?*, 40 Hastings Center Report (2010), http://www.thehastingscenter.org/Publications/HCR/Detail.aspx?id=4537.

42. *See, e.g.*, June Carbone & Paige Gottheim, Markets, Subsidies, Regulation, and Trust: Building Ethical Understandings into the Market for Fertility Services, 9 J. Gender Race & Just. 509, 510, 538 (2006) (tying gamete shortage in Australia to the prohibition on compensation).

43. Viviana Zelizer, *How People Talk about Money*, 41 Am. Beh. Sci. 1373 (1998).

44. *See id.*; Julie Nelson, *One Sphere or Two?* 41 Am. Beh. Sci. 1467, 1468 (1998) (noting that economists who believe in efficient, rational self-acting and sociologists who condemn markets for objectifying social relationships are nonetheless still reifying "The Market as a *supra*social entity").

45. Joan Williams, Unbending Gender: Why Family and Work Conflict and What to Do About It 118 (2000).

46. Margaret Somerville, *Life's Essence: Bought and Sold*, The Globe and Mail, July 9, 2010, http://www.theglobeandmail.com/news/opinions/lifes-essence-bought-and-sold/article1635165/page2.

47. Senate Legal and Constitutional Affairs References Comm., *Donor Conception Practices in Australia* 99, para. 7.42 (2011), http://www.aph.gov.au/senate/committee/legcon_ctte/donor_conception/report/report.pdf.

48. Martha Ertman, *What's Wrong with a Parenthood Market? A New and Improved Theory of Commodification*, 82 N.C. L. Rev. 1, 35-36 (2003).

49. *Id.* at 35.

50. *See* Viviana Zelizer, The Social Meaning of Money (1994); Viviana A. Zelizer, Pricing the Priceless Child: The Changing Social Value of Children (1985).

51. *See, e.g.*, Jeanne Boydston, Home and Work: Housework, Wages, and the Ideology of Labor in the Early Republic (1990).

52. Milton Regan, Alone Together: Law and the Meanings of Marriage 23 (1999).

53. Margaret Radin, Contested Commodities 138 (1996).

54. *Id.* at 21.

55. Zelizer, Pricing the Priceless Child, *supra* note 50, at 11, 21.

56. *E.g.*, Radin, *supra* note 53, at xiii, 107. She does make clear that it is possible for "incomplete commodification" to serve as a "substitute for a complete noncommodification that might accord with our ideals." *Id.* at 104; *see* Katharine Silbaugh, *Commodification and Women's Household Labor*, 9 Yale J.L. & Fem. 81, 86-87 (1997).

57. *See generally* Viviana Zelizer, *The Purchase of Intimacy*, 25 L. & Soc. Inquiry 817, 832 (2000).

58. *See* Silbaugh, *Commodification*, *supra* note 56.

59. *See* Zelizer, The Social Meaning of Money, *supra* note 50, at 27 (1994) ("Even when the sums earned may be comparable, different systems of payments are not equivalent forms of income: wages, for instance, differ from commissions").

60. *See* Silbaugh, *Commodification*, *supra* note 56, at 120 (With respect to a particular topic that is "almost entirely non-market, however, the objection to commodification seems much weaker, because it fails to consider the potential benefits that economic understandings can bring to the social relations surrounding that non-market phenomenon.").

61. *See* Susan Himmelweit, *Caring Labor*, 561 Annals Am. Acad. Pol. & Soc. Sci. 27 (1999).

62. Rhadika Rao, *Property, Privacy, and the Human Body*, 80 B.U. L. Rev. 359, 458-59 (2000).

63. *See, e.g.*, Hendrik Hartog, Someday All This Will Be Yours: A History of Inheritance and Old Age (2012); Lawrence E. Mitchell, *Trust and Team Production in Post-Capitalist Society*, 24 J. Corp. L. 869 (1999).

64. For further analysis of payment for caretaking services, *see* Hartog, *supra* note 63.

65. Joan Williams & Viviana Zelizer, *To Commodify or Not to Commodify: That Is Not the Question*, in Rethinking Commodification 362, 376 (Martha Ertman & Joan Williams eds. 2006).

66. Danielle Groen, *Down for the Count*, The Grid, May 20, 2011, http://www.thegridto.com/city/local-news/down-for-the-count/3.

CHAPTER 3

1. David M. Schneider, American Kinship: A Cultural Account 25 (1968).

2. *The Switch* (Mandate Pictures, 2010), http://www.miramax.com/theswitch.

3. Judith Stacey, Unhitched: Love, Marriage, and Family Values from West Hollywood to Western China 75-76 (2011).

4. *How Co-ParentMatch.com Works* (2011), http://www.co-parentmatch.com/how.php.

5. Helen Croydon, *Meet the Co-Parents: Friends Not Lovers*, The Telegraph, July 31, 2011, at 28.

6. Cheryl Shuler, Sperm Donor=Dad: A Single Woman's Story of Creating a Family with an Unknown Donor 18 (2010).

7. The World Egg Bank, *View Our Donors*, http://www.theworldeggbank.com/frozen-egg-database.html (last visited May 20, 2011).

8. Growing Generations, *Sperm Donation Questions & Answers* (2011), http://www.growinggenerations.com/sperm-donor-program/questions-and-answers.

9. Lindsay Powers, *Bundle of Joy's Just a Click Away*, N.Y. Post, March 12, 2006, at 21.

10. Liza Mundy, Everything Conceivable: How Assisted Reproduction Is Changing Men, Women, and the World 163-64 (2007).

11. Shuler, *supra* note 6, at 21.

12. Liza Mundy, *Re-Evaluating the Meaning of Family: Fertility Industry Fails to Acknowledge Genes' Roles in Children's Conception, Upbringing*, The Mercury News, Dec. 31, 2006, at 1.

13. Jeremy Hubbard & Kinga Janik, *Celebrity Look-Alike Sperm Donors: A Superficial Service?* Oct. 20, 2009, http://abcnews.go.com/Nightline/celebrity-alike-sperm-donors-resemble-stars-david-beckham/story?id=8781583.

14. California Cryobank, *Donor Look-A-Likes*, http://www.cryobank.com/Donor-Search/Look-A-Likes (last visited December 5, 2011).

15. Michelle Ottey, *Sperm Banks Help Grow Your Family, Not Design a Baby*, Aug. 26, 2010, http://www.fertilityauthority.com/blogger/michelle-ottey/2010/08/26/sperm-banks-help-grow-your-family-not-design-baby.

16. *See* Hubbard & Janik, *supra* note 13.

17. *See* Charis Thompson, *Strategic Naturalizing: Kinship in an Infertility Clinic*, in New Directions in Kinship Study: A Core Concept Revisited 175, 198-99 (Sarah Franklin & Susan McKinnon eds. 2001).

18. Ottey, *supra* note 15.

19. Amie Klempnauer Miller, She Looks Just Like You: A Memoir of (Nonbiological Lesbian) Motherhood 14 (2010).

20. Mundy, *supra* note 10, at 141.

21. Diane Ehrensaft, Mommies, Daddies, Donors, Surrogates: Answering Tough Questions and Building Strong Families 84 (2005).

22. Laura Mamo, Queering Reproduction: Achieving Pregnancy in the Age of Technoscience 218 (2008).

23. Theresa M. Erickson, Surrogacy and Embryo, Sperm, and Egg Donation: What Were You Thinking? Considering IVF and Third-Party Reproduction 45 (2010).

24. Madeline Licker Feingold, *Heterosexual Couples Considering Egg, Sperm, or Embryo Donation* (2011), http://www.madelinefeingoldphd.com/family-building-with-donors-and-surrogates/heterosexual-couples-considering-egg-sperm-or-embryo-donation.

25. *Id.*

26. *Lesbian Couples Considering Sperm Donation* (2011), http://www.madelinefeingoldphd.com/family-building-with-donors-and-surrogates/lesbian-couples-considering-sperm-donation.

27. *Gay Couples Considering Egg Donation and Surrogacy* (2011), http://www.
    madelinefeingoldphd.com/family-building-with-donors-and-surrogates/
    gay-couples-considering-egg-donation-and-surrogacy.

28. Peggy Orenstein, Waiting for Daisy: A Tale of Two Continents, Three Religions, Five
    Infertility Doctors, an Oscar, an Atomic Bomb, a Romantic Night, and One Woman's
    Quest to Become a Mother 179 (2007).

29. Melanie Thernstrom, *Meet the Twiblings*, N.Y. Times, Dec. 29, 2010, http://www.
    nytimes.com/2011/01/02/magazine/02babymaking-t.html?pagewanted=1&_r=1.

30. *Id.*

31. Iris Waichler, *Nurturing the Nature of My Child*, Jan. 5, 2011, http://www.eggdonors-
    now.com/egg-donation-and-recipient-blog.html.

32. *Fertility*, http://www.planethospital.net/fertility.html (last visited Dec. 3, 2011).

33. Tamara Audi & Arlene Chang, *Assembling the Global Baby*, Wall St. J., Dec. 10, 2010,
    http://online.wsj.com/article/SB10001424052748703493504576007774155273928.html.

34. Stacey, *supra* note 3, at 56-58.

35. *Id.* at 59.

36. Melinda Arons & Chris Connelly, *Ultra Modern Family: Dad + Dad +
    Baby*, ABC Nightline, Sept. 29, 3010, http://abcnews.go.com/Nightline/
    growing-generations-surrogacy-agency-gay-families/story?id=11749014.

37. Daily Mail Reporter, *"We Don't Know Who the Daddy Is": Sir Elton John and David
    Furnish Reveal How They Left Baby Zachary's Conception to Chance*, Mail Online, Jan.
    19, 2011, http://www.dailymail.co.uk/tvshowbiz/article-1348208/Sir-Elton-John-David-
    Furnish-reveal-truth-baby-Zacharys-conception.html#ixzz1MuxN4895.

38. *See* Mamo, *supra* note 22, at 223.

39. Orenstein, *supra* note 28, at 170.

40. *See* Charis Thompson, Making Parents: The Ontological Choreography of Reproduc-
    tive Technologies 156 (2005).

41. *Uterine Health More Important Than Egg Quality*, Feb. 4, 2011, http://www.medical-
    newstoday.com/releases/215614.php.

42. *See, e.g.,* Rosanna Hertz, Single by Chance, Mothers by Choice: How Women Are
    Choosing Parenthood without Marriage and Creating the New American Family 64-65
    (2006); Vasanti Jadva, Tabitha Freeman, Wendy Kramer & Susan Golombok, *Sperm
    and Oocyte Donors' Experiences of Anonymous Donation and Subsequent Contact with
    Their Donor Offspring*, 26 Hum. Rep. 638 (2011).

43. Rosanna Hertz, *The Father as an Idea: A Challenge to Kinship Boundaries by Single
    Mothers*, 25 Symbolic Interaction 1, 9 (2002).

44. Wendy Kramer, *Impact of Egg, Sperm, and Embryo Donor Conception on Families: The
    Role of Fertility Clinics*, http://infertilitypronews.com/content/impact-egg-sperm-
    and-embryo-donor-conception-families (last visited Dec. 2, 2011).

45. *See id.*

46. Erhensaft, *supra* note 21, at 16.

47. Diane Ehrensaft, *Who Am I?* http://www.infertilitynetwork.org/files/Who_Am_I.pdf
    (last visited Dec. 3, 2011).

48. *See, e.g.,* Hollee McGinnis, *Ten Questions to Ask Yourself* (2000), http://www.holtinter-
    national.org/mcginnis.shtml (last visited Dec. 3, 2011).

49. Rainbow Flag Health Services, *Known Donor Insemination*, http://www.gayspermbank.
    com/index.html (last visited June 13, 2011).

50. Lawrie McFarlane, *Donor Case Strikes at Basic Family Foundation*, Times Colonist, July 15, 2011, http://www.timescolonist.com/news/Donor+case+strikes+basic+family+foundations/5107457/story.html.

51. J. David Velleman, *The Gift of Life*, 36 Phil. & Public Affairs 245, 263 (2008).

52. Cryos Denmark, *Reservation of Donor Sperm*, http://dk.cryosinternational.com/private-customers/reservation.aspx (last visited June 14, 2011).

53. *E.g.*, Cryogenic Laboratories, *Ordering & Shipping* (2010), http://www.cryolab.com/ordering.shtml#howmany.

54. Family Services (2011), http://www.thespermbankofca.org/pages/page.php?pageid=37.

55. Mundy, *supra* note 10, at 165.

56. Thernstrom, *supra* note 29.

57. Charlotte Gill, *Why I'm Happy to Tell My Child I Don't Know Who Her Father Is . . .* , MailOnline, March 14, 2011, http://www.dailymail.co.uk/femail/article-1365913/Sperm-donors-Why-Im-happy-tell-child-I-dont-know-father-.html#ixzz1PG1Vq9xX.

58. Malathy Iyer, *One Mother, Gay Couple, and Twin Joy*, The Times of India, May 23, 2011.

59. *Id.*

60. Brette McWhorter Sember, Gay and Lesbian Parenting Choices: From Adoptions or Using a Surrogate to Choosing the Perfect Father 150 (2006).

61. Gay Becker, The Elusive Embryo 78 (2000).

62. *Id.* at 240.

CHAPTER 4

1. Courtney Sheinmel, My So-Called Family (2008).

2. *Id.* at 7.

3. *Id.* at 78.

4. The difficulties of collecting information about donor-conceived offspring begin with the fact that there is not even an official record of how many children are born each year as a result of donor sperm in the United States. Studies of the donor-conceived world can only draw on subjects who know they are donor conceived as well as donors and gamete recipients who are willing to discuss their experiences. Consequently, this chapter uses the few studies that do exist as well as anecdotes and stories from a variety of sources, including the Donor Sibling Registry and media.

5. *See id.* at 529.

6. Peggy Orenstein, Waiting for Daisy: A Tale of Two Continents, Three Religions, Five Infertility Doctors, an Oscar, an Atomic Bomb, a Romantic Night, and One Woman's Quest to Become a Mother 177-78 (2007).

7. *Id.* at 177.

8. Melanie Thernstrom, *Meet the Twiblings*, N.Y. Times, Dec. 29, 2010, http://www.nytimes.com/2011/01/02/magazine/02babymaking-t.html?pagewanted=1&_r=1.

9. Ken Daniels & Karyn Taylor, *Secrecy and Openness in Donor Insemination*, 12 Polit. Life Sci. 155, 157 (1993); Katrina Hargreaves & Ken Daniels, *Parents' Dilemmas in Sharing Donor Insemination Conception Stories with Their Children*, 21 Children & Soc. 420, 420 (2007).

10. Jennifer Readings, Lucy Blake, Polly Casey, Vasanti Jadva & Susan Golombok, *Secrecy, Disclosure and Everything In-Between: Decisions of Parents of Children Conceived by Donor Insemination, Egg Donation, and Surrogacy*, 22 Reprod. BioMedicine Online 485, 491, 493 (2011).

11. Eve Kosofsky Sedgwick, Epistemology of the Closet 22 (2d ed. 2008).
12. *See* Ann Pellegrin, *Eve Kosofsky Sedgwick*, The Chronicle Review, May 8, 2009.
13. *See* Sedgwick, *supra* note 11, at 72.
14. *See, e.g.*, Rikke Rosholm, Rikke Lund, Drude Molbo & Lone Schmidt, *Disclosure Patterns of Mode of Conception among Mothers and Fathers: 5-Year Follow-up of the Copenhagen Multi-Centre Psychosocial Infertility (COMPI) Cohort*, 25 Human Rep. 2006 (2010).
15. *See id.* at 2007.
16. Susan Golombok, et al., *The European Study of Assisted Reproduction Families: Family Functioning and Child Development*, 11 Hum. Reprod. 2324, 2329 (1996).
17. *Id.* at 2330.
18. Susan Golombok, Fiona MacCallum, Emma Goodman & Michael Rutter, *Families with Children Conceived by Donor Insemination: A Follow-up at Age Twelve*, 73 Child Dev. 952 (2002), http://www.ncbi.nlm.nih.gov/pubmed/12038562?dopt=Abstract.
19. Susan Golombok et al., *Children Conceived by Gamete Donation: Psychological Adjustment and Mother-Child Relationships at Age 7*, 25 J. Fam. Psych. 230-231 (2011).
20. Ken Daniels, Wayne Gillett & Victoria Grace, *Parental Information Sharing with Donor Insemination–Conceived Offspring: A Follow-up Study*, 24 Hum. Reprod. 1099 (2009).
21. Vasanti Jadva, Tabitha Freeman, Wendy Kramer & Susan Golombok, *Sperm and Oocyte Donors' Experiences of Anonymous Donation and Subsequent Contact with Their Donor Offspring*, 26 Hum. Reprod. 638 (2011).
22. Readings et al., *supra* note 10.
23. Madeline Licker Feingold, *Building Healthy, Donor-Conceived Families*, Am. Fertility Ass'n (2008), http://www.theafa.org/library/article/building_healthy_donor_conceived_families.
24. ASRM, *Patient Fact Sheet, Gamete Donation: Deciding Whether to Tell* (2008), http://www.asrm.org/uploadedFiles/ASRM_Content/Resources/Patient_Resources/Fact_Sheets_and_Info_Booklets/GameteDonation.pdf (last visited July 12, 2011).
25. Fiona MacCallum & Susan Golombok, *Embryo Donation Families: Mothers' Decisions Regarding Disclosure of Donor Conception*, 22 Hum. Reprod. 2888, 2891 (2007).
26. Liza Mundy, Everything Conceivable: How Assisted Reproduction Is Changing Men, Women, and the World 103 (2007).
27. Jadva et al., *supra* note 21.
28. *See* Joanna E. Scheib & Alice Ruby, *Contact among Families Who Share the Same Sperm Donor*, 90 Fertility & Sterility 33, 39 (2008).
29. Vasanti Jadva et al., *The Experiences of Adolescents and Adults Conceived by Sperm Donation: Comparisons by Age of Disclosure and Family Type*, 24 Hum. Reprod. 1909 (2009)..
30. Even in the absence of information disclosure and often, even in the absence of a child having been told of her origins, the donor remains a presence in the donor family. *See* Diane Ehrensaft, Mommies, Daddies, Donors, Surrogates: Answering Tough Questions and Building Strong Families 136-40 (2005).
31. Diane Beeson, Patricia Jennings & Wendy Kramer, *Offspring Searching for Their Sperm Donors: How Family Type Shapes the Process*, 26 Hum. Reprod. 2415, 2417 (2011).
32. *Id.* at 2419-20.
33. *See* Patricia P. Mahlstedt, Kathleen LaBounty & William Thomas Kennedy, *The Views of Adult Offspring of Sperm Donation: Essential Feedback for the Development of Ethical*

Guidelines within the Practice of Assisted Reproductive Technology in the United States, 93 Fertility & Sterility 2236, 2236 (2010); E. Lycett et al., *School-Aged Children of Donor Insemination: A Study of Parents' Disclosure Patterns*, 20 Hum. Reprod. 810, 811 (2005).

34. *E.g.*, Eric Blyth, Darren Langridge & Rhonda Harris, *Family Building in Donor Conception: Parents' Experiences of Sharing Information*, 28 J. Reprod. & Infant Psych. 116 (2010); Readings et al., *supra* note 10.

35. MacCallum & Golombok, *supra* note 25, at 2892.

36. Blyth et al., *supra* note 34, at 119.

37. Daniels et al., *supra* note 20, at 1104 (59 percent had told others).

38. Britta Dinsmore, *Disclosure Decisions*, http://www.parentsviaeggdonation.org/v2/disclosure.html (last visited June 13, 2011).

39. Anonymous, *How My Mother Told Me* (2010), http://anonymousus.org/stories/index.php?cid=2.

40. Henny Bos & Frank van Balen, *Children of the New Reproductive Technologies: Social and Genetic Parenthood*, 81 Patient Educ. & Counseling 429 (2010).

41. *Id.* at 433.

42. *Id.* The authors note various potential imitations, including that the studies used data collected from the parents and children, rather than from other informants, such as teachers. *Id.*

43. *Id.*

44. Susan Golombok et al., *Families with Children Conceived by Donor Insemination: A Follow-Up at Age Twelve*, 73 Child Dev. 952, 966 (2002); Susan Golombok et al., *The European Study of Assisted Reproduction Families: Family Functioning and Child Development*, 11 Hum. Reprod. 2324, 2324 (1996); *see also* Ellen Waldman, *What Do We Tell the Children?* 35 Cap. U. L. Rev. 517, 538-40 (2006) (summarizing Golombok's conclusions). For later studies, *see*, for example, Vasanti Jadva et al., *The Experiences of Adolescents and Adults Conceived by Sperm Donation: Comparisons by Age of Disclosure and Family Type*, 24 Hum. Reprod. 1909 (2009); Lucy Owen & Susan Golombok, *Families Created by Assisted Reproduction: Parent-Child Relationships in Late Adolescence*, 32 J. of Adolescence 835 (2009); but *see* Elizabeth Marquardt, Norval D. Glenn & Karen Clark, *My Daddy's Name Is Donor: A New Study of Young Adults Conceived through Sperm Donation* 51 (2010), http://www.familyscholars.org/assets/Donor_FINAL.pdf.

45. *See* Nanette Gatrell & Henny Bos, *U.S. National Longitudinal Lesbian Family Study: Psychological Adjustment of 17-Year-Old Adolescents*, 126 Pediatrics 1 (2010), http://pediatrics.aappublications.org/content/early/2010/06/07/peds.2009-3153.full.pdf+html.

46. Bos & van Balen, *supra* note 40, at 433-34.

47. Mahlstedt et al., *supra* note 33, at 2238.

48. *Id.* at 2237.

49. *See id.*

50. *See id.* at 2243.

51. *See id.* at 2242.

52. Beeson, *supra* note 31.

53. Golombok et al., *Children Conceived, supra* note 44. They note that children in nondisclosing families did not seem to be affected by this result, as children who had been donor conceived did not differ from natural-conception children with respect to psychological problems.

54. Jesús Palacios & David Brodzinsky, *Adoption Research: Trends, Topics, and Outcomes*, 34 Int'l J Behav. Dev. 270 (2010).
55. Golombok et al., *Children Conceived, supra* note 44.
56. Marquardt et al., *supra* note 44, at 51.
57. *See, e.g.,* Beeson, *supra* note 31, at 2418.
58. Marquardt et al., *supra* note 44, at 83. Seventy-six percent of the donor-conceived individuals strongly or somewhat agreed that the technologies are good, compared to 65 percent of the adopted adults and 61 percent of those raised by their biological parents; 73 percent of the donor-conceived children strongly, or somewhat strongly, agreed that society should encourage gamete donation, compared to 50 percent of adopted adults and 42 percent of children raised by their biological parents. *Id.*
59. *Id.* at 100.
60. *Id.* at 88.
61. *Id.* at 90.
62. *Id.* at 97–98.
63. *Id.* Interestingly, approximately one-quarter of the donor-conceived offspring did not believe that they should have access to nonidentifying information about the donor (25 percent) or to identifying information (24 percent), or that they should have the opportunity to have a relationship with the donor (27 percent) or know the existence (26 percent) or identity (27 percent) of half-siblings. *Id.*
64. Beeson et al., *supra* note 31.
65. *See, e.g.,* Vardit Ravitsky & Joanna E. Scheib, *Donor-Conceived Individuals' Right to Know,* 40 Hastings Center Bioethics Forum 40, 4 (2010).
66. Waldman, *supra* note 44, at 544. As she notes, however, the studies show that relationships can be improved by openness even if the children are not "suffering." *Id.*
67. *See* MacCallum & Golombok, *supra* note 25, at 2889.
68. *Id.* at 33–34.
69. Janet L. Dolgin, *Biological Evaluations: Blood, Genes, and Family,* 41 Akron L. Rev. 347, 385–86, 388 (2008).
70. Ken M. Gatter, *Genetic Information and the Importance of Context: Implications for the Social Meaning of Genetic Information and Individual Identity,* 47 St. Louis U. L.J. 423, 427 (2003).
71. Sagit Ziskind, *The Genetic Information Nondiscrimination Act: A New Look at an Old Problem,* 35 Rutgers Computer & Tech. L.J. 163, 168–69 (2008).
72. *See, e.g.,* Dolgin, *supra* note 69, at 390; *see generally* Jessica D. Gabel, *Probable Cause from Probable Bonds: A Genetic Tattle Tale Based on Familial DNA,* 21 Hastings Women's L.J. 3 (2010) (examining familial DNA testing by law enforcement agencies); Jessica L. Roberts, *Preempting Discrimination: Lessons from the Genetic Information Nondiscrimination Act,* 63 Vand. L. Rev. 439 (2010) (examining a federal statute prohibiting employment and insurance discrimination based on genetic information).
73. Rochelle Cooper Dreyfuss & Dorothy Nelkin, *The Jurisprudence of Genetics,* 45 Vand. L. Rev. 313, 319-21 (1992).
74. *Pratten v. British Columbia,* 2011 BCSC 656, Paras. 51-52 (B. Col S. Ct. 2011), http://www.canlii.org/en/bc/bcsc/doc/2011/2011bcsc656/2011bcsc656.html.
75. Scheib & Ruby, *supra* note 28, at 35–36. The fourteen surveys comprising this study were returned by fourteen mothers who were contacted because of their participation in a family-matching service run by the Sperm Bank of California. *Id.* at 35. Of the

responding families, seven were headed by single women, six were headed by lesbian couples, and one was headed by a heterosexual couple. *Id.* Seven out of eight single-mother households that were invited to participate returned the survey, as did six out of eight lesbian-couple households and one out of two heterosexual-couple households. *Id.*

76. Rosanna Hertz & Jane Mattes, *Donor-Shared Siblings or Genetic Strangers: New Families, Clans, and the Internet*, 20 J. Fam. Issues 1, 7 (2011).
77. *Id.* at 37.
78. *Id.*
79. *Id.* at 38.
80. *Id.*
81. *See* Tabitha Freeman et al., *Gamete Donation: Parents' Experiences of Searching for Their Child's Donor Siblings and Donor*, 24 Hum. Reprod. 505, 506-8 (2009). This survey was conducted by sending out a questionnaire to all registrants of the Donor Sibling Registry. *Id.* at 506. A total of 791 parents of donor children responded out of a possible 4,140 donor parent respondents, the vast majority of whom were women. *Id.* at 507. Seven hundred and seventy-five respondents were women, while only sixteen were men. *Id.* Seventy-four percent of respondents were single or lesbian mothers. *Id.* at 514.
82. *Id.* at 508 tbl.1.
83. *Id.*
84. *Id.* at 509 tbl.3.
85. *Id.*
86. *Id.* at 514.
87. *The Kids Are All Right* (Mandalay Vision 2010).
88. Alessandra Rafferty, *Donor-Conceived and Out of the Closet*, Newsweek, Feb. 25, 2011, http://www.newsweek.com/2011/02/25/donor-conceived-and-out-of-the-closet.html.
89. Vasanti Jadva et al., *Experiences of Offspring Searching for and Contacting Their Donor Siblings and Donor*, 20 Reprod. BioMedicine Online 523, 525-26 (2010).
90. *Id.* at 527–28.
91. *Id.* at 528 tbl.4.
92. *Id.*
93. *Id.* at 528.
94. Cheryl Shuler, Sperm Donor=Dad: A Single Woman's Story of Creating a Family with an Unknown Donor 57 (2010).
95. Jadva et al, *supra* note 89.
96. *Id.* at 529.
97. *Id.* at 529 tbl.5.
98. Beeson, *supra* note 31, at 2420.
99. Beeson, *supra* note 31, at 2421-22.
100. Lucy Blake, Polly Casey, Jennifer Readings & Susan Golombok, *"Daddy Ran out of Tadpoles": How Parents Tell Their Children That They Are Donor Conceived, and What Their Seven- Year-Olds Understand*, 25 Hum. Reprod. 2527-28 (2010).
101. Jadva et al., *supra* note 89, at 529.
102. Katrina Clark, *My Father Was an Anonymous Sperm Donor*, Wash. Post, Dec. 17, 2006, http://www.washingtonpost.com/wp-dyn/content/article/2006/12/15/AR2006121501820.html.

103. *See* Scheib & Ruby, *supra* note 28, at 34.

104. *See* Freeman et al., *supra* note 81, at 506; Jadva et al., *supra* note 89, at 523.

105. *See* Jeff DeGroot, COLAGE Donor Insemination Guide 33 (2010).

106. California Cryobank, *California Cryobank's Sibling Registry*, http://www.sibling-registry.com/whocan.cfm (last visited June 1, 2011).

107. Fairfax Cryobank, *Welcome to Private Donor Forums*, http://www.fairfaxcryobank.com/forums/viewtopic.php?f=5&t=44 (last visited June 1, 2011).

108. The Sperm Bank of California, *Family Contact List FAQs* (2011), http://www.thespermbankofca.org/pages/page.php?pageid=69&cat=14.

109. The Sperm Bank of California, *Donor Information-Releases: Tracking Outcomes*, http://www.thespermbankofca.org/content/research-and-identity-release®-program (last visited Dec. 3, 2011). This may underrepresent the actual number of those interested in matching because half-siblings and donors may have already found each other on the Donor Sibling Registry before they are eligible to connect through the Sperm Bank of California.

110. The Sperm Bank of California, *Addressing TSBC Donor & Family Needs: Findings from the Identity-Release Task Force & Studies (1997–Present)*, http://www.thespermbankofca.org/pages/page.php?pageid=49&cat=9 (last visited Nov. 8, 2010).

111. *Id.*

112. Scheib & Ruby, *supra* note 28, at 35.

113. *See id.* Only fourteen families returned completed surveys for this study. *Id.*

114. Amber L. Cushing, *"I Just Want More Information about Who I Am": The Search Experience of Sperm-Donor Offspring, Searching for Information about Their Donors and Genetic Heritage*, 15 Inform. Res. (2010), http://informationr.net/ir/15-2/paper428.html.

115. Craig Mallsow, *Donor Babies Search for Their Anonymous Fathers*, Houston Press, Nov. 5, 2008, http://www.houstonpress.com/2008-11-06/news/donor-babies-search-for-their-anonymous-fathers.

116. Kathleen R. LaBounty, *My Story*, Nov. 13, 2008, http://childofastranger.blogspot.com/2008/11/my-story.html.

117. Alison Motluk, *The Anonymous Donor Dilemma: To Google or Not to Google*, Globe and Mail, April 18, 2010, http://www.theglobeandmail.com/life/family-and-relationships/the-anonymous-donor-dilemma-to-google-or-not-to-google/article1538635.

118. *See* Rachel Lehmann-Haupt, *Are Sperm Donors Really Anonymous Anymore?* March 1, 2010, http://www.slate.com/id/2243743.

119. Girl Conceived, *Am I Absorbed or Obsessed?* June 7, 2011, http://connectitblog.blogspot.com.

120. *Family Finder* (2011), http://www.familytreedna.com/family-finder-compare.aspx.

121. Lehmann-Haupt, *supra* note 118.

122. Alice Crisci, *Protecting a Sperm Donor's Privacy in the Digital Age* (2011), http://www.huffingtonpost.com/alice-crisci/protecting-a-sperm-donors_b_844524.html.

123. *Donor Sibling Registry*, http://donorsiblingregistry.com (last visited Nov. 8, 2010).

124. Family Tree DNA, *Donor Conceived: Background*, http://www.familytreedna.com/public/donor_conceived/default.aspx (last visited July 14, 2011).

125. *See* Scheib & Ruby, *supra* note 28.

126. *Id.* at 35–36.

127. *Id.* at 37.

128. *Id.*

129. Freeman et al., *supra* note 81, at 511 tbl. 8.

130. *Id.*

131. *Id.*

132. *Id.*

133. *Id.*

134. *See* Jadva et al., *supra* note 89, at 530.

135. *Id.*

136. *Id.* at 530 tbl.6. It is important to note that the number of people in each category was small.

137. *See* Rene Almeling, Sex Cells: The Medical Market in Eggs and Sperm 166-67 (2011).

138. *See* Nancy E. Levine, *Alternative Kinship, Marriage, and Reproduction*, 37 Ann. Rev. Anthropology 375, 377, 382 (2008).

139. Almeling, Sex Cells, *supra* note 137, at 178.

140. *Id.* at 179-80

141. *E.g.,* Jadva et al., *supra* note 21, at tbls. VI and VII.

142. Wendy Kramer et al., *U.S. Oocyte Donors: A Retrospective Study of Medical and Psychosocial Issues*, 24 Hum. Reprod. 3144, 3146–48 (2009). The authors point out that the group had already self-selected toward seeking contact; "[t]he chief limitation of this study is that participants were recruited from a website that attracts those donors who wish information about their donor-conceived offspring (and vice versa)." *Id.* at 3147.

143. Almeling, *supra* note 137, at 184, 190.

144. Marcia C. Inhorn & Daphna Birenbaum-Carmeli, *Assisted Reproductive Technologies and Culture Change*, 37 Ann. Rev. Anthropology 177, 183 (2008).

145. *See* David Plotz, *Donor White Meets His Daughter*, Slate (2002), http://www.slate.com/id/2069027 ("The donor and his wife rushed over to meet his baby daughter. . . . When the visit ended, [the donor] told Vaux he 'would live on that moment for the rest of his life.'"); *see also* David Crary, *The Search for the Donor She Calls "Dad,"* Virginian-Pilot, Aug. 16, 2010, at A3 (describing a happy relationship between a donor and his three separately raised children); Amy Harmon, *Sperm Donor Father Ends Anonymity*, N.Y. Times, Feb. 14, 2007, at A18 (reporting on one donor's successful meeting with his children).

146. Cushing, *supra* note 114.

147. *The Reality of Reunion . . . and What the Media Doesn't Tell You* (2010), http://cryokidconfessions.blogspot.com/2010/03/reality-of-reunionand-what-media-doesnt.html.

148. *Confessions of a Cryokid*, http://cryokidconfessions.blogspot.com (last visited Feb. 23, 2012).

149. Rosanna Hertz, *Turning Strangers into Kin (Half Siblings and Anonymous Donors)*, in Who's Watching? Daily Practices of Surveillance among Contemporary Families 156, 169 (Margaret K. Nelson & Anita Ilta Garey eds. 2009).

150. Telephone interview with Wendy Kramer, Director, Donor Sibling Registry (Sept. 15, 2011).

151. Carey Goldberg, *The Search for Donor DGM 2598: More Children of Anonymous Sperm Donors Want to Know Who Fathered Them*, Bos. Globe, Nov. 23, 2008, at A1 *See generally* Joanna E. Scheib & Rachel A. *Cushing, Open-Identity Donor Insemination in the United States: Is It on the Rise?* 88 Fert. & Steril 231 (2007).

152. Motluk, *The Anonymous Donor Dilemma, supra* note 117.

153. Rick Montgomery, *Donor-Conceived Siblings Connect, Online Registry Matches Relatives*, San Jose Mercury News, April 19, 2009.
154. *See* Hertz & Mattes, *supra* note 76, at 22-23.
155. *See* Wendy Kramer, *Questions and Answers*, in Behind Closed Doors: Moving Beyond Secrecy and Shame 24, 30-31 (Mikki Morrissette ed. 2006).
156. *See* Jadva et al, *supra* note 21 (reporting on mother who cut off contact with donor).
157. Pim M. W. Jansens, *Colouring the Different Phases in Gamete and Embryo Donation*, 24 Hum. Rep. 502 (2009); *see Donor-Conceived Kids Connect with Half Siblings*, Nat'l Pub. Radio, Feb. 26, 2009, http://www.npr.org/templates/transcript/transcript.php?storyId=101198830 ("'It's a new form of family,' says sociologist Tabitha Freeman. . . . 'It's not, perhaps, what people traditionally understand by family—sort of mum, dad, child. And yes, they do describe each other as brothers and sisters.'").
158. *See, e.g.*, Shuler, *supra* note 94, at 81.(describing the time when "we truly started to become a family. The kids acted like siblings.").
159. Hertz & Mattes, *supra* note 76, at 21.
160. Amy Hatch, *Donor Conceived Children, Parents Redefining Family* (Apr. 9, 2009), http://www.parentdish.com/2009/04/09/donor-conceived-children-parents-redefining-family.
161. *Id.*
162. Emily Bazelon, *The Children of Donor X*, O, The Oprah Magazine, Aug. 2008, http://www.oprah.com/relationships/Autism-Aspergers-and-the-Donor-Sibling-Registry
163. Freeman et al., *supra* note 81, at 513.
164. Anthea Gerrie, *Six Children, Four Mothers—and One Father None of Them Has Met*, Sept. 13, 2008, http://www.dailymail.co.uk/news/article-1055600/Six-children-mothers--8211-father-met-Meet--8216-family-8217-Donor-66.html.
165. Jadva et al., *supra* note 21, at tbl. VI.
166. *See* Rachel Lehmann-Haupt, *Are Sperm Donors Really Anonymous Anymore? DNA Testing Makes Them Easier to Trace*, Slate.com, March 1, 2010, http://www.slate.com/id/2243743.
167. Jadva et al., *supra* note 21.
168. *See* Naomi Cahn, Test Tube Families: Why the Fertility Markets Need Legal Regulation 119 (2009).
169. *Sperm-Donors' Kids Seek More Rights, Respect*, Aug. 16, 2010, http://www.foxnews.com/health/2010/08/16/sperm-donors-kids-seek-rights-respect/#ixzz1NeuzpRx7.
170. Bridgid O'Connell, *Egg Donor Won't Stop at 19 Bubs*, Herald Sun (Australia), June 5, 2011, at 8.
171. *See* Hertz, *supra* note 149, at 168-69.
172. *E.g.*, Jadva, et al., *supra* note 21, at 643 (tbl. VIII).
173. *Id.*

CHAPTER 5
1. *Goodright v. Moss*, 98 Eng. Rep. 1257, 1258 (K.B. 1777).
2. *See, e.g.*, June Carbone & Naomi Cahn, *Marriage, Parentage, and Child Support*, 45 Fam. L.Q. 219, 224 (2011).
3. Unif. Parentage Act, § 5 (1973).
4. Alabama, California, Colorado, Delaware, Hawaii, Illinois, Kansas, Minnesota, Missouri, Montana, Nevada, New Jersey, New Mexico, North Dakota, Ohio, Rhode Island, Washington, and Wyoming. *See* Table of Jurisdictions Where Act Has Been Adopted. Uniform Parentage Act (1973), 9B U.L.A. 378 (2001).

5. *Id.*, Art. 7 Prefatory Comment.
6. *Id.*, Art. 7, §§ 703-4 .
7. *Id.* §§ 102(4), 702.
8. *Id.* § 702 cmt.
9. *Id.*, Art. 7, §702 comment.
10. Alabama, Delaware, New Mexico, North Dakota, Oklahoma, Texas, Utah, Washington, Wyoming. *See* Uniform Law Commissioners, *Legislative Fact Sheet: Parentage Act*, http://www.nccusl.org/LegislativeFactSheet.aspx?title=Parentage%20Act (last visited May 27, 2011).
11. Nancy D. Polikoff, *A Mother Should Not Have to Adopt Her Own Child: Parentage Laws for Lesbian Couples in the Twenty-First Century*, 5 Stan. J. Civ. Rts. & Civ. Lib. 201, 245 (2009).
12. N. R. Kleinfeld, *Baby Makes Four, and Complications*, N.Y. Times, June 19, 2011, http://www.nytimes.com/2011/06/19/nyregion/an-american-family-mom-sperm-donor-lover-child.html?pagewanted=1&_r=2&hp.
13. E.g., N.H. Rev. Stat. Ann. §§168-B:3 I(e), 168-B:11 (2011); *see* Carlos A. Ball, The Right to Be Parents: LGBT Families and the Transformation of Parenthood 131 (2012).
14. Tex. Fam. Code Sec. §160.7031 (2011). There appear to be no similar provisions with respect to an egg donor.
15. *In re Mullen*, 924 N.E.2d 448 (Ohio App. 1 Dist., 2009).
16. *E.g.*, Roderick M. Hills Jr., *The Political Economy of Cooperative Federalism: Why State Autonomy Makes Sense and "Dual Sovereignty" Doesn't*, 96 Mich. L. Rev. 813 (1998); *see also* Heather Gerken, *Foreword: Federalism All the Way Down*, 124 Harv. L. Rev. 4 (2010) (arguing for expanded visions of federalism including other decision-making entities beyond states).
17. Of course, some states do allow the donor and intending parent to enter into enforceable agreements. *See* Polikoff, *supra* note 11.
18. This contrasts with the situation in other countries. *See, e.g,* Yaniv Heled, *The Regulation of Genetic Aspects of Donated Reproductive Tissue—The Need for Federal Regulation*, 11 Colum. Sci. & Tech. L. Rev. 243, 282-87 (2010) (discussing the paucity of state regulation).
19. *See* Naomi Cahn & June Carbone, Red Families v. Blue Families: Legal Polarization and the Creation of Culture (2010).
20. Elizabeth Marquardt, Norval D. Glenn & Karen Clark, *My Daddy's Name Is Donor: A New Study of Young Adults Conceived through Sperm Donation* 21, 28 (2010), http://www.familyscholars.org/assets/Donor_FINAL.pdf. Data were collected through Web interviews from 1,687 respondents, with equal numbers of individuals who were (or believed they were) donor conceived (n = 562), adopted (n = 562), or raised by their biological parents (n = 563). *Id.* at 119. The study has received some criticism. *See, e.g.,* Eric Blyth & Wendy Kramer, *"My Daddy's Name Is Donor": Read with Caution!* (July 9, 2010), http://www.bionews.org.uk/page_65970.asp; Julie Shapiro, *Choosing Studies: Eenie Meenie or Something More?* Related Topics (June 7, 2010), http://julieshapiro.wordpress.com/2010/06/07/choosing-studies-eenie-meenie-or-something-more. Indeed, two of the study's authors stated that their "findings suggest that openness alone does not resolve the complex risks to which children are exposed when they are deliberately conceived not to know and be known by their biological fathers." Karen Clark & Elizabeth Marquardt, *The Sperm-Donor Kids Are Not Really All Right*, Slate

(June 14, 2010, 11:23 a.m.), http://www.slate.com/articles/double_x/doublex/2010/06/ the_spermdonor_kids_are_not_really_all_right.html; Marquardt et al., *supra* note 20, at 61.

21. *See* Janet L. Dolgin, *Biological Evaluations: Blood, Genes, and Family*, 41 Akron L. Rev. 347, 385–86, 386 (2008).

22. *See* Rosanna Hertz, *Turning Strangers into Kin (Half Siblings and Anonymous Donors)*, in Who's Watching? Daily Practices of Surveillance among Contemporary Families 156, 159 (Margaret K. Nelson & Anita Ilta Garey eds. 2009).

23. Courtney Sheinmel, My So-Called Family 129 (2008).

24. Cal. Welf. & Instit. Code Sec. 388(b)(2011).

25. *Roberts v. U.S. Jaycees*, 468 U.S. 609, 615-17 (1984).

26. *Id.*

27. *Id.* at 619-20.

28. Christopher D. Vanderbeek, *Oh, Brother! A California Appeals Court Reaffirms the Denial of Necessary Access for Separated Children to Build and Maintain Sibling Relationships*, 13 U.C. Davis J. Juv. L. & Pol'y 349, 358 (2009); *but see* William Wesley Patton, *The Status of Siblings' Rights: A View into the New Millennium*, 51 DePaul L. Rev. 1, 30-33 (2001) (noting that *Troxel* established that case law regarding sibling association rights is unsettled, and the Court is not necessarily opposed to such rights. The "plurality never articulates why the breadth of potential visitation applicants or the liberality of such visitation schedules, at least without a showing of additional constitutional infirmities, violates parents' liberty interest" and instead focuses on two other problematic aspects of the visitation statute.).

29. Wash. Rev. Code Ann. § 26.10.160 (West 1989).

30. *Troxel v. Granville*, 530 U.S. 57, 66 (2000).

31. *Id.* at 67.

32. *Hugo P. v. George P.*, 526 U.S. 1034 (1999).

33. An example of a circuit court avoiding the issue is *31 Foster Children v. Bush*, 329 F.3d 1255 (11th Cir. 2003), in which the court relied on standing grounds and the fact that some of the children had other remedies available in state courts to rule that foster children in custody of the state of Florida failed to show that their due process rights were violated when they were unnecessarily separated from their siblings.

34. *Trujillo v. Bd. of Cnty. Comm'rs*, 768 F.2d 1186, 1188-89 (10th Cir. 1985) (The plaintiffs, a mother and daughter, sued public agencies and officials claiming that the wrongful death of their son and brother, who died while in a county jail's custody, deprived them of their constitutionally founded family association rights under the First and Fourteenth Amendments.); *Rivera v. Marcus*, 696 F.2d 1016, 1024-25 (2nd Cir. 1982); *see also Patel v. Searles*, 305 F.3d 130, 136 (2nd Cir. 2002) (noting that the relationship between the plaintiff, who was suing the police chief for portraying him as the murderer of his mother and sister, and his "father, siblings, wife, and children—receive the greatest degree of protection because they are among the most intimate of relationships"). A contrasting case is *Sun v. Ashcroft*, 370 F.3d 932, 944 (9th Cir. 2004).

35. *Aristotle P. v. Johnson*, 721 F. Supp. 1002, 1005 (N.D. Ill. 1989). However, the *Aristotle P.* decision is arguably flawed because "siblings do not choose to enter into their relationships with each other." Lisa Westergaard, Note: *What's Going to Happen to Us? The Legal Right of Half-Siblings to Remain Together Once Their Custodial Parent Has Succumbed to a Terminal Illness*, 70 U. Mo. Kan. City L. Rev. 471, 481 (2001).

36. *Black v. Beame*, 419 F. Supp. 599 (S.D.N.Y. 1976).
37. *Id.* at 605.
38. Vanderbeek, *supra* note 28, at 361-62.
39. *Id.* at 362.
40. *Id.* at 363-64.
41. *See, e.g.,* Ariz. Rev. Stat. Ann. § 8-872 (2010) ("Any party to a dependency proceeding may file a motion for permanent guardianship."); Del. Code Ann. tit. 31, § 3814 (West 2010) ("Administrative review procedures for a Review Committee must include, but are not limited to, consideration and evaluation of the following. . . . The opportunity for parents, legal guardians and siblings to visit regularly with the child"); S.C. Code Ann. § 63-3-530 (2010) ("The family court has exclusive jurisdiction . . . to order sibling visitation where the court finds it is in the best interest of the children.").
42. Vanderbeek, *supra* note 28, at 364.
43. James G. Dwyer, *A Taxonomy of Children's Existing Rights in State Decision Making about Their Relationships*, 11 Wm. & Mary Bill of Rts. J. 845, 967 (2003).
44. *Id.* at 968.
45. Conn. Gen. Stat. § 45a-726 (2010) ("Whenever possible, siblings should be placed with the same prospective adoptive parent unless it is determined not to be in the best interests of a sibling.").
46. 102 Mass. Code Regs. 5.08 (2010) ("Siblings shall be placed in the same foster or adoptive home unless the licensee documents a written explanation in the children's record as to why such placement is not in the best interest of the children.").
47. N.Y. Comp. Codes R. & Regs. tit. 18, § 421.18 (2010) (The authorized agencies must "[m]ake placement decisions on the basis of the best interests of the child, including but not limited to . . . the requirement of authorized agencies to place minor siblings or half-siblings together.").
48. Dwyer, *supra* note 43, at 968-69.
49. *See In re Tamara R.*, 764 A.2d 844 (Md. Ct. Spec. App. 2000).
50. *Id.*
51. *Id.* at 854.
52. *New Jersey Division of Youth & Family Services v. S.S.*, 902 A.2d 215, 218 (N.J. 2006) (quoting *L.v G.*, 497 A.2d 215, 222 (N.J. Super. Ct. Ch. Div. 1985)).
53. Cal. Family Code § 3102(a) (West 1992), *invalidated by Herbst v. Swan*, 125 Cal. Rptr. 2d 836 (Cal. Ct. App. 2002).
54. *Herbst*, 125 Cal. Rptr. 2d at 842.
55. *Pennington v. Pennington*, 711 P.2d 254 (Utah 1985).
56. *Pennington*, 711 P.2d at 256. The New York Supreme Court similarly denied a grandmother visitation rights with her grandchild because she had never seen the child before. *People ex rel. Wilder v. Dir., Spence-Chapin Servs. to Families and Children*, 403 N.Y.S.2d 454 (N.Y. Sup. Ct. 1978); *see* Judy E. Nathan, Note: *Visitation after Adoption: In the Best Interests of the Child*, 59 N.Y.U. L. Rev. 633, 645 (1984) (observing that visitation is designed to encourage relationships that benefit the child).
57. *State v. Jeffrey H.*, 798 N.W.2d 96, 107 (Neb. 2011).
58. Angela Ferraris, Comment: *Sibling Visitation as a Fundamental Right in* Herbst v. Swan, 39 New Eng. L. Rev. 715, 730-31 (2005).
59. *Roberts v. United States Jaycees*, 468 U.S. 609, 617-18 (1984).
60. Ferraris, *supra* note 58, at 732-33 (2005).

61. Ellen Marrus, *"Where Have You Been, Fran?" The Right of Siblings to Seek Court Access to Override Parental Denial of Visitation*, 66 Tenn. L. Rev. 977, 984-87 (1999).

62. Westergaard, *supra* note 35, at 478.

63. *Id.* at 477.

64. *In re Tamara R.*, 764 A.2d 844, 854 (Md. Ct. Spec. App. 2000).

65. *Lyons v. Lyons*, 490 N.Y.S.2d 871, 872 (N.Y. App. Div. 1985) (citing *Ebert v. Ebert*, 346 N.E.2d 240, 243 (N.Y. 1976) (noting that "the separation of siblings, where, as here, the custodial parent in whose care all three had been entrusted is fit and willing and able to function as such, is to be frowned upon. Close familial relationships are much to be encouraged. By building identity, countering feelings of isolation, and encouraging healthy adjustments to and with others, they provide an important additional dimension to long-term stability.").

CHAPTER 6

1. The Fertility Clinic Success and Certification Act, 42 U.S.C. § 263a (2008); *see* Lori Andrews & Nanette Elster, *Regulating Reproductive Technologies*, 21 J. Leg. Med. 35, 49 (2000).

2. *See* Naomi Cahn, Test Tube Families: Why the Fertility Markets Need Legal Regulation 119 (2009).

3. *See, e.g.*, the ASRM ethics reports, http://www.asrm.org/Media/Ethics/ethicsmain.html.

4. *See* Naomi Cahn & Jana Singer, *Adoption, Identity, and the Constitution: The Case for Opening Closed Records*, 2 U. Pa. J. Const. L. 187 (1999) (exploring similarities and differences); Ellen Waldman, *What Do We Tell the Children?* 35 Cap. U. L. Rev. 517, 533-34 (2006).

5. *See* Madelyn Freundlich, Adoption and Ethics: Adoption and Assisted Reproduction (2001); Naomi Cahn & Evan B. Donaldson Adoption Institute, *Old Lessons for a New World: Applying Adoption Research and Experience to ART*, 24 J. Am. Acad. Matrimonial Law 1 (2011).

6. A. M. Homes, The Mistress's Daughter 102 (2007).

7. *See* Nanette Elster, *All or Nothing? The International Debate over Disclosure to Donor Offspring, Inst. on Biotech. & the Human Future*, http://www.thehumanfuture.org/commentaries/assisted_reproductive_technology/art_commentary_elster01.html.

8. Elizabeth Samuels, *The Idea of Adoption: An Inquiry into the History of Adult Adoptee Access to Birth Records*, 53 Rutgers L. Rev. 367, 369 (2001).

9. Professor Gaia Bernstein reports that it was not until 1909 that the first publication concerning donor sperm appeared, discussing "an 1848 case in Philadelphia involving a forty-one year old merchant and his wife . . . [who was inseminated with] semen collected from the best looking member of the medical school class. . . . Neither the merchant nor his wife knew what was done. The physician confided in the merchant after the fact. The merchant was delighted but arranged for his wife to remain in ignorance." Gaia Bernstein, *The Socio-Legal Acceptance of New Technologies: A Close Look at Artificial Insemination*, 77 Wash. L. Rev. 1035, 1056 (2002). It appears that the resulting child never knew, either.

10. Uniform Parentage Act Section 5(a) (1973), http://www.law.upenn.edu/bll/archives/ulc/fnact99/1990s/upa7390.htm.

11. The analogies and comparisons between adoption and reproductive technology are not entirely synchronous. *See* Freundlich, *supra* note 5; Cahn & Donaldson Adoption

Institute, *supra* note 5; Melanie B. Jacobs, *Procreation through ART: Why the Adoption Process Should Not Apply*, 35 Cap. U. L. Rev. 399 (2006).

12. *See, e.g.*, June Carbone, *The Role of Adoption in Winning Public Recognition for Adult Partnerships*, 35 Cap. U. L. Rev. 341, 357-59 (2006).

13. Wilfred Finegold, Artificial Insemination 25 (1964). Alan Guttmacher wrote the introduction.

14. *Id.* at 40.

15. *Id.* at 33-35.

16. *See* Naomi Cahn, *Perfect Substitutes or the Real Thing?* 52 Duke L.J. 1077 (2003).

17. Evan B. Donaldson Adoption Institute, *For the Records: Restoring a Legal Right for Adult Adoptees* 3 (2007), http://www.adoptioninstitute.org/publications/2007_11_For_Records.pdf; *see* Jeanne A. Howard et al., *For the Records II: An Examination of the History and Impact of Adult Adoptee Access to Original Birth Certificates*, Evan B. Donaldson Adoption Institute (Adam Pertman ed., July 2010), http://www.adoption-institute.org/publications/7_14_2010_ForTheRecordsII.pdf. Virtually all states allow adoptees access to their original birth certificates based on a showing in court of good cause, and a number of states allow access without requiring adoptees to go to court. *Id.*

18. *Id.* (2007), (2010).

19. Evan B. Donaldson Adoption Institute, *Adoption Registries and Inter-mediaries by State* (2008), http://www.adoptioninstitute.org/resources/openrecord_stratergies_intermediary_programs.pdf (last visited Apr. 22, 2012).

20. Children's Bureau, U.S. Dept. of Health & Human Serv., Child Welfare Information Gateway, *Access to Adoption Records: Summary of State Laws* (2009), http://www.childwelfare.gov/systemwide/laws_policies/statutes/infoaccessapall.pdf (last visited Nov. 26, 2011).

21. Cahn & Singer, *supra* note 4, at 165.

22. *Access to Adoption Records, supra* note 20.

23. Evan B. Donaldson Adoption Institute, Deborah H. Siegel and Susan Livingston Smith, *Openness in Adoption: From Secrecy and Stigma to Knowledge and Connections* (2012), http://www.adoptioninstitute.org/publications/2012_03_OpennessInAdoption.pdf.

24. Uniform Parentage Act, §5(a) (1973) (emphasis added); *see also* Colo. Rev. Stat. § 19-4-106 (2008) (example of enacted state statute)

25. Uniform Parentage Act §700 (2002), http://www.law.upenn.edu/bll/archives/ulc/upa/final2002.htm; *see also* Wash. Rev. Code § 26.26.011 (2002) (example of state that enacted the Uniform Parentage Act of 2002).

26. *See* Elster, *All or Nothing? supra* note 7, at 3-4 (listing New York and Ohio, and noting that the ASRM recommends maintaining permanent records). About half of the states have established laws concerning the supervision of sperm banking. Dawn R. Swink & J. Brad Reich, *Caveat Vendor: Potential Progeny, Paternity, and Product Liability Online*, 2007 BYU L. Rev. 857, 872 (2007).

27. *Johnson v. Superior Court*, 80 Cal. App. 4th 1050, 1057 (2d Dist. 2000), *modified*, 101 Cal. App. 4th 869 (2d. Dist. 2002).

28. *Id.* at 1066.

29. *Id.* at 1067.

30. For courts' interpretation of good cause in the adoption context, *see, e.g.*, Samuels, *supra* note 8, at 427-29; Cahn & Singer, *supra* note 4, at 161-62.

31. *Sutton v. Diane J.*, 2007 Mich. App. Lexis 754 (2007).

32. Murray Davis, *Child Should Have Right to Know Genetic Information*, Detroit Free Press, Mar. 6, 2007, at 9; Christina Stolarz, *Teen Fighting to Find Real Dad*, Detroit News, Nov. 20, 2006, at 1B.

33. Elizabeth Suh & Ashbel S. Green, *Who Gets the Baby?* The Oregonian, Sept. 22, 2006, at A1.

34. Ashbel S. Green, *Judge Rules in OHSU Sperm Sample Mix-Up*, The Oregonian, Apr. 17, 2007, at B2.

35. Tamsyn Burgmann, *Woman Asks Courts to Grant Children of Sperm or Egg Donors Parent's Identity*, Canadian Press, Oct. 25, 2010.

36. *Daughter of Sperm Donor Seeks to Know Identity of Biological Father*, Vancouver Sun, Oct. 27, 2008, http://www.canada.com/vancouversun/news/story. html?id=3146c8d6-d2a6-4d3b-a911-6eaaa3732558.

37. Olivia Pratten, Blog entry, http://www.canadiandonoroffspring.ca/cdo_DCA_olivia. html (last visited May 22, 2011).

38. Hayley Mick, *Who's Your Donor?* Globe and Mail, July 24, 2007, at L1.

39. *Pratten v. British Columbia (Attorney-General)*, 2011 BCSC 656.

40. Paras. 215, 232.

41. Jacqueline Mroz, *One Sperm Donor, 150 Children*, N.Y. Times, Sept. 6, 2011.

42. *See* HFEA, *Infertility: The HFEA Guide* 31 (2007), http://www.hfea.gov.uk/docs/Guide2. pdf.

43. ASRM, *2006 Guidelines for Gamete and Embryo Donation*, 86 Fertility & Sterility S38 (2006); *see* Naomi Cahn, *Accidental Incest: Drawing the Line—or the Curtain—for Reproductive Technology*, 32 Harv. J. Gender & L. 59 (2009).

44. Libby Purves, *Whose Body Is It Anyway?* Times Online, Jan. 15, 2008, http://www. timesonline.co.uk/tol/comment/columnists/libby_purves/article3187337.ece; Steven Kotler, *The God of Sperm: In an Industry Veiled in Secrecy, a Powerful L.A. Sperm Peddler Shapes the Nation's Rules on Disease, Genetics—and Accidental Incest*, L.A. Weekly, Sept. 27, 2007.

45. Dept. Health & Soc. Security, *Report of the Committee on Human Fertilisation and Embryology* 22 (1984) ("The Warnock Report"), http://www.hfea.gov.uk/docs/ Warnock_Report_of_the_Committee_of_Inquiry_into_Human_Fertilisation_and_ Embryology_1984.pdf.

46. *See* Mroz, *supra* note 41.

47. *See* Michael Grossberg, Governing the Hearth: Law and the Family in Nineteenth-Century America 111, 145 (1985).

48. *See, e.g.*, Cal. Penal Code § 285 (2009) (criminalizing incest); Cal. Fam. Code § 2200 (2009) (defining void marriages); *see also* Brett H. McDonnell, *Is Incest Next?* 10 Cardozo J. L & Gender 337, 348 n.73 (2004) ("In a number of states, the two laws are structurally interrelated: the statute criminalizing incestuous acts will refer to the statute voiding incestuous marriages to define which types of relationships are covered.").

49. *State v. Fischer*, 493 N.E.2d 1265 (Ind. Ct. App. 1986).

50. *State v. Bohall*, 546 N.E.2d 1214, 1215 (Ind. 1989). In *Bohall*, the Indiana Supreme Court upheld an incest conviction against a man who sexually molested his biological

daughter, who had been adopted by another family, but who had returned to live with her biological father. *Id.* at 1215-16.

51. *State v. Sharon H.*, 429 A.2d 1321 (Del. 1981).

52. William Saletan, *Incest Repellant?* Slate.com, April 23, 2003, http://www.slate.com/id/2081904.

53. *See* Naomi Cahn, *Accidental Incest: Drawing the Line—or the Curtain?—for Reproductive Technology*, 32 Harv. J.L. & Gender 59 (2009).

54. *See id.*

55. *See* Sigmund Freud, Three Essays on the Theory of Sexuality (James Strachey trans., 1949). *But see* Amy Adler, *The Perverse Law of Child Pornography*, 101 Colum. L. Rev. 209, 221–22 (2001) (explaining scholarly critiques of Freud's theory).

56. *See, e.g.*, Adler, *supra* note 55, at 221–22; H. Spain, *The Westermarck-Freud Incest-Theory Debate: An Evaluation and Reformulation*, 28 Current Anthropology 623, 625 (1987).

57. *See* William Saletan, *The Love That Dare Not Speak Its Name*, Slate.com, April 10, 2002, http://www.slate.com/id/2064227/; Robin L. Bennett, Louanne Hudgins, Corrine O. Smith & Arno G. Motulsky, *Inconsistencies in Genetic Counseling and Screening for Consanguineous Couples and Their Offspring: Recommendations of the National Society of Genetic Counselors*, 11 J. Genetic Counseling 97, 104 (2002) (providing examples of studies determining baseline population estimates for major birth defects and genetic disorders); Bernadette Morrell & Aamra Darr, *Genetic Counseling and Customary Consanguineous Marriage*, 3 Nature Reviews Genetics 225 (2002), http://www.nature.com/nrg/journal/v3/n3/full/nrg754.html (estimating 2-2.5 percent of nonconsanguineous matings produce children with birth defects, while first-cousin matings produce double that number, but pointing out numerous flaws in the way data are collected).

58. *See* Helen V. Firth, Jane A. Hurst & Judith G. Hall, Oxford Desk Reference: Clinical Genetics 370 (2005); Bennett, et al., *supra* note 57; Saletan, *supra* note 57. Firth et al. point out that the estimated risk is actually lower than the observed, empirical risks; the estimated risk is 12.5 percent for recessive disorders, while the observed risk is 30 percent. Apart from physical abnormalities, the empirical risk for mental disability is closer to 50 percent in sibling-sibling and parent-child unions. *See* Firth et al., *supra.* The estimated rate for half-siblings is approximately one-half that of full-blooded siblings. Other studies vary dramatically on the actual genetic risks.

59. Lukas F. Keller & Donald M. Waller, *Inbreeding Effects in Wild Populations*, 17 Trends Ecology Evolution 230, 230 (2002) http://www.homepage.montana.edu/~wwwbi/staff/creel/bio480/keller.pdf ("Data from bird and mammal populations suggest that inbreeding depression often significantly affects birth weight, survival, reproduction and resistance to disease, predation and environmental stress."); *see also* John T. Hogg, Stephen H. Forbes, Brian M. Steele & Gordon Luikart, *Genetic Rescue of an Insular Population of Large Mammals*, 273 Proc. Royal Soc'y B. 1491 (2006) (discussing the benefits of outbreeding in improving fitness of a small, isolated population of bighorn sheep, and contrasting the benefits to the effects of inbreeding).

60. *See* Patrick Bateson, *Inbreeding Avoidance and Incest Taboos*, in Inbreeding, Incest, and the Incest Taboo: The State of Knowledge at the Turn of the Century 24, 25 (Arthur P. Wolf & William H. Durham eds. 2004).

61. Courtney Megan Cahill, *Same-Sex Marriage, Slippery Slope Rhetoric, and the Politics of Disgust: A Critical Perspective on Contemporary Family Discourse and the Incest Taboo*, 99 Nw. U. L. Rev. 1543, 1570 (2005).

62. Certainly, by 1873, one of the leading family law treatises noted, "Marriages between persons closely allied in blood are apt to produce an offspring feeble in body, and tending to insanity in mind." Grossberg, *supra* note 47, at 145 (quoting Joel Bishop, Commentaries on Marriage and Divorce 273–74 (5th ed. 1873)).

63. The increasing use of screening tests before and during pregnancy can help in reducing this risk.

64. Edward Westermarck, The History of Human Marriage 320 (1891). For one application of the hypothesis in legal literature, *see* David J. Herring, *Foster Care Placement: Reducing the Risk of Sibling Incest*, 37 U. Mich. J.L. Reform 1145, 1146–62 (2004) (discussing Westermarck's thesis, and two studies of Irene Bevc and Irwin Silverman showing that opposite-sex siblings who live together before the age of three develop a strong aversion to incestuous behavior).

65. These studies are discussed later in this chapter.

66. *See* William Ian Miller, The Anatomy of Disgust 15 (1997). A full discussion of the significance of emotion to legal reasoning is well beyond the scope of this article, although it is an issue that must be recognized. For useful commentary on this issue *see*, for example, The Passions of Law (Susan A. Bandes ed.1999) and Jonathan Haidt, *The Moral Emotions*, in Handbook of Affective Sciences 852 (Richard J. Davidson, Klaus R. Scherer & H. Hill Goldsmith eds. 2003), http://faculty.virginia.edu/haidtlab/articles/haidt.the-moral-emotions.manuscript.html.

67. John Witte Jr., *Can America Still Ban Polygamy?* Christianity Today Mag., May 23, 2008, http://www.christianitytoday.com/ct/article_print.html?id=55605.

68. *See* Miller, *supra* note 66, at 2. Miller provides a social history and defense of disgust.

69. *See* Miller, *supra* note 66, at 15. Miller hypothesizes that some elements of incest definitions, such as the prohibition on parent-child relationships, are in fact universal. *Id.* at 260, note 39.

70. *See generally* Dan M. Kahan, *The Anatomy of Disgust in Criminal Law*, 96 Mich. L. Rev. 1621 (1998) (calling for criminal law to take account of disgust); Dan M. Kahan, *The Progressive Appropriation of Disgust*, in The Passions of Law 63 (Susan A. Bandes ed. 1999).

71. Kahan, *The Progressive Appropriation, supra* note 70, at 71.

72. *See* Martha C. Nussbaum, Hiding from Humanity: Disgust, Shame, and the Law 125, 171 (2004). The philosopher Leon Kass has used repugnance as a means for limiting various new uses of reproductive technology, including cloning. *See, e.g.*, Leon R. Kass, *Defending Human Dignity*, in Human Ethics and Human Dignity: Essays Commissioned by the President's Council on Bioethics 297, 298 (2008), http://www.bioethics.gov/reports/human_dignity/human_dignity_and_bioethics.pdf.

73. *See* Haidt, *supra* note 66, at 852.

74. *See* Nussbaum, *supra* note 72, at 81.

75. Dan Markel, Jennifer M. Collins & Ethan J. Leib, Privilege or Punish: Criminal Justice and the Challenge of Family Ties (2009); Clare Huntington, *Repairing Family Law*, 57 Duke L.J. 1245, 1277 (2008).

76. Cahill, *supra* note 61, at 1611.

CHAPTER 7

1. *See* June Carbone & Naomi Cahn, *Embryo Fundamentalism*, 18 Wm. & Mary Bill Rts. L.J. 1015 (2010).

2. *See* Ruth Padawer, *Unnatural Selection*, N.Y. Times, Aug. 14, 2011, at MM22.

3. *See generally* Clare Huntington, *Repairing Family Law*, 57 Duke L.J. 1245 (2008).

4. *See Donor Sibling Registry*, http://donorsiblingregistry.com (last visited Nov. 8, 2010). While no donor-conceived individual has yet brought suit in the United States to discover information about a donor or potential half-siblings, the Canadian Supreme Court has considered these issues in an appeal from Olivia Pratten's successful suit ending donor anonymity in British Columbia. In the United States, as discussed earlier, donor gamete recipients, but not their children, have brought suit on the basis of medical issues. *Johnson v. Superior Court*, 95 Cal. Rptr. 2d 864 (Cal. Ct. App. 2000); *Doe v. XYZ*, 914 N.E.2d 117 (Mass. App. Ct. 2009).

5. The British system, for example, allows for disclosure once the offspring reach the age of eighteen. *See For Donor-Conceived People and Their Parents*, http://www.hfea.gov.uk/23.html (last visited Feb. 13, 2011).

6. David Crary, *Sperm-Donors' Kids Seek More Rights and Respect*, Times-Argus, Aug. 19, 2010, at News 01(quoting Dr. Jamie Grifo, former president of the Society for Assisted Reproductive Technologies).

7. *See generally*, Naomi Cahn, Evan B. Donaldson Adoption Inst., Old Lessons for a New World: Applying Adoption Research and Experience to Assisted Reproductive Technology 14 (Adam Pertman et al. eds. 2009), http://www.adoptioninstitute.org/publications/2009_02_OldLessons.pdf (contrasting differing orientations of adoption and ART); Annette R. Appell, *Reflections on the Movement Toward a More Child-Centered Adoption*, 32 W. New Eng. L. Rev. 1 (2010) (urging greater attention to children in adoption).

8. *See, e.g.*, Naomi Cahn, *Necessary Subjects: The Need for a Mandatory National Donor Gamete Databank*, 12 DePaul J. Health Care L. 203 (2009); Michelle Dennison, *Revealing Your Sources: The Case for Non-Anonymous Gamete Donation*, 21 J.L. & Health 1, 8 (2008); *but see* Julie L. Sauer, *Competing Interests and Gamete Donation: The Case for Anonymity*, 39 Seton Hall L. Rev. 919, 939-43 (2009).

9. *See* Naomi Cahn & Jana Singer, *Adoption, Identity, and the Constitution: The Case for Opening Closed Records*, 2 U. Pa. J. Const. L. 150, 162 (1999); Jeanne A. Howard et al., *For the Records II: An Examination of the History and Impact of Adult Adoptee Access to Original Birth Certificates*, Evan B. Donaldson Adoption Institute (Adam Pertman ed., July 2010), http://www.adoptioninstitute.org/publications/7_14_2010_ForTheRecordsII.pdf. Virtually all states allow adoptees access to their original birth certificates based on a showing in court of good cause, and a number of states allow access without requiring adoptees to go to court. *Id.*

10. *See, e.g.*, Complaint at X, *Pratten v. Atty Gen. of British Columbia* (Complaint) (2008); http://www.arvayfinlay.com/news/Writ%20of%20Summons%20and%20Statement%20of%20Claim.pdf; *see also* Eric Blyth & Lucy Frith, *The UK's Donor Gamete "Crisis": A Critical Analysis*, 28 Critical Soc. Pol'y 74, 87 (2008) ("[T]here is . . . an argument concerning parity and non-discrimination that can be advanced in favour of disclosure of donor identity: that donor-conceived people should not be the only group of people *legally* prevented from finding out their biological parentage."). Indeed, illegal discrimination between the rights of adopted and donor-conceived individuals to access information about their biological parents was at the core of the British Columbia Supreme Court's decision in *Pratten*. Pratten v. British Columbia (Attorney-General), 2011 BCSC 656, at paras. 230–34. A few courts in the United States have considered

requests to disclose a donor's identity, but never in the context of offspring's liberty claims; so far, no court has ordered disclosure. *See, e.g., Johnson v. Superior Court*, 95 Cal. Rptr. 2d 864 (Cal. Ct. App. 2000); *Doe v. XYZ*, 914 N.E.2d 117 (Mass. App. Ct. 2009); Cahn, *Necessary Subjects, supra* note 8, at 212.

11. *See* Nancy D. Polikoff, *Breaking the Link between Biology and Parental Rights in Planned Lesbian Families: When Semen Donors Are Not Fathers*, 2 Geo. J. Gender & Law 57 (2000).

12. *See Troxel v. Granville*, 530 U.S. 57 (2000); Naomi Cahn, *Models of Family Privacy*, 67 Geo. Wash. L. Rev. 1225 (1999); *cf.* Barbara Bennett Woodhouse, *Who Owns the Child? Meyer and Pierce and the Child as Property*, 33 Wm. & Mary L. Rev. 995 (1992).

13. *See* Cahn & Singer, *supra* note 9, at 172–75. The child's right to an identity is protected internationally as well. *See generally* Jennifer Baines, Note: *Gamete Donors and Mistaken Identities: The Importance of Genetic Awareness and Proposals Favoring Donor Identity Disclosure for Children Born from Gamete Donations in the United States*, 45 Fam. Ct. Rev. 116, 120–21 (2007).

14. Barbara Bennett Woodhouse, *"Are You My Mother?": Conceptualizing Children's Identity Rights in Transracial Adoptions*, 2 Duke J. Gender L. & Pol'y 107, 128 (1995) *see* Mary Lyndon Shanley, Making Babies, Making Families: What Matters Most in an Age of Reproductive Technologies, Surrogacy, Adoption, and Same-Sex and Unwed Parents 1-33 (2001) (discussing need to see child in context, as both individual and part of previous family unit). Professor Woodhouse speaks of the need for children to claim rights with respect to two aspects of their identity: one involves their identity in the context of their functional, social family, and the second is their "'identity of origin.'" Woodhouse, *supra*, at 127-28. Maxine Eichner notes that the state has an obligation to ensure "the development of children's civic virtues and autonomy." Maxine Eichner, The Supportive State: Families, Government, and America's Political Ideals 173 (2010).

15. *See* Eric Blyth & Lucy Frith, *Donor-Conceived People's Access to Genetic and Biographical History: An Analysis of Provisions in Different Jurisdictions Permitting Disclosure of Donor Identity*, 23 Int'l. J. Law, Policy & Fam. 174, 182-83 (2009); Human Fertilisation & Embryology Authority, *HFEA to Help Donor-Conceived Siblings Contact Each Other* (Apr. 6, 2010), http://www.hfea.gov.uk/5838.html.
    If the government is collecting this information, there is a risk that genetic prescreening may be required in order to prevent inadvertent incest. The government's role here, however, should be as a registry, rather than an active intervenor.

16. *See, e.g.*, Clare Huntington, *Familial Norms and Normativity*, 59 Emory L.J. 1103, 1156-59 (2010); *see also* Richard H. McAdams, *The Origins, Development, and Regulation of Norms*, 96 Mich. L. Rev. 338, 340 (1997).

17. As Elizabeth Emens points out in a different context, "Even when seemingly uninvolved in intimate discrimination, the state creates infrastructure and influences hierarchies in ways that determine whom we meet (accidents) and how we view those we meet (calculations)." Elizabeth F. Emens, *Intimate Discrimination: The State's Role in the Accidents of Sex and Love*, 122 Harv. L. Rev. 1307, 1401 (2009).

18. *See generally* Eichner, *supra* note 14 (discussing the relationship between supporting families and the public good); Huntington, *supra* note 3 (addressing the role of family law in healing families).

19. *For the Records II, supra* note 9, at 12.

20. *See* Jennifer A. Baines, Note: *Gamete Donors and Mistaken Identities: The Importance of Genetic Awareness and Proposals Favoring Donor Identity Disclosure for Children Born from Gamete Donations in the United States*, 45 Fam. Ct. Rev. 116, 126 (2007).

21. *See, e.g.*, Naomi Cahn, Test Tube Families: Why the Fertility Markets Need Legal Regulation, chapter 12 (2009).

22. Shanley, *supra* note 14.

23. Peter Conrad, The Medicalization of Society: On the Transformation of Human Conditions into Treatable Disorders (2007); Rene Almeling, Sex Cells: The Medical Market in Eggs and Sperm (2011).

24. Indeed, paradigm shifting is one of the themes of this book.

25. *E.g.*, William N. Sage, *Relational Duties, Regulatory Duties, and the Widening Gap between Individual Health Law and Collective Health Policy*, 96 Geo. L.J. 497 (2008) (discussing medical ethics); William D. White, *Market Forces, Competitive Strategies, and Health Care Regulation*, 2004 U. Ill. L. Rev. 137 (2004) (discussing market competition); Stephanie N. Sivinski, Note: *Putting Too Many (Fertilized) Eggs in One Basket: Methods of Reducing Multifetal Pregnancies in the United States*, 88 Tex. L. Rev. 897, 913 (2010).

26. Adoption law has moved toward increasing recognition of the child's right to learn about her biological parents, and toward enforcement of agreements for contact between the biological parents and the child. *See, e.g.*, Annette R. Appell, *The Endurance of Biological Connection: Heteronormativity, Same-Sex Parenting, and the Lessons of Adoption*, 22 BYU J. Pub. L. 289 (2008); Annette Ruth Appell, *Reflections on the Movement toward a More Child-Centered Adoption*, 32 W. New Eng. L. Rev. 1 (2010).

27. *See, e.g.*, Eichner, *supra* note 14, at 157-82.

28. In a series of cases beginning in 1972, the Supreme Court held that biological, non-marital fathers had a constitutionally protected interest in establishing a relationship with their children, and later cases have clarified that this right exists when the men had taken some steps to develop a relationship with the children. *See, e.g., Stanley v. Illinois*, 405 U.S. 645, 658 (1972); Alice Ristroph & Melissa Murray, *Disestablishing the Family*, 119 Yale L.J. 1236, 1252-53 (2010); Nelson Tebbe & Deborah A. Widiss, *Equal Access and the Right to Marry*, 158 U. Pa. L. Rev. 1375, 1400 (2010).

29. *See* Huntington, *supra* note 3, at 1287-94.

30. *See* Melissa Murray, *The Networked Family: Reframing the Legal Understanding of Caregiving and Caregivers*, 94 Va. L. Rev. 385 (2008); Huntington, *supra* note 3, at 1304. As Clare Huntington notes in the context of dissolved familial relationships, "Rather than wishing that a clear legal name—spouse/legal stranger, parent/nonparent—will resolve the underlying psychological issues, the new legal status acknowledges the ongoing connection that exists and thus conceives of a place beyond rupture." *Id. See generally* Clare Huntington, *Happy Families? Translating Positive Psychology into Family Law*, 16 Va. J. Soc. Pol'y & L. 385 (2009) (exploring how the law can respect positive emotions within the family).

31. *See* Huntington, *Happy Families, supra* note 30, at 408.

32. *See, e.g., In re K.M.H.*, 169 P.3d 1025 (Kan. 2007); Nancy D. Polikoff, *A Mother Should Not Have to Adopt Her Own Child: Parentage Laws for Lesbian Couples in the Twenty-First Century*, 5 Stan. J. Civ. Rts. & Civ. Lib. 201, 241-42 (2009).

33. For a discussion of benefits based on marital status, *see, e.g., Gill v. Office of Personnel Man.*, 699 F. Supp. 2d 374 (D. Mass. 2010); *Goodridge v. Dep't of Pub. Health*, 798 N.E.2d 941, 948 (Mass. 2003); Letter from Dayna K. Shah, Associate General Counsel,

United States General Accounting Office, to Honorable Bill Frist, Majority Leader, United States Senate (Jan. 23, 2004), http:// www.gao.gov/new.items/d04353r.pdf. Surrogate decision making most commonly takes the form of substituted judgments when one partner is medically incapacitated.

34. These are some of the benefits that might be accorded to legally recognized friendships. *See, e.g.*, Laura Rosenbury, *Friends with Benefits*,106 Mich. L. Rev. 179, 191 (2007); see also Ethan J. Leib, *Friendship & the Law*, 54 UCLA L. Rev. 631, 632–33 (2007) (documenting the absence of legal regulation of friendship more generally).

CHAPTER 8

1. At a conference in Chicago, Dr. Charles Sims circulated a proposal for a national voluntary registry. *See also* DSR, Draft Proposal for a National Donor Gamete Databank (unpublished, on file with author, 2008) (coauthored by Christina Ayiotis, Naomi Cahn & Wendy Kramer) (counterproposal).
2. Nanette R. Elster & Andrea Braverman, *The Future Is Now: A* Voluntary *Gamete Donor Registry Is Feasible*, 12 DePaul J. Health Care L. 195 (2009).
3. Stephanie Nano, *Few Fertility Clinics Follow Embryo Guidelines*, SFGATE.COM, Feb. 21, 2009, http://www.sfchronicle.us/cgi-bin/article.cgi?f=/c/a/2009/02/21/MN2A161S2S.DTL.
4. Wendy Kramer, *Donor Sibling Registry*, http://www.donorsiblingregistry.com/chicago-talk.pdf at 6.
5. 42 U.S.C. §263a-1 (2008); *see* 70 Fed. Reg. 5187 (2005).
6. *See* Centers for Disease Control and Prevention, *Assisted Reproductive Technology Success Rates: National Summary Report: 2009 National Summary* (2011), http://apps.nccd.cdc.gov/art/Apps/NationalSummaryReport.aspx.
7. 21 Fed. CFR 1271 et seq. (2008).
8. *See, e.g.*, Jennifer A. Baines, Note: *Gamete Donors and Mistaken Identities: The Importance of Genetic Awareness and Proposals Favoring Donor Identity Disclosure for Children Born from Gamete Donations in the United States*, 45 Fam. Ct. Rev. 116, 126 (2007).
9. *Uniform Parentage Act* (2011), http://apps.leg.wa.gov/documents/billdocs/2011-12/Pdf/Bills/Session%20Law%202011/1267-S2.SL.pdf .
10. This is discussed later in this chapter.
11. Bonnie Rochman, *Where Do (Some) Babies Come From? In Washington, a New Law Bans Anonymous Sperm and Egg Donors*, Time, July 22, 2011, http://healthland.time.com/2011/07/22/where-do-some-babies-come-from-in-washington-a-new-law-bans-anonymous-sperm-and-egg-donors/#ixzz1U3bIw8sH.
12. Sara Cotton et al., *Model Assisted Reproductive Technology Act*, 9 J. Gender Race & Just. 55, 79-80 (2005).
13. Pino D'Orazio, *Half of the Family Tree: A Call for Access to a Full Genetic History for Children Born by Artificial Insemination*, 2 J. Health & Biomedical Law 249, 267 (2006).
14. Human Fertilisation and Embryology Authority, *HFEA Code of Practice* (2011), http://cop.hfea.gov.uk/cop/COPContent.aspx?M=0&S=71&SM=83&P=58#content.
15. *See* Naomi Cahn, Test Tube Families: Why the Fertility Markets Need Legal Regulation, chapter 12 (2009).
16. A second objection relates to the privacy interests of all involved, an issue discussed later, in chapter 10.

17. Surrogacy contracts, for example, have been struck down as contrary to public policy. *E.g., Baby M*, 537 A.2d 1227, 1234 (N.J. 1988) (invalidating surrogacy agreement); Elizabeth Scott, *Surrogacy and the Politics of Commodification*, 72 Law & Contemp. Probs. 109 (2009). Similarly, where agreements violate legal rights, they are struck down; perhaps the best known example involves racially restrictive covenants. *Shelley v. Kraemer*, 334 U.S. 1 (1948); *see* Mark D. Rosen, *Was* Shelley v. Kraemer *Incorrectly Decided? Some New Answers*, 95 Cal. L. Rev. 451 (2007); Russell Korobkin, *Bounded Rationality, Standard Form Contracts, and Unconscionability*, 70 U. Ch. L. Rev. 1203, 1229-30 (2003).

18. *See* E. Wayne Carp, *Does Opening Adoption Records Have an Adverse Social Impact? Some Lessons from the U.S., Great Britain, and Australia, 1953–2007*, 10 Adoption Q. 29 (2007); Elizabeth J. Samuels, *The Idea of Adoption: An Inquiry into the History of Adult Adoptee Access to Birth Records*, 53 Rutgers L. Rev. 367, 380 (2001); Jennifer Butch, Note: *Finding Family: Why New Jersey Should Allow Adult Adoptees Access to Their Original Birth Certificates*, 34 Seton Hall Legis. J. 251, 257-59 (2010).

19. *See Johnson*, 80 Cal. App. 4th at 1057; Uniform Parentage Act §§700 et seq. (2002); Naomi Cahn & Jana Singer, *Adoption, Identity, and the Constitution: The Case for Opening Closed Records*, 2 U. Pa. J. Const. L. 150, 162 (1999).

20. *See* Eric Blyth & Marilyn Cranshaw, Comment: *Countdown Begins for Ending Donor Anonymity in British Columbia: Lessons for Us All?* Bionews, June 6, 2011, http://www.bionews.org.uk/page_96105.asp.

21. UK DonorLink, *Donor Conception, Find the Missing Piece* (2011), http://www.ukdonorlink.org.uk/information.asp.

22. Sonia Allen, *Submission to Senate Committee Inquiry into Donor Conception, Access to Information by Donor Conceived Individuals about Their Donors* 21-22 (2010), http://www.parliament.vic.gov.au/images/stories/committees/lawrefrom/donor-conceived/DCP05-Sonia_Allan.pdf.

23. This has been done by some states for adoptees, allowing the biological parents and the adoptee to indicate their interest in contacting one another. *See* Cahn & Singer, *supra* note 19, at 162-63. Approximately thirty states have established these registries. Children's Bureau, U.S. Dept. of Health & Human Serv., Child Welfare Information Gateway, *Access to Adoption Records: Summary of State Laws* (2009), http://www.childwelfare.gov/systemwide/laws_policies/statutes/infoaccessapall.pdf (last visited Nov. 26, 2011). Although Senator Carl Levin repeatedly introduced proposals for a national registry (and I testified in favor of such a registry), the legislation has never been enacted. *See* Cahn & Singer, *supra* note 19, at 163 n. 59.

24. Lucy Frith, *Beneath the Rhetoric: The Role of Rights in the Practice of Non-Anonymous Gamete Donation*, 15 Bioethics 473,476 (2001).

25. Vardit Ravitsky, *A Child's Right, a Family's Secret*, Globe and Mail, May 26, 2011, http://www.theglobeandmail.com/news/opinions/opinion/a-childs-right-a-familys-secret/article2034905.

26. *See id.* A report from the Ethics Committee of the American Society for Reproductive Medicine on the topic of disclosure observed,

> Clinicians, mental health professionals, academics, and children themselves have in recent years called for more openness in donor conception in order to protect the interests of offspring. Because of persons' fundamental interest in knowing their genetic heritage and the importance of their ability to make

NOTES TO CHAPTER 8   >>   219

informed health care decisions in the future, the Ethics Committee supports disclosure about the fact of donation to children. It also supports the gathering and storage of medical and genetic information that can be provided to offspring if they ask. It recognizes, however, that disclosure is a personal matter to be decided by the participants. . . .

Ethics Committee of the ASRM, *Informing Offspring of Their Conception by Gamete Donation*, 81 Fertility & Sterility 527, 530 (2004).

27. *See* Alison Motluk, *Okay, So Who's Really Your Daddy?* Toronto Star, Feb. 16, 2008, at D6.
28. *See* David Derbyshire, *Children of Egg Donors "Should Have Birth Certificates Stamped,"* Daily Mail, Dec. 11, 2007, §1, at 4; Amy Iggulden & Sophie Goodchild, *Symbol to Identify Donor Babies on Birth Certificates*, Evening Standard, Dec. 10, 2007, at A10.
29. Caroline Jones, *The Changing Face of Families: A Controversial New Proposal Would Mean a Special Stamp on the Birth Certificates of Babies from Donor Eggs or Sperm; How Will This—and Other New Laws—Affect Families?* The Mirror (London), Jan. 10, 2008, at 40.
30. *But see* IFFS Surveillance '07, *Anonymity*, 87 Fertility & Sterility S33, S34 (2007) (tbl. 9.2, "Specific Modifications to Anonymity," highlighting variations in national programs for release of gamete donor information).
31. *See* Evonne Barry, *Donor Secrecy "Could Lead to Incest,"* Aust. Donor Conception Forum, Aug. 13, 2008, http://australiandonorconceptionforum.org/index.php?topic=165.0; Sonia Allan, *Submission to the Senate Legal and Constitutional Affairs Committee Inquiry into Donor Conception, Access to Genetic Information and Donor Identification* 23 (2010), http://www.parliament.vic.gov.au/images/stories/committees/lawrefrom/donor-conceived/DCP05-Sonia_Allan.pdf. Professor Allan notes a variety of different ways of marking a child's donor-conceived status, including (1) annotating the birth certificate of a donor-conceived person with his or her donor-conceived status; (2) providing a separate certificate to a donor-conceived child to let the individual know that there is more information about the child's birth status; (3) issuing dual birth certificates; or (4) placing a special code on the birth certificate. *Id.*
32. *See, e.g.,* Richard Thaler & Cass Sunstein, Nudge (2008); Dan Ariely, *3 Main Lessons of Psychology*, http://danariely.com/2008/05/05/3-main-lessons-of-psychology (last visited Aug. 3, 2011).
33. *See* Ariely, *supra* note 32.
34. *See* Dan Markel, Jennifer M. Collins & Ethan J. Leib, Privilege or Punish? Criminal Justice and the Challenge of Family Ties (2009); Jana Singer, *The Privatization of Family Law*, 1992 Wis. L. Rev. 1443 (1992).
35. *See, e.g.,* Melissa Murray, *The Networked Family: Reframing the Legal Understanding of Caregiving and Caregivers,* 94 Va. L. Rev. 385, 451-52 (2008) (discussing costs and benefits of such a proposal). Ethan Leib suggests a "'Friends and Medical Leave Act.'" *See* Ethan J. Leib, *Friendship & the Law,* 54 UCLA L. Rev. 631, 682 (2007); see also Ethan J. Leib, *Friend v. Friend: The Transformation of Friendship—and What the Law Has to Do with It* 99 (2011) (further exploration).
36. For issues involving surrogate decision making and guardianship, *see* Jerry Borison, Naomi Cahn, Susan Gary & Paula Monopoli, Contemporary Trusts and Estates Law, chapter 13 (2011).

37. *See* Angela Ferraris, *Sibling Visitation as a Fundamental Right in* Herbst v. Swan, 39 New Eng. L. Rev. 715, 744-47 (2005) (sibling association rights might affect child custody and visitation as well as the child welfare system).

38. Colo. Rev. Stat. § 15-22-105 (2009); *see* David D. Meyer, *Fragmentation and Consolidation in the Law of Marriage and Same-Sex Relationships*, 58 Am. J. Comp. L. 115 (2010).

39. For a nice accounting of how the state recognizes the rights accorded to family partners, *see Appling v. Doyle* (Wi. Cir. Ct. 2011), http://data.lambdalegal.org/in-court/downloads/appling_wi_20110620_decision-and-order.pdf.

CHAPTER 9

1. *See* Naomi Cahn, *Necessary Subjects: The Need for a Mandatory National Donor Gamete Databank,* 12 DePaul J. Health Care L. 203, 218-19 (2009).

2. Although there is relatively little literature on this in the reproductive technology world, there is a significant amount of comparable discussion in the adoption world. Anecdotal accounts in the reproductive technology world also abound, however. *See, e.g., Nightline: Making Babies, Sperm Donor Regrets* (ABC online television broadcast Sept. 1, 2006) (one sperm donor stating that "I think the people who had children who are now eighteen would want to know, did he get heart disease, did he go bald, I mean, what happened to this guy? I think the kids should be told, and I think that the donors should be told that they exist, and that they're healthy or not").

3. For further analysis of the commodification issues, *see generally* Rethinking Commodification: Cases and Readings in Law and Culture (Martha Ertman & Joan Williams eds. 2005); Baby Markets: Money and the New Politics of Creating Families (Michele Goodwin ed. 2010); Martha Ertman, *What's Wrong with a Parenthood Market? A New and Improved Theory of Commodification*, 82 N.C. L. Rev. 1, 35-36 (2003); Sonia M. Suter, *Giving In to Baby Markets: Regulation without Prohibition*, 16 Mich. J. Gender & L. 217, 275 (2009). *See, e.g.*, Ruth Ragan, Where Are My Eggs?, Motherlodes: Adventures in Parenting, July 22, 2011, http://parenting.blogs.nytimes.com/2011/07/22/an-egg-donor-responds/.

4. Judy Norsigian, *Risks to Women in Embryo Cloning*, Boston Globe, Feb. 25, 2005, at A13; *see also* Judy Norsigian, *Egg Donation for IVF and Stem Cell Research: Time to Weigh the Risks to Women's Health,* Etopia News, 2005, http://www.etopiamedia.net/empnn/pdfs/norsigian1.pdf; *see also* Barbara Seaman, *Is This Any Way to Have a Baby?*, O Mag., Feb. 2004, http://www.gilliansanson.com/articles/infertility.htm (outlining, through anecdotal evidence, the negative medical effects that women have experienced after undergoing in vitro fertilization and fertility treatments. Seaman was the cofounder of the National Women's Health Network.).

5. *See* Natalie Adsuar, Julianne E. Zweifel, Elizabeth A. Pritts, Marie A. Davidson, David L. Olive & Steven R. Lindheim, *Assessment of Wishes Regarding Disposition of Oocytes and Embryo Management among Ovum Donors in an Anonymous Egg Donation Program*, 84 Fertility & Sterility 1513, 1514 (2005).

6. *See generally* Julia Derek, Confessions of a Serial Egg Donor (2004).

7. Ruth Farrell, Susannah Baruch & Kathy Hudson, *IVF, Egg Donation, and Women's Health*, Genetics & Public Policy Center (2006), http://www.dnapolicy.org/resources/IVF_Egg_Donation_Womens_Health_final.pdf.

8. Committee on Assessing the Medical Risks of Human Oocyte Donation for Stem Cell Research, Assessing the Medical Risks of Human Oocyte Donation for Stem Cell Research: Workshop Report 18 (Linda Guidice, Eileen Santa & Robert Pool eds. 2007).

9. Advisory Group on Assisted Reproductive Technologies, Task Force on Life and the Law, New York State Dep't of Health, *Becoming an Egg Donor,* http://www.health.state.ny.us/community/reproductive_health/infertility/eggdonor.htm.

10. *See* Farrell, Baruch & Hudson, *supra* note 6.

11. *See* Practice Comm. of the Am. Soc'y for Reprod. Med., *Repetitive Oocyte Donation,* 90 Fertility & Sterility S194, S195 (2008).

12. *See* Farrell, Baruch & Hudson, *supra* note 6.

13. *See id.*

14. *See, e.g.,* Alison Venn, Lyndsey Watson, Fiona Bruinsma, Graham Giles & David Healy, *Risk of Cancer after the Use of Fertility Drugs with In-Vitro Fertilisation,* 354 Lancet 1586 (1999).

15. *See* Louise A. Brinton, Kamran S. Moghissi, Bert Scoccia, Carolyn L. Westhoff & Emmet J. Lamb, *Ovulation Induction and Cancer Risk,* 83 Fertility & Sterility 261, 262 (2005).

16. *See* Sarah B. Angel, *The Value of the Human Egg: An Analysis of Risk and Reward in Stem Cell Research,* 22 Berkeley J. Gender L. & Just. 183, 207 (2007).

17. *See* Committee on Assessing the Medical Risks of Human Oocyte Donation for Stem Cell Research: Workshop Report, *supra* note 7, at 25–26.

18. *See* Stanford University Egg Donor Information Project, *The Medical Procedure of Egg Donation* (2002), http://www.stanford.edu/class/siw198q/websites/eggdonor/procedures.html (last visited Dec. 3, 2011).

19. *See* Angel, *supra* note 15.

20. *See Repetitive Oocyte Donation, supra* note 10, at S194–95.

21. *See, e.g.,* Norsigian, *Egg Donation for IVF and Stem Cell Research, supra* note 3; Seaman, *supra* note 3; Heidi Mertes & Guido Pennings, *Oocyte Donation for Stem Cell Research,* 22 Human Reprod. 629, 630 (2007). Moreover, there are risks of coercion and exploitation. *See* Loane Skene, *Human Cloning and Stem Cell Research: Engaging in the Political Process,* 21 J. Med. & L. 119, 125 (2008).

22. *See Repetitive Oocyte Donation, supra* note 10, at S195 (also recommending that, as with sperm donors, the number of families given any one donor's eggs be limited to twenty-five per every eight hundred thousand people).

23. *See, e.g.,* Ova the Rainbow, Inc., *FAQs,* http://ovatherainbow.com/FAQs%20egg%20donors.htm (last visited Dec. 3, 2011).

24. *See generally Derek, supra* note 5.

25. Given the purpose of collecting DNA records, whether any genetic data collected would thereafter be available to offspring presents entirely different issues; certainly, non-donor-conceived offspring do not have access to such data about their parents.

26. 21 CFR § 1271.290 (2011).

27. For a comprehensive discussion, *see* Lisa M. Luetkemeyer, Note: *Who's Guarding the Henhouse and What Are They Doing with the Eggs (and Sperm)? A Call for Increased Regulation of Gamete Donation and Long-term Tracking of Donor Gametes,* 3 St. Louis U. J. Health L. & Pol'y 397, 421-24 (2010).

28. Practice Comm., ASRM & Soc'y for Assisted Reprod. Tech., *2008 Guidelines for Gamete and Embryo Donation,* 90 Fertility & Sterility S30, S35 (2008); *Repetitive Oocyte Donation, supra* note 10, at S195.

29. Eric Blyth & Lucy Frith, *Donor-Conceived People's Access to Genetic and Biographical History: An Analysis of Provisions in Different Jurisdictions Permitting Disclosure of Donor Identity,* 23 Int'l. J. Law, Policy & Fam. 174, 178-79 (2009).

30. *See, e.g.*, Naomi Cahn, *Accidental Incest: Drawing the Line—or the Curtain—for Reproductive Technology*, 32 Harv. J. Gender & L. 59 (2009).

31. *See, e.g.*, Maxine Eichner, The Supportive State: Families, Government, and America's Political Ideals 68 (2010) (discussing possibility of changing "the state's role from neutral protector of individual rights to active supporter of caretaking and human development").

32. *2008 Guidelines, supra* note 28. For example, they provide that donors "[s]hould not have any significant familial disease with a major genetic component." *Id.* at S44.

33. Charles A. Sims et al., *Genetic Testing of Sperm Donors: Survey of Current Practices*, 94 Fertility & Sterility 126 (2010).

34. *Id.* at 127.

35. N.H. Rev. Stat. Ann. §168-B:10 (2011).

36. Susan Donaldson James, *Sperm Donor's 24 Kids Never Told about Fatal Illness*, ABC News, July 21, 2011, http://abcnews.go.com/Health/sperm-donors-24-children-told-fatal-illness-medical/story?id=14115344; Bonnie Rochman, *Where Do (Some) Babies Come From? In Washington, a New Law Bans Anonymous Sperm and Egg Donors*, Time, July 22, 2011, http://healthland.time.com/2011/07/22/where-do-some-babies-come-from-in-washington-a-new-law-bans-anonymous-sperm-and-egg-donors/print/#ixzz1fUtrNj5V.

37. *See* Michael L. Eisenberg et al., *Perceived Negative Consequences of Donor Gametes from Male and Female Members of Infertile Couples*, 94 Fertility & Sterility 921, 926 (2010). For example, women believed that using donor eggs would be more emotionally stressful than using donor sperm, and men believed that both would be emotionally stressful (although they believed donor sperm would be more stressful). *Id.* at 924.

38. The Senate Legal and Constitutional Affairs References Committee, *Donor Conception Practices in Australia* 60-61 (2011), http://www.aph.gov.au/senate/committee/legcon_ctte/donor_conception/report/report.pdf.

39. Kate Kelland, *Unequal Access Drives Fertility Tourism, Experts Say*, Reuters UK, Sept. 14, 2010, http://uk.reuters.com/article/2010/09/13/health-us-fertility-tourism-idUKTRE68C57P20100913.

40. *Id.*

41. NCSL, *State Laws Related to Insurance Coverage for Infertility Treatment* (2011), http://www.ncsl.org/default.aspx?tabid=14391.

42. Iva Skoch, *Should IVF Be Affordable to All?* Newsweek, July 21, 2010, http://www.newsweek.com/2010/07/20/should-ivf-be-affordable-for-all.html.

43. Report of the Committee of Inquiry into Human Fertilisation and Embryology 26–27 (1984).

44. *Id.* at 26. The commission recommended ongoing review of whether ten was the appropriate number. *Id.* at 27.

45. *See* Human Fertilisation Embryology Authority, *Using Donated Sperm, Eggs, or Embryos: The HFEA Guide to Infertility* 29, 31 (2007-2008), http://www.hfea.gov.uk/docs/Guide2.pdf (last visited Nov. 21, 2008).

46. *See* Howard W. Jones Jr. & Jean Cohen, *IFFS Surveillance 07*, 87 Fertility & Sterility S1, S28 (2007), http://www.iffs-reproduction.org/documents/surveillance_07.pdf.

47. *See* Ella Lee, *Database to Track Sperm and Offspring; Records Kept to Avoid Incest, Unethical Acts*, S. China Morning Post, Feb. 13, 2008, at 3.

48. *See* Jones & Cohen, *supra* note 46, at S31.

49. *In re Marriage Cases*, 43 Cal. 4th 757, 829 n.52 (Cal. 2008) (emphasis added).

50. The state's interests—other than disgust—are discussed later in this article. For further discussion of the constitutional implications, *see* Brett H. McDonnell, *Is Incest Next?* 10 Cardozo J. L. & Gender 337, 350-52 (2004).

51. The definition of "family" is highly contested. *See, e.g.,* Note, *Inbred Obscurity: Improving Incest Laws in the Shadow of the "Sexual Family,"* 119 Harvard L. Rev. 2464, 2483 (2006). Here, I am referring to intergenerational relationships of caretaking.

52. *See Clark v. Jeter*, 486 U.S. 456, 461 (1988) ("To withstand intermediate scrutiny, a statutory classification must be substantially related to an important governmental objective."); *Vance v. Bradley*, 440 U.S. 93, 97 (1979) (Applying rational basis review, the court said, "[W]e will not overturn such a statute unless the varying treatment of different groups or persons is so unrelated to the achievement of any combination of legitimate purposes that we can only conclude that the legislature's actions were irrational.").

53. This formulation is based on *Inbred Obscurity, supra* note 51, at 2484 ("The determination whether two people were 'family members' [subject to the incest law] would be an inquiry into whether there was a natural dependency relationship involved.").

54. Some members of the Supreme Court have questioned the parameters of the constitutional right to privacy. *See, e.g., Lawrence*, 539 U.S. at 593 (Scalia, J., dissenting) (emphasizing that while laws infringing on *fundamental* liberty interests are subject to strict scrutiny under substantive due process jurisprudence, fundamental rights are limited to those "deeply rooted in this Nation's history and tradition"; all other liberty interests may be infringed by valid state laws that are rationally related to a legitimate state interest). Therefore, even if incest falls within the right to privacy, the right to privacy may fall outside the scope of substantive due process fundamental interest protections.

55. For one suggestion, *see, e.g.,* Joanna L. Grossman, *The Consequences of* Lawrence v. Texas, FindLaw's Writ, July 8, 2003, http://writ.news.findlaw.com/grossman/20030708. html (suggesting that bans on marriage between adoptive siblings who share no genes and who are similar in age or between cousins might be suspect under *Lawrence's* privacy analysis).

56. For differing perspectives on the applicability of a privacy analysis to issues of restricting choices within the reproductive technology world, such as by limiting the freedom of donors to sell gametes as frequently as they would like, the freedom of numerous consumers to purchase the one "best" donor, and the freedom of fertility clinics and banks to buy and sell without limits, *see, e.g.,* Michele Goodwin, Black Markets: The Supply and Demand of Body Parts (2006); Radhika Rao, *Equal Liberty: Assisted Reproductive Technology and Reproductive Equality*, 76 Geo. Wash. L. Rev. 1457 (2008); I. Glenn Cohen, *The Constitution and the Rights Not to Procreate*, 60 Stan. L. Rev. 1135 (2008); John A. Robertson, *Procreative Liberty in the Era of Genomics*, 29 Am. J.L. & Med. 439 (2003); Cass Sunstein, *Is There a Constitutional Right to Clone?* 53 Hastings L.J. 987, 994 (2002) ("[N]one of this means that there is a presumptive right to do whatever might be done to increase the likelihood of having, or not having, a child."); Radhika Rao, *Reconceiving Privacy: Relationships and Reproductive Technology*, 45 UCLA L. Rev. 1077, 1083–84 (1998).

57. *See Repetitive Oocyte Donation, supra* note 10, at S194.

58. *Nightline: Making Babies, Sperm Donor Regrets, supra* note 1.

59. *See, e.g.,* Staff Editorial, *Incest: A Needed Taboo,* Daily Targum, Jan. 24, 2008.

60. *2008 Guidelines, supra* note 28, at S36.

61. Zosia Bielski, *Sperm Shortage Possible after Landmark Decision,* Globe and Mail (Can.), Nov. 13, 2008, at L5; Denise Grady, *Shortage of Sperm Donors in Britain Prompts Call for Change,* N.Y. Times, Nov. 12, 2008, at A10; James Randerson, *Shortage Brings Call to Let Sperm Donors Father More Children,* The Guardian, Nov. 12, 2008, at 13.

62. *See* Judith Graham, *When a Disease Is Donated: Mom's Quest to Warn Daughter's Offspring Goes to the Heart of a Thorny Debate on Sperm, Egg Donors,* Chi. Trib., March 27, 2008, at C1. For further discussion of observed links between unlimited sperm donations and disease transmission, *see* Emily Bazelon, *The Children of Donor X,* O, The Oprah Magazine, Aug. 2008, http://www.oprah.com/relationships/Autism-Aspergers-and-The-Donor-Sibling-Registry (discussing the transmission of autism); Denise Grady, *As the Use of Donor Sperm Increases, Secrecy Can Be a Health Hazard,* N.Y. Times, June 6, 2006, at F6.

63. *Swedish Women Warned over Danish Sperm,* The Local (Sweden), May 31, 2011, http://www.thelocal.se/34102/20110531; *Nine Children Conceived with Donated Sperm Found to Have a Neurological Disease,* Helsingin Sanomat (International Edition), http://www.hs.fi/english/article/Nine+children+conceived+with+donated+sperm+found+to+have+a+neurological+disease/1135266584832 (last visited June 3, 2011).

64. *See 2008 Guidelines, supra* note 28, at S35.

65. *See id.*

66. *2008 Guidelines, supra* note 28, at S35. Although this recommendation is focused on sperm donors, the ASRM has made the same recommendation for egg donors. *See Repetitive Oocyte Donation, supra* note 10, at S194.

67. For a discussion of the federal regulations applicable to sperm banks and egg clinics, *see* chapter 1.

68. *See id.*

69. There have been several reported cases of embryos that were mistakenly implanted in the wrong woman, for example. *See* Leslie Bender, *Genes, Parents, and Assisted Reproductive Technologies: ARTs, Mistakes, Sex, Race & Law,* 12 Colum. J. Gender & L. 1 (2003); Leslie Bender, *"To Err Is Human": ART Mix-Ups; A Labor-Based, Relational Proposal,* 9 J. Gender Race & Just. 443 (2006) (focusing on ART-related mix-ups).

70. *See* Bender, *"To Err Is Human," supra* note 69, at 486 (discussing a new approach to deciding parentage where there has been a mix-up because other alternatives "do not work"). For someone who has had the wrong embryo implanted, monetary damages are a poor substitute for the desired result.

71. *See 2008 Guidelines, supra* note 28 (using eight hundred thousand as a baseline population for determining limits on donation to avoid inadvertent consanguinity).

72. The Donor Sibling Registry, as discussed earlier, facilitates mutually desired contact and connections between donor-conceived individuals, their families, and their donors, and provides education and support, including by hosting various discussion groups. See *The Donor Sibling Registry,* https://www.donorsiblingregistry.com/ (last visited Sept. 24, 2012).

73. *See* P. M. W. Janssens, *Spreading of Hereditary Diseases through Donor Sperm: Not a Reason for Reducing the Number of Offspring per Donor in the Netherlands,* 146 Ned Tijdschr voor Geneeskd 1215 (2002).

74. *See* Eric Blyth and Marilyn Crawshaw, *"Think of a Number, Then Double It": Playing a Numbers Game with Donor Conception,* Bionews, Nov. 24, 2008, http://www.bionews.org.uk/page_38032.asp.

75. *See* Human Fertilisation & Embryology Authority, *For Donor-Conceived People,* http://www.hfea.gov.uk/en/1183.html#can_i_find_out_if_there_are_other_donor_conceived_people_who_are_genetically_related_to_me (last visited Nov. 23, 2008).

CHAPTER 10

1. Jamie Grifo, *Room for Debate: A Rush to Pass Laws,* N.Y. Times, Sept. 13, 2011, http://www.nytimes.com/roomfordebate/2011/09/13/making-laws-about-making-babies/well-intentioned-regulators-can-harm-patients.

2. For an information-privacy analysis of donors' interests, *see, e.g.,* Sunni Yuen, Comment: *An Information Privacy Approach to Regulating the Middlemen in the Lucrative Gametes Market,* 2 U. Pa. J. Intl . L. 527 (2007).

3. For a discussion of these remedies, *see, e.g.,* Shahar Lifshitz, *Married against Their Will? Toward a Pluralist Recognition of Spousal Relationships,* 66 Wash. & Lee L. Rev. 1565 (2009).

4. *See, e.g.,* Naomi Cahn & June Carbone, Red Families v. Blue Families: Legal Polarization and the Creation of Culture (2010) (discussing the changes in the American family and calculation of the divorce rate).

5. Laura Kessler, *Community Parenting,* 24 Wash U. J.L. & Pol'y 47, 73 (2007).

6. Charles A. Sims*, Room for Debate: A Private-Sector Problem,* N.Y. Times, Sept. 13, 2011, http://www.nytimes.com/roomfordebate/2011/09/13/making-laws-about-making-babies/the-fertility-industry-can-solve-donor-concerns.

7. *See* Judith F. Daar, *Accessing Reproductive Technologies: Invisible Barriers, Indelible Harms,* 23 Berkeley J. Gender L. & Just. 18, 51- 54 (2008); Vanessa L. Pi, Note: *Regulating Sperm Donation: Why Requiring Exposed Donation Is Not the Answer,* 16 Duke J. Gender L. & Pol'y 379, 381, 395 (2009); Stephanie N. Sivinski, Note: *Putting Too Many (Fertilized) Eggs in One Basket: Methods of Reducing Multifetal Pregnancies in the United States,* 88 Tex. L. Rev. 897, 908-9 (2010); *see generally* John Robertson, *Assisting Reproduction, Choosing Genes, and the Scope of Reproductive Freedom,* 76 Geo. Wash. L. Rev. 1490 (2008).

8. *See* Gaia Bernstein, *The Socio-Legal Acceptance of New Technologies: A Close Look at Artificial Insemination,* 77 Wash. L. Rev. 1035, 1056 (2002).

9. *See, e.g.,* Eric Blyth & Lucy Frith, *The UK's Gamete Donor "Crisis": A Critical Analysis,* 28 Critical Soc. Pol'y 74 (2008); Neroli Sawyer, *Who's Keeping Count? The Need for Regulation Is a Relative Matter,* 92 Fertility & Sterility 1811 (2009).

10. *See* Eric D. Blyth, Lucy Frith & Abigail Farrand, *Is It Possible to Recruit Gamete Donors Who Are Both Altruistic and Identifiable?* 84 Fertility & Sterility (Supp. 1) S21 (2005), http://www.sciencedirect.com.

11. *See* June Carbone & Paige Gottheim, *Markets, Subsidies, Regulation, and Trust: Building Ethical Understandings into the Market for Fertility Services,* 9 J. Gender, Race & Just. 509, 540 (2006); K. Daniels & O. Lalos, *The Swedish Insemination Act and Availability of Donors,* 10 Hum. Reprod. 1871 (1995).

12. Carbone & Gottheim, *supra* note 11.

13. K. Daniels & O. Lalos, *supra* note 11; F. Shenfield, *Privacy versus Disclosure in Gamete Donation: A Clash of Interest, of Duties, or an Exercise in Responsibility?* 14 J. Assisted

Reprod, & Genetics 371 (1997); A. Lalos, K. Daniels, C. Gottlieb & O. Lalos, *Recruitment and Motivation of Semen Providers in Sweden*, 18 Hum. Reprod. 212 (2003).

14. *See* Bernstein, *supra* note 8. Where payment is allowed, the sperm business functions like other market commodities. *See, e.g.*, Kimberly Krawiec, *Sunny Samaritans and Egomaniacs: Price-Fixing in the Gamete Market*, 72 Law & Contemp. Probs. 59 (2009). Restricting anonymity, but not payment, might affect both supply and demand, but would probably result in higher prices for sperm.

15. Shenfield, *supra* note 13, at 371. Other scholars affirm the idea that drop-offs in donations may occur, but need not be permanent. *See* Sonia M. Suter, *Giving In to Baby Markets: Regulation without Prohibition*, 16 Mich. J. Gender & L. 217, 275 (2009) ("A period of readjustment might be necessary as we make the cultural shift toward greater openness.").

16. *See* Rebecca Camber, *Britain Faces Fertility Crisis as Loss of Donor Anonymity Sees Sperm and Egg Donor Numbers Plummet*, The Daily Mail, June 26, 2008, http://www.dailymail.co.uk/health/article-1029712/Britain-faces-fertility-crisis-loss-donor-anonymity-sees-sperm-egg-donor-numbers-plummet.html.

17. HFEA, *Who Are the Donors? An HFEA Analysis of Donor Registrations and Use of Donor Gametes Over the Last 10 Years* 2 (2005), http://www.hfea.gov.uk/docs/Who_are_the_donors_factsheet.pdf.

18. *See* Posting by wendykr, *Banning Egg and Sperm Donor Anonymity Does Not Result in a Drop of Donors* (Feb. 13, 2012), http://www.donorsiblingregistry.com/blog/?p=359; Marie Woolf, *Sperm Bank Asks Rival Football Fans to Lend a Hand*, Sunday Times, Jan. 10, 2010, at 13; Kate Foster, *Scots Giving Sperm . . . to Get Their Oats*, Daily Star, March 19, 2010, at 22; Human Fertilisation & Embryology Authority, *New Donor Registrations*, http://www.hfea.gov.uk/3411.html (last modified July 21, 2009) (reporting on new sperm and egg donor registrations).

19. Liza Mundy, *Shortage? What Shortage? How the Sperm Donor Debate Missed Its Mark*, Sept. 19, 2010, http://www.guardian.co.uk/commentisfree/2010/sep/19/sperm-donors-shortage-market-forces.

20. Posting by wendykr, *Banning Egg and Sperm Donor Anonymity Does Not Result in a Drop of Donors*, Feb. 12, 2012, http://www.donorsiblingregistry.com/blog/?p=359.

21. Sarah Guy, *Sperm, Smoking, Screening, and More*, BioNews, July 11, 2011, http://www.bionews.org.uk/page_101473.asp.

22. *Id.* Figures from the British Human Fertilisation and Embryology Authority show that numbers on new donors have gone up almost every year since the new law went into effect, keeping pace with or exceeding the yearly rate of increase before the implementation of the law. Mundy, *supra* note 19.

23. Blyth et al., *supra* note 9.

24. HFEA, *Fertility Regulator Launches Strategy to Boost Egg and Sperm Donation*, April 4, 2012, http://www.hfea.gov.uk/7142.html.

25. *See, e.g.*, Ken Daniels, *Anonymity and Openness and the Recruitment of Gamete Donors: Part I*, 10 Human Fertility 151 (2007); Lucy Frith, Eric Blyth & Abigail Farrand, *UK Gamete Donors' Reflections on the Removal of Anonymity: Implications for Recruitment*, 22 Human Rep. 1675 (2007).

26. *Sperm Donor Crisis: Researchers Find Sharp Fall Requires Urgent New Recruitment Strategies* (Nov. 10, 2005), http://www.oxfordjournals.org/eshre/press-release/nov051.pdf (quoting Dr. Jane Stewart).

27. Joanna E. Scheib & Alice Ruby, *Contact among Families Who Share the Same Sperm Donor*, 90 Fertility & Sterility 33, 18 (2008).

28. "Sperm Donor Shortage Hits Canadian Fertility Clinics," *CBC News* (Dec. 19, 2006), http://www.cbc.ca/health/story/2006/12/19/sperm-shortage.html.

29. *See* Debora L. Spar, *As You Like It: Exploring the Limits of Parental Choice in Assisted Reproduction*, 27 Law & Ineq. 481, 491 (2009) (noting that adoption requires some entity to "deem[] that the parent is fit and that the proposed adoption is in the best interests of the child. . . . The underlying principle, however, could easily be extended into the realm of assisted reproduction.").

30. *See, e.g.*, Ken R. Daniels & Darel J. Hall, *Semen Donor Recruitment Strategies: A Non-Payment-Based Approach*, 12 Hum. Reprod. 2230 (1997).

31. *See* Naomi Cahn & Jana Singer, *Adoption, Identity, and the Constitution: The Case for Opening Closed Records*, 2 U. Pa. J. Const. L. 150, 187 (1999).

32. *See, e.g.*, Martha Ertman, *What's Wrong with a Parenthood Market? A New and Improved Theory of Commodification*, 82 N.C. L. Rev. 1, 35-36 (2003); Katherine M. Franke, *The Domesticated Liberty of* Lawrence v. Texas, 104 Colum. L. Rev. 1399, 1419 (2004); Katherine M. Franke, *Longing for* Loving, 76 Fordham L. Rev. 2685, 2688 (2008).

33. Franke, *Longing for* Loving, *supra* note 34, at 2703.

34. Emily Galpern, *Assisted Reproductive Technologies: Overview and Perspectives Using a Reproductive Justice Framework*, Reproductive Health and Human Rights, Gender and Justice Program, Center for Genetics and Society, Oakland, CA (Dec. 2007), http://www.geneticsandsociety.org/downloads/ART.pdf; *see* Elizabeth Marquardt, principal investigator, *The Revolution in Parenthood: The Emerging Global Clash between Adult Rights and Children's Needs*, Institute for American Values (2006), http://www.americanvalues.org/pdfs/parenthood.pdf (last visited Feb. 25, 2012) (calling for a five-year moratorium).

35. Elizabeth Marquardt, Norval D. Glenn & Karen Clark, *My Daddy's Name Is Donor: A New Study of Young Adults Conceived through Sperm Donation* 21, 78 (2010), http://www.familyscholars.org/assets/Donor_FINAL.pdf.

36. *Goals*, Institute for American Values, http://www.americanvalues.org/intro/index.php#goals (last visited Feb. 25, 2012).

37. Vince Londini, *My Daddy's Name Is Adoption*, May 16, 2011, http://www.bionews.org.uk/page_93262.asp.

38. Radhika Rao, *Equal Liberty: Assisted Reproductive Technology and Reproductive Equality*, 76 Geo. Wash. L. Rev. 1457, 1475-76 (2008).

39. *E.g.*, Md. INSURANCE Code Ann. § 15-810 (2011); Bebe J. Anderson, *Lesbians, Gays, and People Living with HIV: Facing and Fighting Barriers to Assisted Reproduction*, 15 Card. J. L. & Gender 451, 460-61 (2009).

40. Andrea D. Gurmankin et al., *Screening Practices and Beliefs of Assisted Reproductive Technology Programs*, 83 Fertility & Sterility 61, 65 (2005).

41. *Same-Sex Couples Given Equal IVF Rights*, Nursing Times, April 6, 2009, http://www.nursingtimes.net/whats-new-in-nursing/primary-care/same-sex-couples-given-equal-ivf-rights/5000272.article.

42. *North Coast Women's Care Med. Group v. San Diego Cty. Sup. Ct.*, 189 P.3d 959, 963 (Cal. 2008); *see* Sumeet Ajmani, North Coast Women's Care: *California's Still-Undefined Standard for Protecting Religious Freedom*, 97 Cal. L. Rev. 1867 (2009) ("In

a landmark ruling, the California Supreme Court recently held that clinic physicians may not deny lesbians access to fertility treatment on the grounds that the procedure violated the physicians' religious beliefs").

43. *See* Katherine Franke, *The Domesticated Liberty of* Lawrence v. Texas, 104 Colum. L. Rev. 1399, 1419-20, 1424 (2004).

44. I credit this argument to my colleague, Dan Solove.

45. Todd Essig, *Balancing the Rights of Donor Offspring with Those of Donors: But What about Parents?* Forbes, June 30, 2011, http://blogs.forbes.com/toddessig/2011/06/30/balancing-the-rights-of-donor-offspring-with-those-of-donors-but-what-about-parents.

46. I. Glenn Cohen, *Regulating Reproduction: The Problem with Best Interests*, 96 Minn. L. Rev. 423 (2011); I. Glenn Cohen, *Intentional Diminishment, the Non-Identity Problem, and Legal Liability*, 60 Hastings L.J. 347 (2008).

47. See *I. Glenn Cohen, Rethinking Sperm Donor Anonymity: Of Changed Selves, Nonidentity, and One-Night Stands*, 100 Geo. L.J. 431, 435 (2012).

48. *Id.*

49. *See* Cohen, *Regulating Reproduction, supra* note 48, at 426 ("[T]he protection of the best interests of existing children serves as a powerful organizing principle that justifies state intervention" in other aspects of family law).

50. *See* Amartya Sen, Development as Freedom 144 (2000); Women, Culture, and Development: A Study of Human Capabilities (Martha C. Nussbaum & Jonathan Glover eds. 1995); Amartya Sen, Choice, Welfare and Measurement 30-31 (1982); *see also* Maxine Eichner, *Dependency and the Liberal Polity: On Martha Fineman's* The Autonomy Myth, 93 Calif. L. Rev. 1285, 1316 (2005) (book review) ("The state's responsibility to protect the well-being of dependents has a special corollary when it comes to children: an intrinsic part of ensuring their well-being involves ensuring that they have adequate conditions to develop their basic capabilities.").

51. Martha Nussbaum, *Human Rights and Human Capabilities*, 20 Harv. Hum. Rts. J. 21, 23 (2007).

52. Elizabeth Marquardt, *On Gratitude for One's Existence*, FamilyScholars.org (May 22, 2010), http://familyscholars.org/2010/05/22/on-gratitude-for-ones-existence.

53. *Pratten*, para. 253 (p. 83).

54. *See* Sonia M. Suter, *Giving In to Baby Markets: Regulation without Prohibition*, 16 Mich. J. Gender & L. 217, 276 (2009).

55. This objection might be resolved by allowing intending parents and donors to choose an open-identity option so that they retain the possibility of connection, by allowing a market in which both disclosure and nondisclosure are available. This does not, however, protect existing children who seek disclosure if they are born to parents who have opted against disclosure; it (somewhat paternalistically) denies that intent might change over time; and, critically, it suggests that, apart, perhaps, from a child's interests, there is no other conceivable state interest in mandating disclosure. My thanks to Professor Cohen for helping me sharpen this argument.

56. Frank Newport, *For First Time, Majority of Americans Favor Gay Marriage*, May 20, 2011, http://www.gallup.com/poll/147662/first-time-majority-americans-favor-legal-gay-marriage.aspx.

57. *See* Seana Valentine Shiffrin, *Wrongful Life, Procreative Responsibility, and the Significance of Harm*, 5 Legal Theory 117, 119-20 (1999).

58. While the corollary—that no one is harmed if he or she is brought into existence with a life worth living—is also true, *see* Cohen, *Regulating Reproduction, supra* note 47, this returns us to the first argument of how to maximize the lives of people, including children, parents, and donors, currently in existence. The comparison, once they are living, is not with nonexistence but with others who are living. *See, e.g., Pratten* (striking down distinction between donor conceived and adoptees with respect to knowledge of their genetic background).

59. Ariela R. Dubler, *Sexing* Skinner: *History and the Politics of the Right to Marry*, 110 Colum. L. Rev. 1348, 1359 (2010) (suggesting how *Skinner* can be read as a case about "disentangling sex from reproduction and the social anxieties raised by that separation"); Cass R. Sunstein, *Is There a Constitutional Right to Clone?* 53 Hastings L.J. 987, 993–94 (2002) (describing ambiguity in Supreme Court jurisprudence on procreational rights relating to reproductive technology); Sonia M. Suter, *The "Repugnance" Lens of* Gonzales v. Carhart *and Other Theories of Reproductive Rights: Evaluating Advanced Reproductive Technologies*, 76 Geo. Wash. L. Rev. 1514, 1520–27 (2008); Elyse Whitney Grant, Note: *Assessing the Constitutionality of Reproductive Technologies Regulation: A Bioethical Approach*, 61 Hastings L.J. 997 (2010).

60. *See* Radhika Rao, *Conflicting Interests in Reproductive Autonomy and Their Impact on New Reproductive Technologies*, 76 Geo. Wash. L. Rev. 1457 (2008); *but see* John A. Robertson, *Liberty, Identity, and Human Cloning*, 76 Tex. L. Rev. 1371, 1441 (1998).

61. Laura Beauvais-Godwin and Raymond Godwin, The Complete Adoption Book: Everything You Need to Know to Adopt a Child 36-37 (2005).

62. Kate Benson, *Fertility Law Change Puts Spotlight on Donors*, Sydney Morning Herald (Australia), Feb. 25, 2009, at 9, http://www.smh.com.au/national/fertility-law-change-puts-spotlight-on-donors-20090224-8guk.html.

63. *See* Cheryl Shuler, Sperm Donor=Dad: A Single Woman's Story of Creating a Family with an Unknown Donor (2010). This was an argument in the adoption context as well. *See* Jeanne A. Howard et al., *For the Records II: An Examination of the History and Impact of Adult Adoptee Access to Original Birth Certificates*, Evan B. Donaldson Adoption Institute (Adam Pertman ed., July 2010), http://www.adoptioninstitute.org/publications/7_14_2010_ForTheRecordsII.pdf.

64. This is another aspect of their difference from other types of families; while you typically choose your adult partner, you do not choose your children—or your parents.

65. Madelyn Freundlich, *For the Records: Restoring a Right to Adult Adoptees* 18-19 (2007), http://www.adoptioninstitute.org/publications/2007_11_For_Records.pdf; *For the Records II, supra* note 65.

66. *See, e.g.*, Dena Shehab et al., *How Parents Whose Children Have Been Conceived with Donor Gametes Make Their Disclosure Decision: Contexts, Influences, and Couple Dynamics*, 89 Fertility& Sterility 189, 193 (2008) (fear of disrupting relationship); Dorothy A. Greenfield & Susan Caruso Klock, *Disclosure Decisions among Known and Anonymous Oocyte Donation Recipients*, 81Fertility& Sterility 1565, 1567 (2004) (women who chose anonymous donors did so to prevent the donor from interfering with their parenting decisions): Susan Caruso Klock & Dorothy A. Greenfield, *Parents' Knowledge about the Donors and Their Attitudes toward Disclosure in Oocyte Donation*, 19 Hum. Reprod. 1675 (2004) (discussing parental concerns that child will become alienated from nongenetic parent); Mundy, *supra* note 22, at 183 (discussing fathers' discomfort with telling child about donor conception).

67. This has certainly been true in the adoption context, where similar fears have been expressed. *See For the Records II, supra* note 65. And, in adoptions that have allowed contact between the birth parents and the adoptive family, there are few regrets. *E.g.*, Harold D. Grotevant et al., *Many Faces of Openness in Adoption: Perspectives of Adopted Adolescents and Their Parents*, 10 Adoption Q. 1544 (2008) (on file with author).

68. *See, e.g.*, Alison Motluk, *Anonymous Sperm Donor Traced on Internet*, New Scientist, Nov. 5, 2005, at 6, http://www.newscientist.com/article/mg18825244.200; Alison Smith-Squire, *Daddy Not Included*, Daily Mail, Mar. 19, 2009 (as a result of DNA test, woman found out she had two half-siblings, and ultimately was able to trace her sperm donor); Elizabeth E. Joh, *Reclaiming "Abandoned" DNA: The Fourth Amendment and Genetic Privacy*, 100 Nw. U. L. Rev. 857 (2006) (describing forms of involuntary genetic testing).

69. *See, e.g.*, Theresa M. Erickson, Surrogacy and Embryo, Sperm & Egg Donation: What Were you Thinking? Considering IVF & Third-Party Reproduction 50-51 (2010).

70. For examples in the adoption context, *see, e.g.*, Ala. Code § 22-9A-12(c)-(d) (2010) (contact preference form); Me. Rev. Stat. Tit. 22, §§ 2765; 2768 (2010); Tenn. Code Ann. § 36-1-128 (2010) (availability of no-contact form). The forms typically provide the opportunity to indicate a preference for contact, contact with an intermediary, or no contact.

71. Daniel Solove, *The Virtues of Knowing Less: Justifying Privacy Protections against Disclosure*, 53 Duke L.J. 967, 1065 (2003).

72. *See* Daniel J. Solove, *A Taxonomy of Privacy*, 154 U. Pa. L. Rev. 477, 532–35 (2006).

73. *Doe v. Sundquist*, 943 F. Supp. 886, 893 (M.D. Tenn. 1996), aff'd 106 F.2d 702 (6th Cir. 1997).

74. And, as discussed in the text, the no-contact forms can provide protection against unwanted communications.

75. *See* Judith Daar, *Accessing Reproductive Technologies: Invisible Barriers, Indelible Harms*, 23 Berkeley J. Gender L. & Just. 18, 23-24 (2008) (discussing "functional" and "structural" infertility).

76. I am frequently privy to conversations involving precisely these issues. The Donor Sibling Registry Yahoo! discussion group also provides a forum for such discussions.

INDEX

Numbers in italics refer to figures.

Adoption: ART and, 107–13, 115–16, 169; attitude changes towards, 110; as biological family substitute, 111–12; birth parent's rights in, 176; as challenge to conventional family, 4; child's rights in, 4, 111, 130; confidential intermediary system in, 113; confidentiality and, 111–13; connection and self-knowledge need in, 109–10, 112; in current form, 107; disclosure in, 110, 111, 112–13, 114, 116, 132; donor-conceived families compared to, 4, 67–68, 69–71, 107–17, 145; donor gamete confidentiality informed by, 116; donor imagined by children of, 56–57; donor rights compared to, 176; as donor world regulation model, 107–8, 132, 143, 170; incest and, 108; legal oversight in, 108, 110, 111, 112–13; mutual voluntary registries in, 112–13; nature of, 4; privacy rights in, 179; regulatory systems for, 108; states with open record policies, 112; surrogacy and, 108; UPA and, 94, 95

Aging, 15

Agreements, 50, 147, 149

AI. *See* Artificial insemination

Allan, Sonia, 141

Almeling, Rene, 28, 82–83

Altruism: in egg donors, 28, 29; money and, 44

American Board of Obstetrics and Gynecology, 23

American Board of Urology, 23

American Society for Reproductive Medicine (ASRM), 21; counseling recommended by, 152; disclosure recommendations of, 65, 117, 140; donor offspring limits from, 160, 161; donor payment guidelines, 40; egg donor health risks from, 153–54;

fertility industry self-regulation through, 27, 109, 155; genetic test standards of, 155; price-fixing claim against, 40–41

Anonymity: banning, 173; countries abolishing, 168; donor, 1, 28, 51, 52, 54, 56, 57–58, 86, 115, 161, 167–70, 172–73, 175, 177; donor sperm and, 25, 111; donor supply and, 167–70; egg and sperm donor, 168–69; gametes and, 54; infertility stigma fostering, 174–75; law addressing, 91; media story on, 5; technology ending, 79, 178. *See also* Disclosure; Donor gamete confidentiality; Donor identity disclosure; *specific topics*

ART. *See* Assisted reproductive technology

Artificial insemination (AI), 111

ASRM. *See* American Society for Reproductive Medicine

Assisted reproductive technology (ART): access expanded to, 157–58; adoption and, 107–13, 115–16, 169; confidentiality in, 113–17; constitutional right to, 175; cost of, 14; as cultural ideology signal, 59; cycle types, *17*; data collection involving, 155; donor egg cycle usage by age, *19*; family altered by, 33; Federal Department of Health and Human Services overseeing, 151–52; genetic testing for, 156; growth of, 14, 18; income and, 16; kinship altered by, 33, 50; morality driving, 125–26; non-donor techniques of, 7; parent over child interests in, 169; private nature of, 111; regulation of, 108–9, 125–27, 135–36, 171; reporting requirements for, 24; uniform standards lacking for, 24, 108–9. *See also* Donor law; Donor world, proposed regulation of; In vitro fertilization

constitutional and family law inclusion
of, 133–36, 148, 181, 182; defining, 1, 3;
disclosure in, 62, 64–66, 68–71, 110–17,
145; equal treatment in law for, 127,
183; friendship justifying, 37–38; IAV
opposition to, 171; identity interests of,
129–31; incest and, 108, 117–21; information sharing in, 154–55; law for, 3, 4, 36,
91–105, 128–29; nature of, 2; parenting in, conventional compared to, 68;
privacy rights of, 177–79; psychological
health of, 68; recombinant, 33; relational
interest for, 151, 181, 182; third-party
gametes creating, 2, 4; types of, 2, 62–63,
75. See also Connections, creating
Donor-conceived families and communities, proposed rights of: designated
beneficiaries as model for, 149; explicit
agreements for, 149; among families,
148–50; in family law, 133–36, 148, 181,
182; family status recognized as, 148–49;
IAV opposition to, 171; intent as deciding factor in, 150; non-specificity in
regulation for, 171–72; "opt-in" nature of,
148, 149, 150; privacy rights and, 177–79;
regulation as interference in, 170, 171–72;
relational interest in, 151, 181, 182; sibling
association as, 149
Donor-conceived family community,
177; analogies for, 164–65; benefits of,
81, 86; challenges of, 84; connection
searching in, 71–72, 73, 81–87; contact
variations in, 84–85, 87, 178; donors
in, 86; extended family feeling in, 85;
family compared to, 164, 165–66, 182;
family defined in, 2–3, 84–85; genes
role in, 52, 84; language framing, 9;
law for acceptance of, 128–29, 166–67;
media portrayal of, 83; recombinant, 33;
rights framework for, 164–65; 66 Club
as, 85; state law recognition of, 134–35;
stories involving, 86–87; technologically
focused regulation for, 165; third-party
gametes and, 2–3. See also Connection
registry; Donor-sibling family
Donor-conceived people: book about,
61, 62; capabilities right of, 173–74;

conception disclosure impact on, 68–71,
174–75; connection need for, 61–62, 70,
76, 109–10, 133, 166; connection searching by, 2, 5, 74–87; extended family
feeling in, 85; genetic connection for,
61–62, 76; half-siblings and, 98–99, 103;
language framing, 8–9; parents for, biological and legal, 57–58; secrecy for, 13,
63–64, 69–70; self-knowledge need of,
61–62, 64, 70, 74–75, 109–10, 130; sibling
contact rating of, 82; stigma faced by, 57
Donor-conceived people, rights of: disclosure, 68–71, 111, 113–17, 129–31, 144–45,
174–75; identity interest, 129–31; law in,
93–94, 103, 113–17; legal focus on, 135–36;
parental rights versus, 145, 146–47;
sibling, 103
Donor conception, 67
Donor conception disclosure: in Australia,
146; donor-conceived people right to,
144–45; through HFEA, 146; methods
for, 146; requiring, 145
Donor eggs: ART cycle usage of, 19; family
created from, 59; fresh versus frozen,
21–22, 25; identified, 21; preference for,
16–17, 18; secrecy involving, 110; statistics, 21; usefulness of, 18
Donor gamete confidentiality, 117; adoption
law as model for, 116; court cases involving, 114–15; landmark case involving,
115–16; marital presumption in, 114–15;
sources for, 113; UPA and, 113–14
Donor gametes. See Donor, egg and sperm
Donor identity disclosure, 116–17, 130, 131–
32, 133, 139, 140, 142, 174–75; in federal
law, 114–15, 129; marital presumption
and, 114–15; privacy rights and, 177–79;
registry, national and mandatory, for,
140, 142; registry, voluntary retrospective, 143; in state law, 129; supply and,
167–68, 169, 170
Donor insemination (DI): first journal
addressing, 20; first use of, 14
Donor law, 3; donor obligations and,
147–48; donor rights in, 94, 95–96, 109;
education and counseling requirement
in, 7; family relationships defined in,

Naomi Cahn is the Harold H. Greene Professor of Law at George Washington University Law School. Her areas of expertise include family law, reproductive technology, and adoption law. She has written numerous law review articles on family law and other subjects, and has coauthored several books, including *Red Families v. Blue Families* (2010) (with Professor June Carbone), *Test Tube Families* (NYU Press 2009), *Families by Law: An Adoption Reader* (NYU Press 2004), and *Confinements: Fertility and Infertility in Contemporary Culture* (1997) (with Professor Helena Michie).